SOCIAL WORK FOR LAZY RADICALS

SOCIAL WORK FOR LAZY RADICALS

RELATIONSHIP BUILDING, CRITICAL THINKING AND COURAGE IN PRACTICE

JANE FENTON

macmillan international
HIGHER EDUCATION

RED GLOBE PRESS

First published 2019 by
RED GLOBE PRESS

Red Globe Press in the UK is an imprint of Springer Nature Limited,
registered in England, company number 785998, of 4 Crinan Street,
London N1 9XW.

Red Globe Press® is a registered trademark in the United States,
the United Kingdom, Europe and other countries.

ISBN 978–1–352–00245–4 paperback

This book is printed on paper suitable for recycling and made from fully
managed and sustained forest sources. Logging, pulping and manufacturing
processes are expected to conform to the environmental regulations of the
country of origin.

A catalogue record for this book is available from the British Library.

A catalog record for this book is available from the Library of Congress.

*This book is dedicated to my much loved, funny,
clever and brave big brother.
Arthur B. McIntosh, 1953–2018.*

CONTENTS

ACKNOWLEDGEMENTS

I would like to thank the School of Education and Social Work at the University of Dundee, and Peter Hooper from Red Globe Press for supporting me in the process of writing this book. Special thanks to my friend, Dr Richard Ingram, for some quality conversations that found their way into the pages of this book, and for some that didn't! Thanks also to my family, Steve, Gina and Adam, who didn't really notice I was writing another book but pretended to be interested now and again. Finally, thanks to the social workers who have inspired me over the years with the heartfelt work they do, especially Lesley, Alex, Rosie and Fiona.

1

Introduction

Welcome to *Social work for lazy radicals: relationship building, critical thinking and courage in practice*. It is very good indeed that the word 'lazy' in the title did not stop you from wanting to read this book, although you may be intrigued by the concept of lazy radical social work practice. I know that social workers, as a group, are not known for their laziness – quite the opposite in fact. Demanding caseloads, difficult and stressful work and often working beyond the call of duty are elements of a more accurate appraisal of social work practice. What exactly is meant by lazy radical practice, then? This chapter will answer that question and by the end of it, you will understand exactly how reading this book is going to help you attain, maintain or develop confident, value-based and courageous practice.

Another unique component of the book is that lazy radical practice will be deconstructed in order to help you understand first principle underpinnings. To explore these, you will be given access to some important ideas from very significant influential thinkers, such as Bauman, Arendt and Mill. Reference to these and other thinkers, will not be in-depth, as that would not be possible within the parameters of the book, but some key ideas will be drawn on, to underscore the foundational thinking of lazy radical practice.

Finally, this book is meant as an accessible text for students and social workers; one which is easy to read and to understand. I hope you find it enjoyable and useful.

What is lazy radical social work practice?

To answer this question, a good starting point is Bailey and Brake's (1975) seminal text on radical practice. As the authors state: 'Radical social work, we feel, is essentially understanding the position of the oppressed in the context of the social and economic structure they live in....Our aim is not, for example, to eliminate casework, but to eliminate casework that supports the ruling class hegemony' (ibid., p. 9). *This* is the positioning of the proposed book rather than fusing that idea of radical social work with the necessity for 'their (social workers') involvement in a programme of political action' (ibid.).

The separation of those two strands of radical social work will be tackled unflinchingly by this book, as from the author's own experience, students and social workers can be put off embracing a radical form of practice because of the perceived pressure to be 'politically active' – going on marches, volunteering for 'good causes' or even posting petitions on facebook. I have seen students balk at the amount of commitment required for activism, just as I have seen very committed, radical students treat their 'lazy' counterparts somewhat disdainfully.

There is pressure on students to be activist, not only from peers, but also from wider influences. For example, Ivory (2017, n.p.), writing about the inception of Social Work Without Borders, quotes the founder as saying 'social workers could be political activists'. The article goes on to discuss changing the curriculum and promoting a different, more active type of social work practice, and ends with a quote from Lisa Hackett, head of a social work training programme, in relation to the attack on an asylum seeker by a gang of teenagers in South London:

> 'You can say it's just mindless violence, but the important thing is to explain it', Hackett says. 'If we just remain outraged, we don't have any understanding. Why do young people feel compelled to take that action? It may be that they feel on the periphery of society in terms of their own life chances'.

Although the article is in support of activism, the quote above is actually about *critical understanding* rather than actually taking action as discussed earlier in the article. This is a key point and critical understanding is something that underpins all lazy radical practice as it influences all case-work and interaction with service users.

Returning to the suggestion that there is pressure from the contemporary radical branch of social work to be activists, Lavalette (2017, p. 19) writing in *Professional Social Work* states that 'social work activism is good for the profession and good for the mental health of practitioners'. He also makes the point that social movements, which were criticised at the time, made huge differences to people's lives, for example voting rights and welfare provision, and the current emphasis on service-user engagement was born out of social movements, not policy making. He claims that agitating for rights is a feature of contemporary life. Lavalette is correct in all of that, and social work activists are crucially important and deserve all of our support. However, the *critical thinking* theme in Lavalette's piece can also be detected: 'social movements challenge the dominant ideas of the

age … including culture, ways of working, welfare and government policies' (ibid.). So again, there are ways to do that actually *in practice* without
necessarily being activist. The *Guardian* ran an article entitled *A guide to
radical social work* (Ioakimidis, 2016, n.p.) which very strongly promotes
activism as an essential part of radical practice:

> Despite recent deviations and misinterpretations of the term, a radical concept
> historically refers to a political theory and practice that aims to understand the
> root causes of social problems. Whilst appreciation of these causes and allevia-
> tion of their detrimental effects on people's lives are important dimensions of
> radical social work, *what really differentiates it from mainstream approaches is its
> emphasis on action that aims at social change* [emphasis added].

Clearly, then, not everyone will agree that a lazy radical practice is
acceptable as 'real' radical practice. And maybe it is not. And maybe it
does not have to be. Lazy radical practice is, perhaps, a slightly separate,
but overlapping form of social work. Lazy radicals are not, as a matter of
course, involved in 'action for social change' (apart from exercising voting rights, I would suggest. No one is too lazy for that!) but are absolutely
concerned with understanding and taking action about structural barriers
and problems, caused by political policy, *within* their practice. Ioakimidis
also states 'The dichotomy between the social worker as a nine-to-five state
agent and a five-to-nine activist is a crucial one' (ibid.), but there is another
way to look at this which refutes that dichotomy – do not simply be a
'state agent' at work, but be a nine-to-five practice activist (a practivist?).

Having recognised, then, that a *requirement* to be an activist might
put some students off the idea of radical practice, it must be explicitly
acknowledged from the outset that activism by social workers is invalu-
able and extremely worthwhile. This book is not intended to degrade that
in any way, and is in fact meant as a complementary and congruent way
to think about casework which should fit with any activist's practice. It is,
however, also a stand-alone way of working for the significant number of
students and social workers who do not want to be an activist due to busy
lives, competing demands or just prioritising real relaxation and/or family
time. This way of working is, as Bailey and Brake (1975) suggest, a casework way of working which does not support the 'ruling class hegemony'.

Getting to grips with the basics

OK, it may be that reading this chapter so far, students are thinking that
it is going to be too 'political' for them or difficult to understand. Be reas-
sured that this is not the case. Everything is explained clearly and you

will be able to develop an understanding of some things that you have maybe not fully understood before. As a handy reminder, there is a glossary of terms at the back of the book, so turn to that any time you are in doubt. Firstly, however, it might be useful just to consider a brief introduction to politics, given that social work, and radical social work in particular, is not politically neutral (Hansford, Ely, Flaherty and Meyer-Adams, 2017). When you think about it, all the legislation and policies that govern social work and frame what social workers have to do, come from the government. This means that the ideology of the particular government has a direct impact on how we think about and work with service users.

What are politics anyway? The Oxford English Dictionary (2018) defines politics as: 'The activities associated with the governance of a country or area, especially the debate between parties having power' and we need to understand this before thinking about anything more complicated. We are thinking about the UK here, and although some powers are devolved to Scotland, Northern Ireland and Wales, we are going to stick to the governance of the UK by the Westminster government. The learning you do, however, will be applicable to all countries and systems of government, because you are going to understand the basic political framework.

A good starting point here is the Political Compass (Political Compass, 2017). Follow this link and have a look at the website. Even do the test and see where you sit in comparison to political parties and historical figures:

www.politicalcompass.org/

Scroll down and click on *Take The Test*.

As you can see, the Political Compass has two axes – the economic scale, and the social scale. Let's look at each of these in turn.

Economic scale

A right wing economic position, associated in the UK with the Conservative Party and UKIP, and in the USA by the Republican Party, means a belief in low taxes and a smaller role for the government. This means less regulation and fewer taxes on the rich – a belief that it is best to let the market run and regulate itself (The Life Guide, 2016). When the market runs itself and regulation and other state interference is removed from business, then companies and corporations are free to pay their employees what they want and to do things as cheaply as possible to create profit. It is worth thinking about what that might mean! Certainly, knowing that this type of economic policy creates inequality (through poor wages and increased profits for owners and share-holders) is important (Ferguson, 2008).

Right wing economic thinking also lends itself to the privatisation of traditionally state-run work such as health care, utilities, social care and education. Once again, profit then becomes the main aim of those areas of civic life hitherto out of market reach (Eagleton-Pierce, 2016).

In contrast to the above, left wing economic policy strives for more equality. There are, therefore, regulations from government about wage levels and other workers' conditions (such as secure contracts and sick pay). Left wing economics also allow for government borrowing of money to invest in industry when there is a decrease in business or an increase in inflation, thus protecting employment and workers' conditions through lean times. The money would then be recouped when business once again picked up (Crouch, 2011). This type of Keynesian demand management, which was economic policy from after World War 2 until the late 1970s, cushioned workers from fluctuations in the market (Crouch, 2011). Businesses are also taxed more under left wing economic policies. So, for all of those reasons, inequality decreases as wages increase and profits and the money made from shares decrease (Garner, Ferdinand and Lawson, 2009).

Left wing economics also takes some areas of life out of the reach of the market and into state ownership. The current shadow Labour government, for example, intends to bring the railways back into state ownership (BBC, 2018a) and would re-invest in the areas of social care, education and so on.

Please see the section on *What happened?* in Chapter 2 for a more in-depth consideration of the political history and consequent changes in social work over time. Chapter 5 also includes a section on *Economics* in the section: *Foregrounded knowledge leading to a world view.*

In the UK, we have been subject to right wing economic policies since 1979 when Margaret Thatcher's Conservative Government came to power. New Labour, in 1997, did not change the direction of right wing economic travel which continued with the coalition government (in 2010), then the current conservative government (in 2015). The basic tenets of right wing economic thinking have now become almost unquestioned and taken-for-granted, including the results of those policies, on: inequality, the emergence of 'the working poor' and the rise of foodbanks (JRF, 2016). This right wing economic ideology is explained further in the forthcoming section in this chapter, *Neoliberalism: the ruling class hegemony*.

So, staying with the political compass, hopefully students will now have some grasp of the economic axis and we can move on to the social axis – much more easily understood!

Social scale

Rather than a spectrum between left and right wing, the social scale is arranged from authoritarian to libertarian. Authoritarian policies are concerned with people being subject to control from the government, usually by way of tough crime control, sanctions for bad behaviour, surveillance and rules and regulations to govern life. Authoritarian can also mean a belief that children should be 'seen and not heard' and be strictly brought up to respect their elders and that the traditional family unit should be encouraged through restrictions on alternatives. As you can see, this sometimes aligns itself well with conservative politics, where a belief in tradition and in hierarchy dominates. More libertarian people believe in equal rights for non-traditional family choices (gay rights, same sex marriage and adoption, abortion choice rights, for example), and are often associated with general left wing thinking (Political Compass, 2017).

However, students also need to understand that extreme governments on both the right (fascism, for example) and on the left (communism, for example) have authoritarian policies due to complete loyalty to the state being demanded of people and the subjugation of freedom to dissent or to vote for another party (Garner et al., 2009). Students need to look out for authoritarianism in all its guises – oppression of people's rights, freedom and individuality as well as erosion of free thought and speech.

It is worth watching this short video called *The Political Spectrum Explained In 4 Minutes* at: www.youtube.com/watch?v=JlQ5fGECmsA (The Life Guide, 2016).

What about you?

Did you do the Political Compass? Where did you find yourself sitting? Has it given you cause for reflection?

A small study by Fenton (2019) found that a cohort of social work students were quite homogenous in their positions on the Political Compass. Most sat in the bottom left (left wing/libertarian) quadrant. This makes sense in terms of social work values where clear principles are laid out in terms of human rights, and respect for difference and choice (libertarian); and for redistribution of resources and support for equality (left wing economically).

If this was the same for you, read on! The thinking in this book will resonate with your beliefs, even if you are not yet quite sure how to articulate those (you soon will be...). Or were you placed somewhere very different on the Political Compass axes? If so, read on too! There may well be some interesting material in this book that will challenge how you think and give you cause for reflection. That can only be for the good.

So, knowing a bit more about political ideologies, it is time to consider the 'ruling class hegemony' (Bailey and Brake, 1975, and see the previous section, *What is lazy radical social work practice*). 'Hegemony' is a term coined by Gramsci, which means a system of governance that permeates all areas of political, public and civic life to the extent that people stop noticing it or are unaware of it, such is its prevalence (Gramsci, 1971). The institutions of life (media, education, social services, church, employment structures etc.) are all underpinned by the hegemony, but it is very hard to see or realise that. Monbiot (2016, n.p.) states:

> Imagine if the people of the Soviet Union had never heard of communism. The ideology that dominates our lives has, for most of us, no name. Mention it in conversation and you'll be rewarded with a shrug. Even if your listeners have heard the term before, they will struggle to define it. Neoliberalism: do you know what it is?
>
> Its anonymity is both a symptom and cause of its power. It has played a major role in a remarkable variety of crises: the financial meltdown of 2007–8, the offshoring of wealth and power, of which the Panama Papers offer us merely a glimpse, the slow collapse of public health and education, resurgent child poverty, the epidemic of loneliness, the collapse of ecosystems, the rise of Donald Trump. But we respond to these crises as if they emerge in isolation, apparently unaware that they have all been either catalysed or exacerbated by the same coherent philosophy; a philosophy that has – or had – a name. What greater power can there be than to operate namelessly?

Neoliberalism, the 'ruling class hegemony'

Lazy radical practice is at odds with this current political ideology, 'neoliberalism', that has characterised our political and civic life since Margaret Thatcher's Government in the UK, and Ronald Reagan's in the USA in the late 1970s (Ferguson, 2008). At this time 'through the IMF, the World Bank, the Maastricht treaty and the World Trade Organisation, neoliberal policies were imposed – often without democratic consent – on much of the world' creating an international implementation of neoliberalism and its attendant austerity policies (Monbiot, 2016, n.p.). In the light of neoliberalism as the ruling class hegemony here in the UK and in much of the world, it is very important to explore a bit more fully what neoliberalism is before going any further. Critical thinking about the problems service users might face, and understanding how they are framed and shaped by the political context within which we exist, takes a foundational understanding of that context. The historical development of social work and the changing political context is explored more fully in the *What happened?* section of Chapter 2. However, since the whole point of lazy radical practice is to ensure that the 'ruling class hegemony', is not simply blindly supported by our practice, and the fact that the 'ruling class hegemony' is currently neoliberalism, it is important to get an initial understanding of what neoliberalism *is* at this early stage.

Neoliberalism is usually associated with 'the expansion of commercial markets and the privileging of corporations; the re-engineering of government as an "entrepreneurial" actor; and the imposition of "fiscal discipline", particularly in welfare spending' (Eagleton-Pierce, 2016). Neoliberalism shares much of its philosophy with classical liberalism (and is a contemporary form of such), developed in the 18th and 19th centuries, and characterised by the following beliefs: 'unfettered laissez-fair capitalism is the ideal economic system' (no government interference), 'unemployment is caused by government interference (giving workers an alternative to employment) and behaviour of unemployed people (voluntary withdrawal from job market)', 'social doctrine espouses individualism, inequality and guaranteed freedoms', 'business should be privately owned', and 'corporate taxes, minimum wages and workplace legislation squeeze out jobs' (Mullaly, 2007, p. 93). These beliefs can be seen playing out in: the de-regulation of markets and financial institutions, in other words governments not 'interfering' to protect jobs or workers' rights (leading to zero-hour contracts and very insecure, poorly paid work); people being 'free' to make a success or failure of their lives, and individual pursuit of success on one's own behalf being the correct way to do that (so erosion of trade unions, for example); and the government's selling off of public utilities such as railways, energy, Royal Mail, care agencies and the probation service. Alongside these features of neoliberalism, we can see that protections traditionally afforded to people under previous economic ideology (Keynesianism) are stripped away and that there is a new emphasis on competition at all levels, even in aspects of social life that had been beyond the reach of competition such as agencies concerned with 'public good' for example, care, protection and the basics of life (Garrett, 2010). Note how neoliberalism is very clearly a right wing economic ideology which resonates with the right wing economic position discussed in the previous section.

Garrett (2010) considers the main features of neoliberalism that have a direct and explicit bearing on social work practice:

➣ The private sector has taken on many traditional social work or public service roles (especially care, prisons, and more recently, the probation service). This means these services are concerned with value for money and profit as a priority – rather than quality care itself.

➤ The growth of privately owned children's services, especially fostering provision and residential care. The same caution above applies.

➤ Regulation of the workforce (see Chapter 3).

➤ A change in the role of the state (rather than a simple 'rolling back') to one which ensures the correct conditions for capital accumulation, and thus facilitates redistribution of wealth towards the wealthiest.

➤ Precariousness in working conditions – and making sure that the 'reserve price' (below which workers will not work) is lowered as far as possible, usually done by cutting benefits. This leaves growing numbers of people in poverty by being on very minimal benefits or belonging to the 'working poor'.

➤ The 'new punitiveness' and the expansion of the penal state – more prisons and secure accommodation for example. There is also a change in ethos within the new punitive approach, as Feeley and Simon (1992) stated: 'the task is managerial, not transformative'. This means there is more control and containment and less working at, or believing in, change. This expansion is, according to Garrett: 'the hidden face of the neoliberal model and the necessary counterpart to the restructuring of welfare' (Garrett, 2010, p. 347).

Garrett also points out, however, that neoliberalism cannot achieve its aims in a straightforward way – it is rather that there is an on-going process of 'neoliberalisation' (ibid., p. 348). The themes above will play out in the rest of the book, but it is important to have a basic sense of neoliberalism and its interface with social work at the outset. Garrett draws on Bourdieu's work to support resistance to neoliberalism in a way that is very apposite for the central thesis in this book:

> One of Bourdieu's ideas is that for a 'field' [of expertise] to maintain sufficient integrity and viability it must be able to define itself and maintain sufficient autonomy to prevent it being entirely subsumed within neoliberalism. Thus, when working in a neoliberal context, practitioners ... become liable 'to two masters: the practices and norms of the discipline and the practices and norms of the market' (Pileggi and Parton, 2003, p. 318)....Given this tension, or competition, individual workers are confronted with a choice as to which 'master' to follow (Garrett, 2010, p. 351).

This is where the emphasis on critical thinking (see especially Chapter 5) is so crucially important, because students need to be equipped to understand and think through any situation and its political, hegemonic context, in order to choose the 'practices and norms of the profession' that is, to do proper social work.

One aspect of neoliberalism that underpins all of the above is the attendant 'moralising self-sufficiency discourse' (Marston, 2013, p. 132). This discourse is *required by* neoliberalism to make sense of, and gain support for, the harsh consequences it has for many, usually poor, people. So blaming poor people's behaviour for the situation they are in is necessary in order that support can be gained for otherwise obviously unfair policies. Marston points out that understanding a social problem relies on how that problem is framed and so, for example, understanding measures that weakened housing security among social tenants can be framed as necessary measures to deal with 'bad tenants' and their bad behaviour. This simple and reductionist 'framing' leaves out of the picture, and diverts attention away from, structural elements such as rising inequality, long waiting lists for housing, rising cost of land and discrimination and unfair treatment in the housing market. Without knowledge, understanding and critical thinking, it is very easy for students to 'buy' a simplistic self-sufficiency explanation for the problems encountered by many of the people they deal with and, of course, looking back to the defining characteristics of neoliberalism, it is easy to see how congruent a self-sufficiency understanding is. As Marston states:

> To engage in these discursive struggles requires a recognition that policy discourses can distort as much as they reveal. For example, it is disingenuous to suggest that persons living in neighbourhoods with poor schools, few shops and dilapidated housing, kilometres away from the best job opportunities, have equal opportunity with persons in the same metropolitan area. Yet this is precisely what a moralising self-sufficiency discourse does. It assumes that the background conditions that these people face are not unjust and that structural difficulties have been overcome through the march of modernity and the achievements of a range of social movements (ibid., p. 132).

This is, unfortunately, exactly what many students *do* espouse and partially answers the question about why we need lazy radical practice.

Why lazy radical social work practice?

Cohen (2017), writing in the *London Evening Standard*, reported on the increased levels of knife crime in London. His analysis centred on black youth gang culture; the Patois language, imported from Jamaica and mixed up with new dialects learned in prison; rap songs and videos; social media and young people following trends; and absent fathers. Absent fathers, of course, or put another way the terrible 'single mother' culture, also featured heavily in Charles Murray's (1990) analysis of the British 'underclass'. Reading this article, and knowing that many of these crimes were committed by young, black men, with their own particular ways of dressing and speaking can make sense and can be understood quite easily – this is an individual behavioural problem. These behaviours – speaking in that way, listening to that music, being a gang member and boasting on social media – are the roots of the problem. As are single mothers' behaviours – getting pregnant irresponsibly outwith marriage. From my experience of social work education, I know that many students would understand and agree with Cohen's analysis. They might also, as a way of implementing 'social work values', discuss at length how they would be anti-discriminatory in their practice with someone as described above. They would build a relationship, learn about the person's culture from them and therefore be anti-discriminatory at the p-level of Thompson's seminal PCS Model (Thompson, 2001).

This is why lazy radical practice is required. Missing from Cohen's analysis, and not recognised by many students, is any kind of structural analysis. Might the following have something to do with the rise in knife crime among young people in London: cuts to benefits, a bleak law-abiding future as a member of the 'working poor' (JRF, 2016), cuts to youth services, closure of drug agencies, housing shortages, poverty and cuts to police numbers? None of those factors feature in any way in Cohen's analysis and many students would simply not think of them, understand what is meant by them or understand *how* there might be a direct link between them and increasing violence. As one young man in Cohen's piece states, being in a gang and involved in knife crime brings 'power, status, girls, especially girls' (Cohen, 2017, n.p.). Even a basic reading of *The Spirit Level* (Wilkinson and Pickett, 2010) provides a different lens on this status seeking and violent behaviour: when young men seek status and try to 'save face', violence often ensues, and this is especially true for young men with little social capital or other means of achieving status and standing in the wider community. Vast levels of inequality exacerbate this and lead to further status-enhancing behaviour such as being 'top dog' in a gang and maintaining this position through violence. Inequality and poverty are also significantly correlated with more anxiety, substance misuse and less trust – the combination of which leads to family strain and difficulty, thus enhancing the attraction of the peer group (gang) and alternative ways of esteem building and status seeking. As Nellis and McNeill state in the foreword to Allan Weaver's book *So you think you know me?* (Weaver, 2008, p. viii), people who can withstand the early brutality of their lives are exceptions and deserve special explanations, 'not the many who became hard and cruel because this is what survival and status-seeking amidst poverty and disadvantage demanded of them'. This idea will be developed later in the book, but suffice to say at this point that *critical understanding* of social problems is a fundamental aspect to lazy radical practice, otherwise the type of casework resulting from a Cohen-esque understanding of the problem would quite simply 'support the ruling class hegemony'.

Structure of the book

The book is designed to help students think through a logical progression of ideas, and its chapters are designed to do just that. The building blocks of lazy radical practice will be explored at the outset, then the 3-step model of practice will be introduced step by step. Each step will, as already mentioned, be deconstructed to first principles rooted in ethical thinking and knowledge, and the work of some great thinkers will be drawn on to assist with that deconstruction. This means that students and social workers will be able to have confidence in their practice framework, built as it will be on a deep critical understanding. Tasks, as required by agencies, will, therefore, be subject to examination and will be viewed through the new 3-step model, thus leading to informed, enlightened and critical practice. This in turn will increase moral courage and the ability to do the right thing (Munro, 2011). Finally, the book will analyse examples of how lazy radical practice can look in the real world.

Throughout, there will be opportunities for readers to think about issues and to consider practice examples. *Stop and think* boxes will feature in each chapter when particularly important or complex issues are raised and when readers might like to take some time to reflect and analyse them for themselves. *Practice examples* will ask the reader to consider the *application* of the ideas to fictional, but not atypical, examples of social work practice.

In a little more detail, the chapters are as follows:

Chapter 2, *Dependence, independence and values* sets out the case for radical social work and explores the fundamentals of such an approach, drawing links with notions of dependency and social democracy. Zygmunt Bauman's work on democracy and dependency will be introduced here, especially in terms of how dependency has become something negative and shameful. His thinking about people as essentially belonging to communities leads to an ethical orientation concerned with common good, ideas of caring for each other and of shared humanity. Links between this ethical orientation, the resultant ethical impulse and political positioning are analysed.

The chapter also explores how and why social work has re-orientated to a position of neoliberal design and managerial measurement and how notions of care, the acceptance of dependency and frailty, and the idea that problems are structurally influenced rather than simply about individual fecklessness or poor behaviour are all features of social work that are dwindling.

Chapter 3 is concerned with *Bureaucracy, regulation and professionalism,* and explores codes of practice and other managerial tools for regulation of behaviour. These are contrasted with social work's fundamental ethics. The idea that newer social workers and students are less critical in their practice, and much more comfortable with managerial and procedure-driven agency requirements is analysed, especially in terms of increasing pre-occupation with bureaucracy as a symptom of neoliberalism and as a dangerous 'distancing' practice. Once again, Bauman's work is drawn on to get to the heart of the matter and to the essence of what is going on. His writing about the Holocaust and the emotionally and cognitively distancing effects of bureaucracy is utilised and applied to the neoliberal direction of social work practice. Hannah Arendt is also introduced, and her work on the dangers of unthinking rule-following is employed to help readers understand the perilousness of this type of practice.

The 3-step model of lazy radical practice is introduced in Chapter 4, *Relationship building, trust and emotional engagement.* In essence, this chapter is about the individual-level of practice that, although not enough on its own, is an essential component of radical practice. As Ferguson (2013, p. 201) states: 'One view, then, is that value-based work prioritizing a worker-client relationship, once regarded as traditional – mainstream – practice, has now become radical in contemporary, managerial environments'. Unless social workers want to engage with the people who use services and try, and are able to, understand and empathise with their feelings (given often grim circumstances) they are likely to sit in judgement of them and their choices. Social workers must embrace the notion that 'there but by the grace of God go I' (John Bradford, 16th century) rather than feeling, in a vaguely superior, 'othering' way, that they would *never* make those choices.

This is a difficult chapter, because how does a person do that, when trying to empathise with, for example, a sexual abuser or someone who has harmed children? There may be limits to empathy, but those limits should not be curtailed unnecessarily. Notions of 'social empathy' (Segal, 2011), compassion, ethics of care and getting to know someone's 'inner world' (Hennessey, 2011) will also be examined.

In my opinion, the most important chapter in the book is Chapter 5 which covers step 2 in the model: *Critical thinking.* This chapter promotes practice that involves knowledge, understanding and critical analysis;

a type of thinking-practice that is really the opposite of the 'dangerous' practice that can be understood by reference to Bauman and Arendt and deconstructed in earlier chapters. Thinking-practice takes knowledge: for example knowledge of the effects of inequality and poverty, knowledge of politics and neoliberal policy choices, economics and *why* those choices are made, and traditional theoretical social work knowledge. Then students need to *understand*: for example, how the above knowledge can be used to see social problems through a different lens than neoliberal hegemony would have us believe is the 'common sense' – that people simply make bad choices and don't take advantage of the opportunities provided by our benign society. Also, students need *critical analytical skills* to explore how a person, family or society's problems can be viewed through different lenses or understood through different discourses, depending on the fundamental underpinning beliefs and assumptions of the analyser.

Finally in this chapter, a further aspect of critical thinking is explored. The idea that really good debate and the advancement of ideas can be inhibited by people being afraid to say what they really think. The censorious nature of university life, in terms of toeing the party line, is raised and explored as an inhibitor to scholarly thinking and debate. The value of ideas and opinions that make us uncomfortable, and, in contrast, the 'dulling' power of any ubiquitous ideology or party-line are analysed. Nothing is more detrimental to critical thinking than only being permitted to think within certain predefined parameters. Mill and Arendt's work will be drawn on in this chapter.

Chapter 6 introduces step 3 of the model: *Moral courage.* Organisational versus occupational professionalism, introduced in Chapter 3, is utilised as the context for thinking about social work knowledge. The link between being an 'occupational' professional and having 'moral courage' is explored. Using concepts such as 'ethical stress' as an impetus to action, and building on the 'ethical impulse' explored earlier is covered in this chapter. Ultimately, lazy radical practice is about 'doing the right thing' and having courage to take action is crucial.

Actually doing lazy radical practice is the subject of Chapter 7: *Doing lazy radical social work.* This chapter confronts an increasing tendency in students to seek non-punitive, yet still individual-level explanations for problems. Identity politics and vulnerability/therapeutic narratives will be critiqued and contrasted with lazy radical practice. Considering a person's social conditions as a priority, as opposed to assuming moral bankruptcy, individual-level discrimination or pathology will be highlighted as the central feature of a lazy radical approach.

Finally, Chapter 8 concludes the book. In *Conclusion* the main ideas are revisited and recapped. The chapter returns to the resurrection of radical social work's ethical impulse and to the thinking of Bauman as introduced in Chapter 2, centring on the belief in the equality of human beings and engaging in human-to-human social work as essential to just practice. The suggestion that just practice cannot happen without moral courage leading to ethical action is revisited.

Swimming against the tide? Lazy radical social work as resistance

Michael Gove, the then Justice Secretary, speaking in 2013 said:

> In too many cases, social work training involves idealistic students being told that the individuals with whom they will work have been disempowered by society. They will be encouraged to see these individuals as victims of social injustice whose fate is overwhelmingly decreed by the economic forces and inherent inequalities which scar our society.

> This analysis is, sadly, as widespread as it is pernicious. It robs individuals of the power of agency and breaks the link between an individual's actions and the consequences. It risks explaining away substance abuse, domestic violence and personal irresponsibility, rather than doing away with them (Gove, 2013, n.p.).

Mr Gove is right, to an extent. This book is an explicit encouragement for social work students to see service users' problems as located within wider, structural issues, to view them as 'disempowered' and 'victims of social injustice'. However, where he goes wrong, in my opinion, is to say that this view (which is overwhelmingly evidence-based, *Guardian*, 2013) leads to a fatalistic and predetermined view of services users' futures, and that it abdicates any attempt to 'do away with' problems such as substance misuse, domestic violence or personal irresponsibility. What it *does* do unapologetically, is to support the premise that students must understand and critically analyse the problems the people they work with have, and therefore must understand that structural issues *do* have an impact as supported by the evidence base. It is not to view people as without agency or as helpless, but to realise that in trying to enact that agency, the barriers and difficulties are very significant. This is especially true if you are poor, living in grim housing, with over-crowded schools and in an environment where there is significant crime, substance misuse and poor health. The people in those environments are *up against it* when it comes to making changes. This issue will be explored in more detail in

Chapter 5, when knowledge and evidence of life at the bottom end of the social hierarchy are explored.

Clearly the view unashamedly promoted in this book is at odds with current government rhetoric and ideology. The neoliberal idea that people should be independent go-getters, and being left behind is their own fault, emanates from Mr Gove's speech.

He is not alone. Malcolm Narey, in his 2014 report *Making the education of social workers consistently effective,* takes issue with social work academic Lena Dominelli as follows:

Anti oppressive practice is vital, she goes on to argue, because social work should be about empowering:

People whose lives are configured by struggles against structural inequalities like poverty, sexism, racism and disablism.

The view of those receiving social work support as being necessarily victims is captured by a recent Community Care blog published in the summer of 2013:

Good practice [in social work] is based on building relationships. It also depends on being given the scope to use them to the benefit of service users whose issues are the product of being at the bottom of a very unequal and oppressive society … the service user is a victim rather than creator of their life situation.

Anti oppressive practice in academic social work is closely linked to concepts of empowerment and working in partnership. While a number of social work academics reject them, these are not extreme notions at the fringes of academic social work. One newly qualified social worker from a well-regarded university told me that the concentration in her course on non-oppressive practice was at the expense of understanding practicalities about the job. I don't believe her experience was unique (Narey, 2014, p. 11).

Once again, it appears that there is a conflation of ideas here. I would argue that we need to critically understand how structural influences affect, for example, choice, behaviour, planning, mental health *and* advantages and disadvantages (see, for example the statistics about percentages of people educated in public schools and now in positions of real power (Jones, 2011) – is this about meritocracy?). I would also argue that this understanding does lead to a different form of social work than the one Mr Narey might view as 'right'. So, for example, it would involve advocacy, help, assistance, support and care *but* would not sap people of agency (it would assist with that by addressing barriers) nor neglect issues of risk to children or others. It is simply that those issues of risk would be understood as being *influenced* by wider issues. To not acknowledge that, whilst knowing first hand stories of grinding poverty, overwhelming debt, esteem-degrading inequality and the likelihood of a bleak future, is to simply be blind to the reality of service users' lives. Does the government have an investment in being blind to that, and in perpetuating the neoliberal hegemonic ideology of individual responsibility? Yes, because it very much justifies cutting benefits, creating a 'working poor' class of people whilst increasing wealth at the top of the hierarchy, where a conservative government has its members, allegiances, funders and, often, family.

Narey also believes that teaching things like anti-oppressive practice dilutes skills training:

> One distinguished Director of Children's Services told me: 'it's beyond me why universities don't work to a common list of need to know issues'. Another suggested that in the uncertainty about exactly what needs to be taught, we have been left with an academic vacuum, which we have filled with attitudinal stuff rather than skills (Narey, 2014, p. 5).

In the extracts above, Narey has cited two individuals who talk about skills and 'the practicalities of the job' suffering due to teaching 'attitudinal stuff' or AOP. This reduction of social work practice to a 'doing of the task' or 'practical work' is absolutely in conflict with the purpose of this book. Social work education must equip students with knowledge, understanding and critical thinking ability (and expectation!) to really understand what is going on for people, in all its complexity. The interplay between the socio-political context, actual material and emotional circumstances, human development and individual agency is something that must be understood in a way that provides a framework for understanding each, different individual that social workers work with. To erode that in favour of learning practical skills would be a significant move towards a type of casework that simply perpetuates neoliberal thinking or 'ruling class hegemony'.

Encouragingly, Croisdale-Appleby's 2014 review of social work education was drawn from thorough and methodical research and consultation (BASW, 2014a), and he concluded that, among other things, social workers *had* to be 'social scientists' (Croisdale-Appleby, 2014, p. 19). To be a social scientist requires knowledge, understanding and critical thinking, so is in keeping with the form of social work advocated for in this book.

Interestingly, both Narey and Croisedale-Appleby recommend attending to the rigour of the entry requirements for social work education, and assessing for analytical ability and critical reasoning (Croisedale-Appleby, 2014, p. 85). Narey also discusses at some length how difficult it might be for students to fail their courses, even if they are unsuitable for social work. Both of these views are congruent with this book – it is essential that students can think critically and politically and grasp difficult, conceptual issues. I do not have confidence that all graduating students possess this ability and would welcome more rigorous entry requirements. On Narey's point, in a neoliberal/managerial target and measurement-driven consumer-led university context, 'retention rates' are one of the metrics for the Teaching Excellence Framework (Higher Education Funding Council, 2017). Student evaluations of modules, courses and in the highly prized National Student Survey count enormously for universities and staff know that poor grades often lead to poor evaluations. In this target-driven and evaluative context it *is* more difficult to fail students who may be given multiple attempts to pass summative assignments and end up passing their degree when, in actual fact, they are not equipped for the kind of thinking-practice explored in this book.

So, in the main, there is a drive for a particular direction of travel in social work education which is counter-intuitive to lazy radical social work practice. It is a neoliberal direction, characterised by the responsibilisation, and often punishment, of those who are really struggling with grim and harsh lives. Worryingly, this direction of travel is now influential among statutory social work agencies, never more so than in child protection. Rogowski (2015, p. 105) states:

> In brief, following several decades of changing conceptions, policies and practice in relation to child maltreatment, concerns include increased bureaucracy and targets enforced by managers and an authoritarian desire to responsibilise parents regardless of their economic and social circumstances.

Nicolas (2015) suggests that social work should desist from 'pretending' it is about social justice when it is actually about risk assessment and management. Nicolas is a very experienced child protection social worker in England.

Even some of the more, on the face of it, benign or even positive directions in social work must be interrogated thoughtfully and critically. For example, the increasing emphasise on 'personalisation' and its espoused definition as a citizen-rights movement, is examined by Lymbery (2014) and uncovered as more complex than simply a 'good thing'. Lymbery draws a distinction between support for people to be able to make their own choices about care, which is positive, and the actual ability to realise that choice. This is where neoliberal principles such as spending less on welfare have an effect because thresholds for entitlement have been raised so significantly. Lymbery also points out that the group of service users most likely to realise their choices is the better educated and more articulate group. Older people in particular often did not want the higher levels of responsibility that being a 'choosing, deciding shaping author' (Ferguson, 2008, p. 77) brings with it. It is very easy to see the promotion of independence and the antipathy towards dependence within this broad movement. Lymbery states that appeals to citizenship as the rationale for increasing personalisation of services might well mask the real consumerist policy goals of neoliberalism.

> The implications of this for social work are both worrying and profound. While it is possible to label such a change as 'transformational', it seems to move to a point where the principles of human rights and social justice that are fundamental to social work are no longer fully applicable, thus cutting out a major element of its role (Lymbery, 2014, p. 303).

So, Lymbery's point above leads nicely on to the idea that neoliberalism is quite simply at odds with social work values, especially in relation to social justice. For example, the British Association of Social Workers (BASW, 2014b, p. 9) states that social workers should:

> ensure that resources at their disposal are distributed fairly, according to need.... Social workers have a duty to bring to the attention of their employers, policy makers, politicians and the general public situations where resources are inadequate or where distribution of resources, policies and practice are oppressive, unfair, harmful or illegal.

Students of social work also must understand and oppose where possible unfair distribution of resources and structural barriers. All of this points quite clearly to a *radical* interpretation of social justice (Doel, 2012), where progressive taxation and other policies would be welcomed and where a recognition that 'moralising self-sufficiency' is *not* the way to understand service users' problems, influenced as they significantly are by structural issues. Clearly then, the radical social justice ideal of social work is at odds with a neoliberal ideology and this, of course, will continue to be explored throughout the book. What it means, however, is that social work in many agencies as outlined earlier is, indeed, only *pretending* to be social work – if the work there is not about a radical form of social justice, then it is not social work. Social work is characterised by radical social justice thinking and we simply need to read any of the value statements to understand that (see Chapter 2 for further analysis).

This neoliberal direction or hegemonic 'common sense' is supported by the UK mainstream tabloid media where negative and salacious stories about individuals are held up as representative of an entire 'underclass' (Jones, 2011). In the aftermath of 'Baby P', for example, the circumstances of his death were held up as explicit indicators of life amongst 'those kinds' of people (Warner, 2015):

> Of course, nothing can ever excuse the unspeakable cruelty of Baby P's mother. But this harrowing Mail investigation lays bare how society's amoral and brutalised underclass breeds such monsters (*Daily Mail*, 2009).

Contrast the above quote with Nellis and McNeill's earlier point that people who can *withstand* the early brutality of their lives are exceptions, not the ones who become hard and cruel; that is, *circumstances and environment* brutalise people. The above quote would have us believe that *these people* are already brutal and 'breed' others just like themselves. A very different and important emphasis. The type of thinking exemplified in the quote above leads to hardening attitudes to people in poverty (JRF, 2014) and skews the public's attitude towards inaccurate, negative views about issues such as crime, benefit claimants etc. (*Independent*, 2013).

At this point then, it is clear that the explicit neoliberal ideology promoted by the government and supported by sensationalist media stories is going strong. It has carried out a concerted assault on current social work education, has infiltrated social work agencies and has, of course, had an extremely significant influence on social work students. For example, Fenton (2014) found that younger workers in Scottish criminal justice social work were significantly less likely to object to neoliberal features of practice such as increasing emphasis on risk assessment, management, monitoring and individual methods of change endeavour and erosion of welfare practices. Indeed, one younger social worker commented 'this offending is through their own choice' (Fenton and Kelly, 2017) and felt there was no other understanding or analysis required: a moralising self-sufficiency discourse clearly underpinning this worker's philosophy. Other authors have found similar issues with students and younger workers (e.g., see: Gilligan, 2007; Woodward and MacKay, 2012; Norstrand, 2017) and Pease (2013, p. 31) states that 'neoliberal ideas have penetrated the psyche of social workers' thus posing a challenge that may have been much less in earlier generations.

In summary, then, this book promotes a form of social work that is anathema to the current neoliberal governmental direction, to the actual reality of practice in many social work agencies and to the kinds of hegemonic attitudes held by the public and many social work students. So, the question might come to mind: why is it worth reading? The real point here, however, is that it is *not* anathema to social work. It is absolutely in tune with social work values – interpersonal level values and wider social justice values. It follows then that resisting the neoliberal direction is something that social workers should do, if they want to consider their daily work as professional social work. Essentially, a form of social work that resists the neoliberal hegemony *is* real social work.

Reasons for optimism

It is important to also note that the picture is perhaps not quite as depressing as it might seem so far. Not only is lazy radical social work in tune with social work values and ethics, but it may also sit naturally with social work students, albeit that many of them cannot see this and have been heavily influenced by neoliberal hegemony and the media. As mentioned earlier, a study by Fenton (2019), found that social work students were strongly in agreement with politics being an important subject to understand *and* scored overwhelmingly in the bottom left quadrant of the Political Compass. This means that the students' natural inclinations were towards libertarian social values (in terms of human rights) and progressive economic policies; in other words left-wing (Political Compass, 2017). This natural political orientation, even although students might not be able to articulate it or properly understand it, is very much congruent with a lazy radical form of social work and thus very hopeful for a comfortable and ethically congruent 'fit' between the theory outlined in this book and students' nascent practice.

Perhaps what currently happens is, without a strong enough message from social work education about radical practice being fundamental to good social work practice, students and new social workers are left without a robust framework for practice. *It is this vacuum that neoliberal ideas, assumptions and managerial practice can very easily fill.*

Conclusion

I hope, then, that the case is made in this book, that a radical approach to social work can be embraced by the most non-active of social workers, *if* they can develop a real empathy and understanding of oppression, of managerialism, of the moral heart of social work, of the importance of human connection, and of the effects of neoliberal hegemony. The importance of John Bradford's humble attitude: 'there but by the grace of God, go I' will hopefully be understood by readers as an essential element in the approach to the people with whom social workers work, as will the fundamental emotional engagement and relationship building required for that.

Summary of main points

➤ Radical social work has two strands and this book focuses on a form of social work practice that does not support the neoliberal hegemony, rather than on the activist strand.

➤ Neoliberalism is based on a free market economy and an attendant self-sufficiency discourse that can be experienced by service users as punitive and harsh.

➤ Lazy radical practice encourages social workers to see the structural and political influences on service users but does not attempt to rob them of agency.

➤ Social work values quite clearly align with lazy radical practice.

➤ Government influences social work in a neoliberal direction, and lazy radical practice is resistant to this. However, the task is significant!

2
Dependence, Independence and Values

This chapter will begin with an introduction to Zygmunt Bauman (1925–2017). Bauman was born in Poland, to Jewish parents, and escaped with his family to the USSR when Germany invaded Poland in 1939. He was perhaps most famous for his concept of 'Liquid Modernity' – the idea that the solid and dependable institutions of the 'modern' world have been replaced by uncertainty, changeability, anxiety and fear (Bauman, 2000a). He also wrote about the Holocaust and how such an atrocity was possible, with bureaucracy as a central concern (Bauman, 1989). This will be revisited in Chapter 3. For the moment, however, we will concentrate on Bauman's work which is directly associated with social work. In 2000, in a special essay, he wrote:

> The proper task of social work ought to be, we are told, getting rid of unemployed, handicapped, invalid and other indolent people who for one reason or another cannot eke out their own living and depend on social help and care for their survival: and this, evidently, is not happening. As social work, we are told, ought to be judged like any other human action by its cost-and-effects balance sheet, it does not, in its present form, make economic sense. It could only justify its continued existence if it made dependent people independent and made the lame people walk on their own two feet. The tacit, rarely spelled out assumption is that for not-independent people, such people as do not join in the game of selling and buying, there is no room in the society of players. 'Dependence' has become a dirty word: it refers to something decent people should be ashamed of (Bauman, 2000b, p. 5).

Bauman raises a fundamental tension here, between social work's ethos and purpose, and the current neoliberal political context. It is worth, at this point, looking at this issue in more detail, especially in terms of the unquestioned acceptance of the neoliberal underpinning assumption that independence is good and, therefore, dependence bad.

Individual responsibility, independence and the welfare state

In the introduction, the connection was made between Michael Gove's assertion that social workers were robbing people of agency by not making them 'stand on their own two feet' and the underpinning assumptions of neoliberalism. This absolutely key issue needs proper exploration because Mr Gove's speech seems to make so much *sense*. It is very easy to be persuaded by notions of dependence as a bad thing, or radical social work as being about making excuses for people – especially when these ideas are unfailingly supported by emotive stories of 'scroungers' in the media.

So, the welfare state came into being post World War 2, when the new 'social democracy' emerged (Crouch, 2011). This was a form of centre-left compromise, where governments would invest and regulate business to protect workers from fluctuations in the market, thus keeping, for example, unemployment low. The system of National Insurance was introduced as was the National Health Service, and, for the first time, unemployment did not mean potential destitution – people would be given enough money to survive. Poverty, of course, declined and has since been shown to decline in correlation with welfare spending (Brady, 2005). This Keynesian form of economics and its socialist character was criticised strongly by thinkers from the right, such as Friedrich von Hayek who felt that pursuing social justice through welfare mechanisms ran the risk of intruding on people's individual freedoms, and that a free market economy was best placed to ensure that freedom (Eagleton-Pierce, 2016).

Perhaps at this juncture we can see the disparity in different political orientations' fundamental philosophies. The key word for the left might be 'care' whilst the key word for the right might be 'freedom' (McCandless and Posavec, 2010). On a cynical note, it is interesting that Giroux (2014) describes the use of the concept of freedom as 'eviscerated' – how can people, as if larger structural issues did not exist, be absolutely responsible for their own fate? This does raise the question of how free people really are if they are in dreadful social circumstances. Classical liberals understood freedom as 'freedom from', that is negative freedom – free from external constraints (like the state). Reformist liberals (who saw a role for the state and understood people could not simply pull themselves out of grinding, absolute, Victorian poverty) came to understand freedom as 'positive' freedom, where the state can remove obstacles to real liberty (e.g., poverty) (Garner et al., 2009). Corporations, then, having negative freedom to accumulate as much capital as possible at any social cost, are the consequence of neoliberal doctrine involving a very limited role for the state, which does not include, or includes in a very minimal way, the protection of the rights of workers and unemployed people (Giroux, 2014).

In the 1980s, the attack on the welfare state had gathered significant momentum. Some conservative academics, journalists and think tank researchers retained the classical liberal emphasis on individual, negative freedom, but (and this is crucial) introduced a stronger moral dimension in relation to welfare, which appeared to resurrect the 'deserving' versus 'undeserving' ideas of the Victorian era (Eagleton-Pierce, 2016). Margaret Thatcher made much of this, and in fact was very explicit in her belief that people were simply to blame for their poor circumstances:

> Nowadays there really is no primary poverty left in this country.... In western countries we are left with the problems which aren't poverty. All right, there may be poverty because they don't know how to budget, don't know how to spend their earnings, but now you are left with really hard fundamental character-personality defect (*Catholic Herald*, 1978, n.p.).

The welfare state was beginning to be viewed as fostering the dreaded *dependence culture* and stereotypes were utilised to very significant influence to perpetuate this idea. For example, this 'culture of dependency' was reported as being an intergenerational malaise where people simply did not want to work, enjoyed being scroungers and needed to be forced into employment. One example of this was given by Tony Blair in 1997 who reported that 'Behind the statistics lie households where three generations have never had a job' (Blair, 1997, in MacDonald, 2015). When this claim, and others, were investigated, there was no evidence that this was true (MacDonald, 2015). Although this seems a dreadful example of misinformation, the image took hold firmly in the mind of the public. The utility of stereotypes and caricatures could also be seen on the other side of the Atlantic, when President Clinton passed the 'workfare' (as opposed to welfare) laws to free people from said culture of dependency (Wacquant, 2009). As Wacquant says, however, this reform of public aid or welfare did:

> Nothing of the sort. First, it was not a reform but a counterrevolutionary measure, since it essentially abolished the right to assistance for the country's most destitute children, which had required a half-century of struggles to fully establish (ibid., p. 78).

To gain support for such significant changes, a sharp distinction was made between 'worthy' or deserving people and 'unworthy' or undeserving, very much akin to the picture in the UK, although the racialised nature of the division was much more acute in the USA. Wacquant considers four stereotypes including:

> The 'welfare queen', a wily and fecund black matriarch who shirks employment, cheats the public aid bureaucracy, and spends her assistance check [sic] high on drugs and liquor, leaving her many children in appalling neglect (ibid., p. 84).

The parallels between the 'welfare queen' and Vicky Pollard, a character invented by Matt Lucas, a British comedian, are easily seen. Although just a 'bit of fun' the character (who tries to swap one of her children for a Westlife CD) smokes, drinks, is promiscuous and neglectful, *and* was believed to be an 'accurate representation of Britain's white working class' by a YouGov poll in 2006! (Jones, 2011, p. 127). Wacquant's other stereotypical characters include an African-American teenage mother; a 'baby having babies', a black, unemployed, 'deadbeat' dad fathering lots of children but abandoning the mothers to the hardworking tax-payer, and an older immigrant from the third world who manipulates welfare into providing a no-cost, comfortable retirement. All of these images would also be perfectly at home in the pages of the UK's right wing tabloid media.

Levitas (2005, p. 14) states that around the time of Tony Blair's statement, an increasingly vociferous 'moral underclass discourse' (MUD) or 'moralising self-sufficiency discourse' (Marston, 2013) from Chapter 1, could be detected in the politics of New Labour and the media. Levitas makes the connection between this discourse and prevailing neoliberal market economics and with the neoconservative strengthening of the law and order arm of the state. She terms this the 'dual character of the new right' and it seems that both aspects fitted well together in pursuit of moral order. Levitas credits this with the shift from welfare as beneficent and necessary, to an undesirable burden on tax-payers, fostering a dependency culture and robbing people of any incentive to work. In turn, Levitas suggests that this fed into the growing idea of an 'underclass'.

So, we can see very clearly the depiction of the 'underclass' (Murray, 1990) with its moral failings, propped up, and even encouraged, by an overly generous welfare state. And all whilst hard-working, honest and 'good' people are just managing and paying taxes which go to fund the lazy lifestyles of the 'scroungers'.

At this point, it is easy to see how cuts to welfare, austerity policies, the introduction of sanctions for claimants, the reduction of state intervention, the privatisation of many public services and the underpinning theme of individual independence and responsibility that ties all of these concepts together, garnered support. Herein is the tension described by

Bauman in the opening quote. How can social work fit into that neoliberal world? Unless we are able to *make* people more independent, to buy into the idea that character flaws are at the bottom of social problems – and therefore we must correct behaviour and to punish the undeserving 'underclass' – then we are at odds with the key ideas of neoliberalism. And if we were to do those things which would support the neoliberal hegemony, we would then *not* be doing social work, because at its core lies social justice. A dilemma!

Neoliberal social justice

There is another question to be raised – why is it that neoliberalism, which undoubtedly sees itself as socially just, does not fit with social work values? If we are to claim that social work cannot be compatible with neoliberalism because of social work's core commitment to social justice, and neoliberals would say 'but our way *is* socially just' then we need to analyse this even further.

First of all, the point was made in Chapter 1 that social work values are based on a radical form of social justice which clearly aligns with a progressive political position where redistribution of wealth (usually via progressive tax policies and support for welfare) is seen as a necessity. Knowing that these measures are an attempt to *reduce* inequality and knowing that increasing inequality is a natural result of neoliberalism working as it should, then it is obvious that there is clear contradiction between neoliberalism and social work's radical ideal of social justice. As was stated in Chapter 1, BASW's *Code of Ethics* (BASW, 2014b) states that we should promote the redistribution of resources. Added to that, the International Federation of Social Workers (IFSW) states that 'social work engages people and structures to address life challenges and enhance wellbeing' (IFSW, 2014, n.p.). Students must also meet certain criteria and demonstrate certain values to qualify in social work by evidencing that they can 'promote social justice, equality and inclusion' and 'be able to use practice to challenge and address the impact of discrimination, disadvantage and oppression' (HCPC, 2017) or 'respond to ... structural inequality' (Scottish Government, 2003, p. 43). Clearly, terms like 'equality', 'structural inequality' and 'the impact of ... disadvantage' are more evidence that there is a clear requirement for social work to embrace a radical form of social justice. These terms and phrases point to an understanding of social justice that goes far beyond a reformist, 'equality of opportunity in a benign society' understanding, to one that engages with structural issues. It is also clear, therefore, that to align with that understanding, one needs a progressive political orientation, although explicitly *requiring* this appears to be unpalatable for many social work educators. Funge (2011), for example, found that social work educators balked at going as far as 'ensuring' an explicit social justice alignment and felt that exposure to different ideas should suffice. Hansford et al. (2017, p. 200), although writing from a USA perspective, state:

> There are certain methods of teaching social justice principles *that may require the abandonment of political neutrality on the part of the social work educator, because the promotion of social justice often allies with progressive, or even liberal, socio-political ideologies* [emphasis added].

Although the case for abandoning political neutrality and explicitly promoting progressive economic ideas seems to be fairly persuasive in terms of social work values and radical social justice, it remains a controversial area. This book, however, provides a framework and basis for radical practice that is explicit in its anti-neoliberal approach as social work without that orientation, is not really social work.

It is useful now, then, to look at what kind of social justice *is* promoted by neoliberal thinking, as it can be assumed that there would be no admittance to being socially *unjust*! Iain Duncan-Smith, a previous leader of the Conservative Party, for example, set up the Centre for Social Justice (CSJ) in 2004. He states:

> I frequently encountered levels of social breakdown which appalled me. In one of the world's largest economies, too many people lived in dysfunctional homes, trapped on benefits. Too many children were leaving school with no qualifications or skills to enable them to work and prosper. Too many communities were blighted by alcohol and drug addiction, debt and criminality, many of them with stunningly low levels of life expectancy (Duncan-Smith, 2017).

Duncan-Smith also states that the CSJ is 'committed to tackling poverty's root causes and recommending life changing solutions'. So far then, we can see that there is, indeed, an assertion from the right that they, too, are concerned with social justice. The question remains, however, is it a redistributive form of social justice which would align with social work values? Here is another illustration:

> The CSJ has pioneered the concept of work as the most effective route out of poverty. In the early part of the century it was not uncommon for children to grow up in households where no one had worked for generations. CSJ policy recommendations have led to a transformation in the way Government approaches poverty, refocusing efforts to help people into work through

the Work Programme, the Universal Credit and support to ensure work always pays more than living a life on welfare and fewer children living in workless households.

It would seem that Mr Duncan-Smith is not talking about redistribution – the mantra is that work should always pay more, and who would disagree with that? However, benefits cuts and austerity whereby the poor have become even poorer (*Guardian*, 2013) means that making work pay more is not hard to achieve. The corollary of that is that work is no longer the route out of poverty. Neoliberal deregulation of business means that the 'working poor' are growing and, in fact, the JRF reported that:

> One in every eight workers in the UK – 3.8 million people – is now living in poverty. A total of 7.4 million people, including 2.6 million children, are in poverty despite being in a working family. This means that a record high of 55% of people in poverty are in working households (JRF, 2016).

Mr Duncan-Smith's claims that 'in the early part of this century it was not uncommon for children to grow up in households where no one had worked for generations' was an oft repeated mantra as described earlier and in 2009 he claimed 'on some deprived estates ... often three generations of the same family have never worked' (Duncan-Smith, 2009, in MacDonald, 2015, n.p.). This was another claim investigated by MacDonald and found to have no evidence upon which it could be based. When challenged, he said it was based on his 'personal observations' (ibid.). Clearly then, as an example of the right's commitment to social justice the CSJ does not align easily with social work values. Once again, understanding is informed by individual behavioural and familial explanations for poverty – structural barriers are ignored and would probably be described by Mr Gove as 'excuses', even in the face of stark figures about people who work hard and yet remain poor. There is also no consideration or mention of redistribution of resources as a way to help more people out of poverty.

So, the first point about the form of social justice promoted by social work values was made in Chapter 1. Codes of ethics and standards for students state quite clearly that a radical form of social justice is intended (Doel, 2012), that is, there is an emphasis on redistribution of resources and tackling structural issues. This, of course, is congruent with a progressive, left wing political orientation with its ethical position of economic redistribution, usually via progressive taxation (paying more if you earn more and having a more generous allowance for people on benefits) and government regulation of business so that people in more poorly paid jobs are paid more generously. It is not congruent with an individual, behavioural analysis of poverty which underpins the right's, including neoliberals', view on social justice. This might be enough on its own to align social work with anti-neoliberal, pro-progressive socio-political thinking, but there are also further compelling reasons.

Further progressive thinking and social work value alignment

Turning, once again, to Bauman:

> When God asked Cain where Abel was, Cain replied, angrily, with another question: 'Am I my brother's keeper?' The greatest ethical philosopher of our century, Emmanuel Levinas, commented: from that angry Cain's question all immorality began. Of course I am my brother's keeper; and I am and remain a moral person as long as I do not ask for a special reason to be one. Whether I admit it or not, I am my brother's keeper because my brother's wellbeing depends on what I do or refrain from doing. And I am a moral person because I recognize that dependence and accept the responsibility that follows. The moment I question that dependence and demand – like Cain did – to be given reasons why I should care, I renounce my responsibility and am no more a moral self. My brother's dependence is what makes me an ethical being. Dependence and ethics stand together and together they fall (Bauman, 2000b, p. 5).

In other words, we should care for each other. To depend on one another is as it should be. Dependency is not bad, it is at the core of morality and is 'the hard core of Judeo-Christian teachings which gestated and weaned our common understanding of humanity and civilised being' (ibid.). Bauman goes on to say that the welfare state came into being for many reasons, but the glue that held things together was the need to keep the 'reserve army' of both soldiers and workers in a healthy and fit state so they could be called on when required. This was in the interests of capitalism and security, but does not apply today. There is unlikely to be mass conscription again, unemployed people are unlikely to be recalled to work places, when businesses are rewarded for slimming down their workforce (and hence their costs) and technology is making this increasingly possible. Instead, people are in very insecure, casualised forms of employment where businesses can make the most from their employees without the job-security commitment that permanent employment requires. And so, beyond that, the 'reserve army' have been redefined as a useless 'underclass' without whom we would all be better off. Bauman concludes this line of thinking by asserting that supporting the welfare state, therefore, makes no economic sense whatsoever. And yet, *this* is where social work does much of its work. Bauman states that we simply do not hear about:

> those hundreds or thousands of human beings whom caring social workers have drawn back from the brink of ultimate despair or collapse; or of those millions for whom welfare provisions made all the difference between wretched poverty and decent life; or of those tens of millions whom the awareness that help will come if needed allowed to face the risks of life with courage and determination without which successful, let alone dignified, life is unthinkable (ibid.).

Instead, we hear about the horrendous caricatures, the 'welfare queens' and the people who live on estates like the one where Baby P had his home. Bauman also states that solidarity with the poor is hard to find in this climate. Although we may be insecure and anxious in a precarious, market driven 'game', the plight of the poor is different – they are secure and do not have worries like us, such as keeping up our material status position. Thus, it is far easier to feel resentful, especially when our hard-earned money is what keeps the unemployed in reasonable circumstances. Might it be better to see them suffer a little more? This is supported by surveys showing hardening attitudes to the poor and especially the unemployed (JRF, 2014; British Social Attitudes, 2017) and, anecdotally, by comments made by some students in class: 'why should we pay for lazy people who do not want to work?' And so the welfare state is unsupported from both sides: the rich and powerful view it as an economic liability with no purpose, whilst the working poor feel little empathy or solidarity with those who depend upon it. How can we defend it? Should we? Defending it on ethical grounds alone sounds flimsy and yet, Bauman argues, it should be enough:

> The human quality of a society ought to be measured by the quality of life of its weakest members. And since the essence of all morality is the responsibility which people take for the humanity of the others, this is also the measure of a society's ethical standard. This is, I propose, the only measure a welfare state can afford, but also the only one it needs (2000b, p. 9).

In terms of social work, Bauman states that remembering this ethical foundation is not without barriers: external in that it is absolutely not aligned to current neoliberal discourse; and internal to social work, such as over bureaucratisation and the emphasis on procedures and rule following. These elements of neoliberal social work, according to Bauman, distance social work from its original 'ethical impulse' as incapsulated in the above quote: taking 'responsibility for the humanity of others'. These barriers to practice will also be examined in later chapters.

Bringing this to some kind of resolution, then, it is not just that the form of social justice enshrined in codes of ethics fits with radical, progressive social work, but so does social work's very roots and enshrinement in its original ethical impulse – to take responsibility for fellow human beings and to help and care.

Respect and social democracy

As well as alignment with redistributive social justice values and the roots and original ethical impulse of social work to take responsibility and care for others, there is a third aspect to an anti-neoliberal stance which aligns very well with radical social work – its central ethical principle of 'respect for persons' – one of Immanuel Kant's categorical imperatives – adopted as core to social work and appearing in social work documents on values and ethics ever since (Banks, 2012). The idea that people are of inherent equal worth and deserving of unfailing respect also lies at the heart of social democracy. This is explored very cogently by Hyslop (2016) who states that social work operates in the space between the respectable and the disenfranchised, sometimes dangerous 'other' and that:

> Practice within this intermediate space combined recognition of the significance of social inequality in determining individual outcomes with an unswerving faith in the capacity for personal redemption.…This aspirational coupling of inherent human worth with unfailing respect for individuals regardless of their shortcomings is consistent with social idealist metaphysics …, which entails 'a concern for others that does not depend on whether they deserve it' (Ellis, 2012, p. 19)' (Hyslop, 2016, p. 23).

The question which then arises is whether 'the value-based structure of social work knowledge – the humanistic storying and re-storying of clients' lives through a process of engagement and dialogue – has been eclipsed by the imposition of neoliberal design, delivery and measurement mechanisms' (ibid.)? To answer this question, Hyslop undertook a study with social workers asking what kinds of knowledge they used in social work interactions and whether the knowledge was related to the socio-political location of social work. He found that social workers still paid deep attention to the social experiences of the 'other', premised upon a central value of respect for persons. This seems to have withstood the powerful neoliberal incursion into practice, and is firmly grounded in 'a discourse of social equality embedded in inclusive social-democratic beliefs' as well as a 'stubborn commitment to the ideal of shared humanity' (ibid., p. 33). It is a form of knowledge which is in direct opposition to neoliberal discourse, and, according to Hyslop, it is the responsibility of social work educators, among others, to reveal and make an explicit claim to this knowledge. Hopefully, this book will help readers do just that.

Hyslop's study, albeit with some attention to knowledge 'in context' (p. 28), has its emphasis on the interpersonal level of practice and it is clear how social democratic thinking informs respect within that. However, when it comes to political knowledge, the findings appear to be less clear, although understanding the grimness of poverty on a human level is obvious. It is when more critical thinking is required that there appears to be a gap. For example, one respondent illustrated how 'the class based nature of child and family work practice remains an uncomfortable reality' (ibid., p. 29) for several of the social workers. She felt that she would like to say her service users came from all classes, but that that was not true. They were mainly poor. The social worker was reluctant to foster class stereotypes, but a deeper knowledge of the *effects* of poverty and inequality, in terms of mental health, anxiety, strain on families, the impetus to turn to substance misuse, despair about the future and so on, would lead to an outrageous proclamation of this injustice, rather than a reluctance. A reluctance could be interpreted as knowing how it might be construed as class stereotyping – the dreadful underclass are just like that – without a real confidence in answering that accusation. Hence a tendency to avoid the debate? Although this is speculation, there is still an imperative for social workers to really be able to face those class stereotypes head on with understanding and confidence.

What happened?

So, there are at least three compelling reasons for social work practice to be characterised by an anti-neoliberal, radical orientation: social work subscribes to a radical form of social justice; the original ethical impulse of social work was to care for others; and social work's central, unifying principle of respect for persons and its connection to social democracy.

How then have we come to the position where government, some agencies, some students and social workers and many of the public believe social work should not 'look' like that, but should be about telling people to 'pull their socks up, or else'?

Thinking about child protection as an illustration of developing and changing narratives, a useful starting point might be the time in history when child welfare first became an issue. According to Parton (2014), this happened in the second half of the 19th century when middle class women used increased leisure time to do charitable work, and as a result drew attention to the welfare of children and to delinquency. The hard winters and famines of the 1850s and 1860s sparked a significant growth in charitable endeavour as the existing provision enshrined in the Poor Law was insufficient. The Charity Organisation Society (COS) was set up to coordinate this work and to investigate whether recipients were 'morally deserving' (Parton, 2014, p. 15). Horner (2012) notes that the distinct approach of the COS was, in effect, casework and the individual targeting of families to work on moral character building. As Horner suggests, 'by adopting this approach, the COS set itself against other bodies which advanced a more structural perspective' (Horner, 2012, p. 24).

Stop and think box 1

Think about the connections between the inception of social work in the emergence of the COS's casework approach and Marston's (2013) 'moralising self-sufficiency discourse' discussed in Chapter 1. Think about the similarities and differences. How are ideas of social change through building moral character in the poor promoted today? In what way was that approach flawed in the 1800s and do these flaws still exist in the moralising self-sufficiency discourse of today?

Horner also notes that in the late 1800s attention was drawn to older adults who were destitute. People at the time agreed that poverty was at the root of the problems afflicting those people: poverty leading to homelessness, drunkenness, child abuse and neglect, and domestic abuse, for example. The difference in opinion, however, was stark in relation to how poverty should be tackled. As already mentioned the COS believed in building moral character in the poor, including self-reliance, self-help groups and thrift. They were against any monetary assistance from the state, believing that such help would remove incentives to work.

Stop and think box 2

Does the above sound familiar? Have you heard, or do you think, that benefit payments dis-incentivise people from working? If not, do you have arguments against that view? If you don't, read on – you will!

On the other side of the debate, the Fabian Society felt very strongly that state intervention was required in relation to welfare, benefit, pensions, housing, health and employment rights. This led to a push for the universal welfare and health provisions that became the essence of the welfare state post World War 2 (Horner, 2012).

Barnard (2008, p. 10) describes this time in the history of social work as the 'morality period' for obvious reasons. The push from the Fabians and others, however, moved concerns from the morality of service users to structural concerns of housing, health and welfare, resulting in the Beveridge report in 1942 that declared a 'War on Want' (ibid.). Barnard states that a class of welfare professionals developed what we would now recognise as traditional social work. Horner (2012), however, draws attention to an interesting, perhaps, unintentional consequence of these developments. The Fabians believed that the need for social work would disappear given the improved circumstances and the reduction in poverty, although conceded that there might be a need for a residual social work service to deal with the lazy and idle, thus promoting the control function of modern social work: an enforcing role, working with those who did not want intervention.

Garrett (2010, p. 340) describes the following period politically as one of 'embedded liberalism', as described briefly in Chapter 1. He describes this as a system of regulation and restraint by governments to curb the excesses of market driven developments and, ultimately, to protect workers' rights, standards of housing and welfare generally. Some areas of life were also regarded as not suitable for market competition, such as health, social care and social work. It can be seen here, then, that the gains won by the introduction of health and welfare provision were protected across political party lines and that a consensus prevailed that this was the right thing to do. Or, perhaps, those who did not agree realised that the population would stand for nothing less, having been promised a brighter future after the total commitment required during the wars (Turbett, 2014).

During the period of political embedded liberalism, however, social work's path was not straightforward. In the 1950s and 1960s, there were advances in science and psychiatry that were very influential in social work. Diagnosing people's problems by looking for signs of maladaptive behaviour, for example, and for underlying explanations within an individual's psyche, prevailed (Fenton, 2016). Bowlby's famous maternal deprivation theory appeared at this time, for example (Bowlby, 1969). So, social workers were in the business of 'diagnosing' and 'treating' and, as Bailey and Brake (1975, p. 6) note: 'the poor and the deviants had progressed from moral inferiority to pathology'. Casework remained as the method of choice which, of course, fitted very well the individualisation of problems and attempts at 'treatment' (see Chapter 7 for some contemporary echoes of this).

Against this backdrop, radical social work emerged. Radical social work is described as 'a broad church' (Barnard, 2008, p. 11) which saw personal problems as resulting from the structural inequalities in society, and which based its approach upon several ideologies including Marxism, feminism and labelling theory. Barnard also notes that the influence of humanism and existentialism became stronger during this period. Carl Rogers (1966), a humanist, suggested his three core conditions for successful relationships between social worker and service user, namely unconditional positive regard, workers should be perceived as genuine and congruent and should have empathy for service users. UK radicals converged in a group called the *Case Con Collective,* comprised of academics and social workers who were disillusioned with their agencies and social work practice methods which they viewed as inadequate for helping with the poverty they saw in their day to day work (Turbett, 2014). The knowledge base for social work was, at the time, becoming heavily influenced by sociology, which augmented the very individual-pathology approaches described above, and asked students of social work to think critically about capitalist societies and the sociological roots of service users' problems (ibid.).

This emerging radical practice was, of course, congruent with the socio-political context of the time – Garrett's 'embedded liberalism' or social democracy. This context was supported by Keynesian economic policy, which allowed for government intervention when the country was performing poorly, to protect jobs or prevent cuts in wages, for example. The government did this by borrowing money, to be repaid when the country recovered and performance improved (Crouch, 2011). However, and this is an absolutely key point, when the economic crisis, caused by rising oil prices, took effect, it uncovered a weakness at the heart of Keynesian economics, namely that there were no agreements between trade unions and employers that, at times of difficulty, the unions would not make demands that would exacerbate inflation (ibid.). The response to this was, not to make the necessary adjustments to Keynesian economics, but to completely abandon it in favour of neoliberalism. The importance of economics will be explored further in Chapter 5, but it is important to understand this particular economic turn, to be able to contextualise the concomitant developments in social work.

Garrett (2010, p. 343) states that at this point, the eradication of embedded liberalism began, and attempts were made to replace it with a new 'common sense' or hegemony. Embedded liberalism, or social democracy, was of course congruent with a radical form of social work practice where difficult social and economic factors were presumed to contribute to people's problems, and therefore the government should legitimately intervene to protect people from the harsh consequences of a completely free market economy. A radical form of social work was operational within a 'mixed economy' of practice where individual level casework was still the most common modus operandi, but where practice *included* significant attention to service users' context, especially in relation to poor material circumstances. The new 'common sense' or hegemony, however, was important to 'ensure that people begin to *think* and *act* in a manner which is conducive to neoliberalism ... even, perhaps, to change the soul' (ibid.).

Remember, 'hegemony' is a Gramscian term that describes how the government elicits agreement to operate in the way it wants to. The government does this by rallying the key players in civic life to agree and perpetuate the hegemonic discourse – in this case free market economic ideology and a self-sufficient, independent individual narrative. As a player in civic life, the media is heavily influential in this regard, as described in Chapter 1, and, as another player in civic life, social work increasingly reflects that agenda. 'Changing the soul' in relation to society, essentially means changing the hegemony. Neoliberalism has done this with significant success, demonstrated by the change in people's attitudes and by the consequent changing character of social work agencies.

PRACTICE EXAMPLE 1

The Forsyth family

You are a social worker in a children and families team and have been allocated the Forsyth family. This is a case of rumbling neglect, things have been bad but never quite bad enough to remove the children. You read the file and identify the key features as follows:

➢ The family are poor and exist on benefits.

➢ They have at times faced benefit sanctions for non-attendance at appointments, and have had to rely on foodbanks.

➢ The parents seem to have enough money for alcohol and cigarettes.

➢ The house is dirty and cold.

➢ The children, aged 6 and 8, are dirty and, sometimes, hungry and the school has expressed concerns.

➢ Despite all of the above, the children have a real bond with their parents.

Think about your starting point and underlying value position with this family. Do you:

1. Tackle the structural issues as a priority: contact the benefits office and maximise income; contact the housing department to see if there is any help to be had/repairs to be done; help materially with furniture, bedding or whatever else you can source from charity or social work budgets?
   OR do you

2. Tackle the behaviour that is undoubtedly contributing to this situation: budget advice about *not* spending on alcohol and cigarettes; routines for the children; spending wisely on food, heating etc. referral to a parenting-skills class to improve the parents' care-taking of the children?
   OR do you

3. Do a bit of both?

Can you see the value/ethical/social justice underpinning of both of these approaches? One is clearly radical and one is neoliberal/individual/behavioural. In reality, you would probably do a bit of both, but it's quite helpful at this stage to think about your practice and the first principles upon which it's based.

Conclusion

To return to the starting point of this chapter, and Bauman's thinking on dependency, it can be seen that if discourses and understandings are only framed in economic definitions of 'value' or 'worth', then the welfare state and social work make no sense. We would be better without them. The only form of social work that would be acceptable in that context is one where service users are told to shape up, to be self-sufficient, to no longer require help or else be punished quite harshly. This chapter, in contrast, makes the case for a moral and social justice framing of problems, underpinned by the fundamental principle that we should care for each other. It is clear that social work values align with radical practice really well, but, again, this framework is only acceptable if there is agreement that values and ethics are important. In social work, these things *are* important, so notions of caring about each other, redistributing wealth in order that people have a reasonable standard of living, understanding that harsh material circumstances can lead to social problems so must be legitimate targets for social work efforts, and that we all depend on each other at times, are absolutely fundamental.

Summary of main points

➤ The current neoliberal context is anathema to any notion of dependency (on the state).

➤ Media stereotypes support this view – the dreaded 'dependency culture'.

➤ Welfare is under attack and ideas of the 'underclass' have a marked purchase.

➤ A neoliberal form of social justice does not align with social work values.

➤ The impulse to care for others makes no sense in economic terms, only in ethical terms.

3
Bureaucracy, Regulation and Professionalism

As Bauman (2000b, p. 9) states: 'When we obscure the essential human and moral aspects of care behind even more rules and regulations we make the daily practice of social work even more distant from its original ethical impulse'.

This chapter will explore the quote above and will deconstruct the seemingly intractable problem of reliance on bureaucracy, managerialism and procedure that permeates contemporary social work, *even* in the face of significant criticism of its consequences. For example, Munro (2011, p. 6), in point 1. of the *Executive summary of the review of Child protection*, states:

> This final report sets out proposals for reform which, taken together, are intended to create the conditions that enable professionals to make the best judgments about the help to give to children, young people and families. This involves moving from a system that has become over-bureaucratised and focused on compliance to one that values and develops professional expertise.

This chapter begins with an exploration of what the problem actually is with bureaucracy and procedure. Why is it anathema to lazy radical practice? Is it really a problem? Does it not keep social workers safe from blame because they can demonstrate they have done what they are meant to do? Social workers do not want to be sacked when things go wrong after all. The chapter will then look at important examples of the consequences of this type of approach and will draw on learning from some important thinkers whose work can be applied to this problem in social work. Finally, the spotlight will focus on contemporary social work, what might be happening and *why* it is so difficult to change.

What is the problem?

One of the key recommendations from the Munro review of child protection is that:

> Practitioners and their managers told the review that statutory guidance, targets and local rules have become so extensive that they limit their ability to stay child centred. The demands of bureaucracy have reduced their capacity to work directly with children, young people and families. Services have become so standardised that they do not provide the required range of responses to the variety of need that is presented. This review recommends a radical reduction in the amount of central prescription to help professionals move from a compliance culture to a learning culture, where they have more freedom to use their expertise in assessing need and providing the right help (Munro, 2011, p. 6).

Munro suggests that bureaucracy inhibits the ability to stay child-centred, to work directly with families and to be responsive to needs. The reason for this could be that form filling and other bureaucratic imperatives take up too much time, therefore not allowing relationship-building or time for direct work. Also, standardised services lead to a one-size-fits-all, codified response that might well be not what the family needs. For example, Featherstone, Broadhurst and Holt (2012) make the point that a family might be in more need of the price of a loaf of bread or help with transport than a dreaded 'parenting skills class'. And yet, student social workers are enthusiastic in their drive to refer on to parenting, anger management or other, standardised and prescribed services. Fazzi (2016) also found that, in Italy, social work students became less imaginative and more standardised in their responses after social work education. They had learned the codified and standard social work 'answers' to problems.

In the body of the Munro report, it can be seen that the problem is as understood above, but is also broader. For example:

> Procedures, however, have a number of weaknesses. The strength mentioned above that newcomers can quickly learn to follow procedures even when they do not understand them is also a weakness. It can lead to people just following procedures and not seeking to understand them or trying to become more effective in their complex tasks (Munro, 2011, p. 39).

So, indeed, time restraints are important, but so is the notion that social workers give primacy to rule-following. Just following rules and procedures without attempting to understand those rules and procedures leads to an unthinking practice that can be ethically hollow and knowledge free. If this is a possibility, then it is vitally important to understand *why* it is a bad, in fact dangerous, way to practise.

This is a good time to introduce Hannah Arendt. Arendt (1906–1975) was born into a German-Jewish family but was forced to leave Germany in 1933. She was a philosopher and probably most famous for the subtitle of her book *Eichmann in Jerusalem*, 'the banality of evil' (Arendt, 1965). This book covered the trial of the eponymous Eichmann, and sparked a very significant debate about Arendt's central thesis which was that evil was not the monstrous conception previously assumed, but was in fact ordinary and banal, as she said, was Eichmann himself. The thinking that Arendt did around the banality of evil, and especially about unthinking behaviour, is the most valuable of her ideas for this section of the book. In Amos Elon's introduction to the book, he states that 'evil comes from a failure to think…that is the banality of evil' (Arendt, 1965, p. xiv).

Preston-Shoot (2011, p. 187) suggests that 'technical rationality, expressed through expert knowledge, regulations and established bureaucratic proce-dures, can promote a sense of legitimacy and routine without the need to engage with social or ethical concerns'. He evokes Arendt's writing to explain:

> Arendt's phrase (1963), banality of evil, spotlights not monstrous actions but ordinary people's conduct derived from conformity interacting with a dulling of conscience. It is rooted in an absence of independent critical thought and in a bureaucratic compact which discourages reflection and dialogue about organ-isational processes and the content of agency rules. She does not attribute evil motives but rather seeks to make sense of breakdowns in personal judgement, to understand moral disintegration and to explore the conclusions reached by those who determine that it is better to act wrongfully than to suffer the conse-quences of behaving morally (Preston-Shoot, 2011, p. 186).

This is a cogent summation of a central thesis of Arendt's and is expanded upon in Chapter 5 when the necessity of critical thinking is discussed. However, to stick with rule following at the moment, Arendt's fascinat-ing analysis of Eichmann's trial reveals a person, of high standing in the Nazi party and who orchestrated the killing of immense numbers of people, who appeared to simply want to follow rules. He was somewhat seduced by hierarchy and being able to consort with people he viewed as important, but running through all of his actions was the desire to stick by the rules and to not really think about them or their ethical basis. So, for example, Arendt states that Eichmann demonstrated his 'utter igno-rance of everything that was not directly, technically and bureaucratically connected with his job' (ibid., p. 54). She also said that it was clear to everyone that he 'was not a "monster" but it was difficult indeed not to suspect he was a clown' (ibid.). Arendt paints a picture of man who seems to be quite stupid, unthinking, lacking in knowledge and finding refuge, security and recognition for becoming almost an 'expert' at the rule-following, bureaucratic imperatives of his (monstrous) job.

It might seem at this point that an exaggerated link is being made between Eichmann's story and poor practice in social work, but there *are* links and, although unlikely to cause death, unthinking, rule-bound and technical social work practice can, indeed, cause untold misery for people. Preston-Shoot (2011) draws on Arendt's thinking and applies it to social work directly, suggesting that social workers should be asked two questions: what is your personal responsibility in this situation and why did you support the organisation? To reply along the lines of 'that's just how we do things around here' would be entirely unacceptable, and could in another context, such as Nazi Germany, lead to mass killing. Arendt insists on a critical engagement with one's actions or practice rather than a blind rule or procedure following. Preston-Shoot (2011, p. 185) points out that the ethical foundations of public administration are *fragile* and states: 'values of procedural correctness contribute to myopia regarding the context in which they are applied and the human consequences for staff and service users of administrative action'. He also states that 'hierarchy is exaggerated, whereby staff defer to their supervisors and choose those standards most likely to be used by their managers evaluating them, meaning that thinking is overshadowed' (ibid.). Both of these theories absolutely resonate with Eichmann's behaviour as instrumental in 'the final solution' (Arendt, 1965, p. 83).

Stop and think box 3

Neil Thompson, writing in *Professional Social Work* (2016, p. 26), notes that in his experience of being an expert witness, he has often heard social workers state: '"That's the way we do it in our team" as if they are just passive victims of the culture in which they work'.

Think about your own practise. Take a standardised assessment form that you use, regardless of which setting you practise in, and have a look at the questions you ask or the topics about which you need to obtain information. Do you really understand why the form requires answers to those questions? Do you know in terms of theory and knowledge? Legislation and policy? Values? See if you really can answer that question.

I worked with someone who was asked at a tribunal why a man convicted of sexual offences had been asked by his supervisor, as part of his court order, not to associate with others outside of the probation group he attended. The worker replied, 'that's just what we do'. It is hoped that you find that shocking! Turn a similar spotlight on your own practice, then. Do you always know why? You always should.

Another important idea from Arendt is that of 'cog-theory' (Arendt, 1964, p. 29). Cog-theory can be recognised in all bureaucracies and civil services and is characterised by the notion that very few people are irreplaceable – most being 'cogs' in a much bigger machine. The idea that, 'if I didn't do it, somebody else would' is central to cog-theory. Clearly, cog-theory could be applied to a techno-rational social work agency where service users are assessed and responded to using standardised assessments and codified responses, and 'referred on'. In such an environment, where social workers have very little autonomy to respond in the way they might want, one social worker might be easily replaced by another. Arendt contradicts this, however, by pointing out that it is a *person, a human*, who stands trial in a court, and this personhood, with its moral obligations, is never lost. She goes on to recognise, however, that the shifting of responsibility onto the system is a characteristic and matter of daily practice within every bureaucracy, because a bureaucracy is the rule of office rather than the rule of people:

> Bureaucracy unhappily is the rule of nobody and for this very reason perhaps the least human and most cruel form of rulership. But in the courtroom, these definitions are of no avail. For to the answer 'Not I, but the system did it in which I was a cog', the court immediately raises the next question: 'And why, if you please, did you become a cog or continue to be a cog under such circumstances?' (ibid., p. 31).

Again, in social work terms, if the bureaucratic system within which a social worker is a cog, is value-poor, punitive and authoritarian, then the social worker *must* question why they continue to be *that kind of cog*. They are obliged as a social work professional and as a human being with morals and values, to decide to be a different sort of cog and to argue with those in the bureaucracy who have the power to define cog duties.

At this point, it is helpful to reintroduce Bauman's work on the Holocaust and the part bureaucracy played within that. Bauman uses Arendt's concept of 'animal pity' – felt when one human witnesses the distress and anguish of another. In some ways, this is at the heart of our perplexity about how something like the Holocaust could have happened. How could people have witnessed such horrendous and unhuman acts and still have gone along with it? Not all were afraid for their lives. As Arendt has pointed out, some were simply following new rules. Bauman talks about the 'social production of moral indifference' (Bauman, 1989, p. 18) and suggests that it requires three conditions: that actions are authorised (by orders, commands or procedures), routinised (role expectations and culture) and that victims are dehumanised (the 'underclass' and 'othering' – the poor are just not like us, for example). Dehumanisation of people is a theme throughout this book (see Chapter 4, for example), but this section is looking at the first two conditions in particular. In relation to these two conditions, Bauman states:

> The demand to obey commands of the superiors to the exclusion of all other stimuli for action, to put the devotion to the welfare of the organisation ... above all other devotions and commitments. Among these other, 'external' influences, interfering with the spirit of dedication and hence marked for suppression and extinction, personal views and preferences are the most prominent (ibid., p. 21).

The supplanting of devotion or commitment to social work values, principles and knowledge by loyalty to agency ways of doing things is significant in terms of authorising the agency-led actions. Devotion or commitment to solidarity with, and advocacy for, service users has a similar fate; it is supplanted by unquestioning loyalty to the agency and line manager which fosters positive feedback, appreciation and respect (and, perhaps, promotion) from the agency. Arguing on behalf of service users, and becoming, perhaps, unpopular and branded as 'idealistic', 'soft', 'naive' or simply 'problematic' is not easy. A current example of this was a report on the BBC News that a social worker, under instructions from her manager, had changed the content of a report and then had lied about it in court (BBC, 2015). A real example of loyalty to the agency, supplanting all external commitments, dedications and even, perhaps, the social worker's personal view. Bauman states that this can become the duty of the civil servant; to carry out instructions in a routinised way and to overcome any moral difficulty by recourse to the definition of the 'task' as simply that – carrying out instructions. Any moral or ethical misgivings which might result can be reconciled by giving the responsibility completely over to the instruction-giver. The idea that internal personal feelings of discomfort about the required task are suppressed in order to comply, is an important theme which will be explored further in Practice example 2.

Bauman (2000b, p. 24) then goes on to consider something even 'more sinister' than the mechanisms used to perpetuate 'moral indifference': 'the social production of moral *invisibility*'. So far, we have considered how a person might overcome 'animal pity' which at least recognises there may be unsettled feelings of ethical or moral questioning – something to be overcome, in any case. However, what if there is a mechanism that means that rather than: 'people in the process face consciously either difficult moral choices or the need to stifle inner resistance of conscience', instead we have a context where, 'the struggle over moral issues never takes place, as the moral aspects of actions are not immediately obvious or are deliberately prevented from discovery and discussion' (ibid.). This moves the discussion on from Arendt's and Bauman's first suggestions about the dangers of following orders or unthinking, uncritical rule and procedure-following, to one which centres on the purposeful concealment or invisibility of the 'moral character of [the] action' (ibid.).

What is Bauman actually getting at here? Well, he is extending the understanding of the dangers of the distancing effects of bureaucracy. He describes a scene of people sitting at desks, composing memoranda, attending meetings, filling in forms and general office bustle. That these office workers could 'destroy a whole people by sitting at their desk' (ibid.) is almost inconceivable, and yet is exactly what happened. These workers were focused on their small, daily tasks with little, if any, causal connection between those tasks and the mass murder that they resulted in. He draws the comparison between this situation and the example of a large arms factory where workers are delighted, and celebrate, that the factory is remaining open thanks to large new orders. At the same time they might also watch, with sadness, news on the television of wars and massacres where the arms from the factory are being used. In other words, people just do not see the 'big picture' or feel it is relevant. Bauman considers this as a distancing between an act and its consequence and illuminates it further by focusing on the place of the middle-man in any action. The person who requests an action is shielded from the consequence (they can only remain imaginary or theoretical) whilst the middle man who actually carries out the action, will always view it as someone else's responsibility. The further this distance, and the more steps there are, the less conflict there is between one's action/task and any moral reluctance about carrying it out:

> The increase in the physical and/or psychic distance between the act and its consequences achieves more than the suspension of moral inhibition; it quashes the moral significance of the act and thereby pre-empts all conflict between personal standard of moral decency and immorality of the social consequences of the act. With most of the socially significant actions mediated by a long chain of complex causal and functionary dependencies, moral dilemmas recede from sight, while the occasions for more scrutiny and conscious moral choice become increasingly rare (ibid., p. 25).

Bauman states that this is why shooting Jews with rifles and having them fall into ditches was quickly redundant as a chosen method of killing – the moral consequences of the actions were too connected to the act. Thus, far more formulaic methods, with many discrete steps, carried out by different people in the 'chain', were preferred.

In terms of social work, think about decisions taken at a multi-agency public protection meeting, for example. Often, only the social worker will know the service user, and decisions taken are deliberately objective, distant and depersonalised. The emotional and ethical consequences of the decision of the meeting are not experienced or witnessed by participants, and the social worker can enact the decisions whilst feeling, and relaying, that they were not responsible for those decisions. Social workers in this situation have told me, anecdotally, that trying to introduce discussion of the emotional consequences for the service user, or to discuss anything that might be interpreted as a version of 'animal pity' is 'embarrassing' for managers who feel it is too 'soft' and 'social-worky' to be aired in the presence of, for example, the police. Might child protection case conferences work in a similar way?

The above invisibility of causal connections comes about due to technical-administrative and bureaucratic processes and can result in people simply not seeing the bigger picture and, in social work terms, simply processing families through a system where being responsive to human feelings hardly exists. To return to Munro, then, who realised the danger in this kind of practice, and equipped with an understanding of Hannah Arendt's caution against rule-following and the 'dulling of conscience', and Bauman's warning against the distancing effects of bureaucracy, it is useful to explore whether the push to reduce bureaucracy and restore autonomy (and, therefore, autonomous critical thinking) has had an effect on social work.

Reduced bureaucracy?

Featherstone et al. (2012) first of all look at what happened to undermine social workers' ability to form relationships and to work properly with families. The authors highlight the issues raised by Munro, in particular increasing numbers of rules, procedures and bureaucracy, but also require the reader to link the practice model to the wider socio-political context. The lack of commitment from successive governments to reduce inequality, promote welfare measures and to tackle poverty must feature in any analysis. The authors go so far as to suggest that this widening inequality, the result of the neoliberal project working as it is intended, will, in fact, cause the recommendations in the Munro report to be undermined. So, for example, requiring social workers to refocus on partnership working, rather than pursuing suspicious 'protection' agendas, is very difficult in a climate of vast inequality, hardship, lack of trust, personal responsibility and the erosion of attention to structural factors, advocacy and help. A neoliberal and managerial approach to social work *makes sense* in that context. Helping families in a holistic way was also made much more difficult because of the division in services between children and adult provision brought about by *Every Child Matters* (Featherstone et al., 2012, p. 622) and parenting was constructed in techniques that could be learned rather than being about relationships, leading to social workers referring on to the, as before – *dreaded* – parenting classes!

Within the above context, performance management techniques became more important and 'quality assured' agency performance by measuring families' performances in terms of how long it took them to shape up and become independent. Helping families on an on-going basis has no place in this context (remember the horror of dependency from Chapter 2?). So much for flexible and responsive work with families! In essence, the authors suggest that decreasing bureaucracy is not possible in isolation – to think systemically about the problem, the neoliberal, self-sufficiency doctrine must also be considered.

Edmondson, Potter and McLaughlin (2013) conducted a study with senior social work practitioners, exploring their views on the Munro report and recommendations. The participants felt that Munro's observation and analysis was congruent with their own experiences, but were pessimistic about whether the recommendations would come to fruition. Their understandings echoed the sophisticated political analysis provided by Featherstone et al. above, and they were very clear that significant political policy choices were the hindrance to the realisation of the recommendations. One participant said:

> Boarder neoliberal contexts, the marketization of welfare and the new managerialist models have all but made it impossible for front line workers to be more than administrative clerks [cogs??] and they have lost power, voice and agency in the work they do (Edmonson et al., 2013, p. 194).

Even when expressed in a less sophisticated way, the political awareness was apparent: 'these suggestions have been swamped by the bigger picture which are the massive cuts and other big changes' (ibid.). Although the study group were experienced and motivated practitioners (undertaking an advanced PQ award) their political analysis stopped somewhat short of the one provided by Featherstone et al. (2012). Cuts to services were flagged as very significant, but the effect of the socio-political context on the *families* in question, and the downgrading of the provision of help, did not really feature. Almost as if the neoliberal 'common sense' had permeated to such a degree that it is taken for granted, albeit that shrinking services were noticeable. What about neoliberalism's consequences for service users? This is the central point of Featherstone's analysis and needs to be kept at the forefront of any critical thinking.

Higgins, Goodyer and Whittaker (2015) point out that there are two underlying assumptions to the way child protection is managed: that the work can be reduced to a series of tasks to be completed and recorded (thus omitting attention to the ethical complexity of the work and the relationship required); and that social workers need targets and audits to motivate them to do the work properly (ignoring altruistic and professional intrinsic drivers). The parallels here with the organisation and administration of the tasks in the mass killing of the Holocaust are undeniable (Bauman, 1989). The qualities outlined by Higgins et al. characterise the managerialism that Munro objects to and is threaded through with risk averse, defensive practice that is about demonstrating social workers have done things correctly. Munro attempts to tackle this head-on with appeals to 'risk sensible' practice (Munro, 2011, p. 60). Aligned to this, once again, is an appeal to reduce bureaucracy and process driven technical-rational practice. Higgins et al. suggest changes to social work education with an increased focus on ethics of care, emotional rather than procedural aspects to practice and an overall approach of relationship based practice. This should echo the practice approach in children's services, concerned with life-story work and relationship building. However, the authors also note that such changes would require a 'paradigm shift' in social work (ibid., p. 337) from a protection model to a relational and ethical one. Although the authors do not analyse this in terms of neoliberal hegemony, it is problematic that a protection model is so conducive to a neoliberal, self-sufficiency, 'pull-your-socks-up-or-else' model. How can a paradigm shift happen when the wider socio-political context supports the existing paradigm to such a degree? Once again, we return to that very question, as posed by Featherstone et al. (2012).

At this point, then, it seems quite clear that implementing Munro's recommendations will not be straightforward given the political context. Reducing bureaucracy and allowing for more autonomous and responsive practice is, of course, a pre-requisite to radical practice and so restrictions on that are very problematic for lazy radical practitioners. However, a first step might be to not allow the bureaucratic imperatives to *supplant* all other practice – especially relationship building and helping with structural issues. Featherstone et al. (2017) reinforce knowledge from sources such as Wilkinson and Pickett (2010) that has demonstrated the destructive and corrosive influence of inequality on many social problems. Featherstone et al. note that the shame and stigma of poverty, inequality, and material deprivation and worry have been left out of the current (neoliberal) understandings of child abuse – individual characteristics and faults are solely to blame. A paradigm shift to allow for practice models that take those factors into account is, according to the authors, unlikely in the current context. The authors also talk about the erosion of trust and the distancing effects of inequality (Wilkinson and Picket, 2010) which, they suggest, leads to an erosion of feelings of solidarity with those who are poor and struggling. Hence the hardening of attitudes towards the poor, witnessed over the last few decades (JRF, 2014). This lack of solidarity and lack of trust also makes relationship building between families and workers very difficult, and, yet again, feeds a managerial, distant and bureaucratic approach – at odds with Munro's ideas.

So, given all of the above, it appears that Munro's suggestions might have a muted impact on children's services. Two years on from the Munro report, *Community Care* ran a story claiming little had changed. The article quoted social work staff, saying:

'In the past year, I have heard virtually no mention of the Munro recommendations from middle or senior management', one social worker in south London told Community Care. On the other side of the capital, a senior social worker in north London confirmed scant progress, saying the feeling is that, 'nothing has changed and nothing will change'.

'I think a lot depends on the attitude of senior managers', the social worker continues. 'Unfortunately, in my authority at least they seem rather wedded to timescales, quantitative measures of compliance, and to have a sense of mistrust that social workers will be able to "do the right thing" unless they are constantly and continually monitored' (Community Care, 2013, n.p.).

More recently, a report by the National Audit Office (2016, p. 10) stated in its conclusion that:

In 2010, the Department commissioned the Munro review because it considered children's services were not good enough. Six years later, far too many children's services are still not good: quality is generally significantly below par and does not correlate to spending levels, access to help or support is not equal across the country, and interventions to improve failed services have been ad hoc. This represents poor progress. The foundations of a cycle of improvement would involve understanding what works, timely measurement of the quality of protection activity across areas, pointing out poor performance and an effective response that improves services quickly. None of these are yet in place to the extent necessary to improve the services quickly enough.

The above conclusion resonates with the kinds of scepticism articulated by social workers in the *Community Care* report. The response of the National Audit Office to lack of improvement triggered by the Munro recommendations, is not to further support agencies to be able to implement the recommendations, but is to undertake more 'timely *measurement*' of performance and *'pointing out poor performance'*: absolutely congruent with being 'wedded to timescales [and] quantitative measures of compliance'.

Advice for newly qualified social workers is also sometimes about acquiescing to this situation:

> It may simply be a salutary exercise to remember that the agency systems were developed in response to valid pressures and that increasing experience will mean that you are able to streamline your approaches to the completion of all the documentation that is required of you (Donnellan and Jack, 2015, p. 122).

In other words, simply get better at coping with managerialism and resultant overwhelming bureaucratic demands; the authors give no advice to critique them. Adapt, don't resist!

All of the above can give rise to a bleak picture, where a reduction in rule and procedure-following unthinking practice seems to be impossible without a paradigm shift. And that paradigm shift seems to be impossible without a socio-political shift. The first step, however, is to be *aware* of this and to be absolutely committed to not simply following rules unthinkingly. Think about Eichmann, Hannah Arendt and Bauman, and remember how easy it is for people to only understand 'that's how we do it around here'. Make a commitment to understand *more* than that.

Stop and think box 4

This calls for honest reflection. Think about Arendt's 'cog-theory'. Have you ever felt like that (in any job or situation)? Really dwell on this – did you abdicate your own responsibility as a human? Was there some comfort and relief in just following the process? Did you agree with what was being done – or did you disagree, but didn't give it much thought (because it is 'just the way it is')? Or did you feel something else? Make some notes and try to really get to the heart of what you felt.

Professionalism – the antidote to managerialism and unthinking rule-following?

Evers (in Munday, 2003, p. 13), in relation to professionalism, states:

> Summing up one can say that professionalism has two sides: one side may be the often-complained arrogance of power while the other side is the burden of responsibility taken. The latter side can be a good point of reference for those

who strive for a better user involvement. To the degree that professionalism puts clients' interests first it can be a strong antidote against old and new ways of putting the interests of authorities, business and providers ahead of the concerns of users and citizens.

This is a very relevant quote in the context of the discussion above. The idea of primary loyalty (or devotion) to the agency, the local authority, the business or the service provider is a condition in which dangerous and oppressive practice can burgeon. Especially when that loyalty supplants social workers' first principle commitment to social justice and the service users with which they work. So, Evers claims that professionalism and being a professional can offer some protection against that dangerous prioritisation of the agency. However, the dangers highlighted by Arendt and Bauman can also lurk and catch out unsuspecting professionals if they are not vigilant. Evetts (2003) draws attention to 'organisational professionalism' which is characterised by loyalty to, and prioritisation of, the agency's rules, culture, hierarchy and procedures. *Occupational* professionalism, on the other hand, means understanding and applying the ethical, legal and knowledge base of social work to one's practice as opposed to simply applying 'how we do things around here'. Whilst it would seem that maintaining an occupational professionalism in one's practice as a social worker should be straightforward, and would afford some protection against technical-rational proceduralism, several authors have outlined how social workers are very readily identifying with 'organisational professionalism'. Preston-Shoot (2011), for example, studied social work students and found that they were overly concerned with bureaucratic imperatives of the agency and discounted social work aims. In 2012, Preston-Shoot also found that social workers did not draw on legal or ethical knowledge (a pre-requisite of being an occupational professional – having a knowledge and value base) and, instead, relied on agency procedures and processes. Reisch (2013) also found that social workers did not consider structural analyses when trying to understand service users' problems, that is, they also did not employ the distinct knowledge-base that occupational professional social work requires. Fenton (2014) also found that, as well as objecting less to the neoliberal and managerial characterisation of social work practice, younger workers also wanted less autonomy than their older colleagues. All of these findings suggest that there is a prevailing tendency for social workers to adopt organisational professionalism as their social work identity. Depressingly, this fits with the kind of organisational behaviour that Arendt and Bauman warn against.

In order to be an occupational professional, then, one must, as Evers states in the quote above, step up to the 'burden of responsibility'.

However, do social workers want to do that? Whittaker (2011), in a study of social workers in child protection, detected real decision-avoidance techniques employed by the social workers, such as describing a situation to their manager, then pausing to allow the manager to fill in what should happen next, and checking decisions with managers. These techniques, the author found, were more prevalent among less experienced workers which might not be a surprise, but which might forge ways of working that then become the norm. The other strategy the author witnessed was an unwavering adherence to agency procedure. All of this meant that the workers were not 'required to make a choice and thus incur the burden of decision-making' (Whittaker, 2011, p. 489), which is absolutely at odds with Evers' definition of professionalism and, in particular, Evett's definition of an 'occupational professional' (see Chapter 6 for more detail on this study).

Another aspect of organisational professionalism is the language or jargon used. Acronyms, agency 'shorthand' language and clichés such as 'the dreaded inappropriate behaviour' (Fox, 2016, p. 84) all serve to foster a feeling of belonging, and thus, allegiance to the agency. Arendt had light to shed on this phenomenon when she discussed the 'language rules' used in the Nazi party. Eichmann himself was a lover of cliché and frequently used trite phrases to explain himself and his actions. In fact, he himself admitted, 'Officialese is my only language' (Arendt, 1964, p. 48). Arendt claims that it became apparent during the trial that Eichmann's inability to speak in any meaningful or original way, 'was closely connected to an inability to *think*' (ibid., p. 49). The Nazi party's 'language rules' included, for example, calling the gassing of the Jews 'a medical matter' (ibid., p. 69) and other words and phrases such as 'final solution', 'evacuation' and 'special treatment' (ibid., p. 85) were commonplace. Eichmann's lack of critical thought, his inability to think about the bigger picture and his love of cliché and stock phrases meant, according to Arendt, that he was an ideal candidate for the use of the 'language rules'.

So, the 'language rules' meant that certain phrases which would accurately pin down the subject under discussion were not allowed and instead, were replaced by stock, codified phrases. This is relevant to social work in two ways. One, the obscuring of real meaning behind words and phrases such as 'inappropriate' or 'meeting needs' or 'high risk' without further explanation or accuracy in meaning. The other, as mentioned, is the sense of belonging that a shared language fosters and the attendant 'organisational professionalism' it fosters.

At this point then, the picture looks quite depressing. The kind of professionalism that might be increasingly characterising social work (Fenton, 2016) is *not* the kind that would offer any protection against the dangerous and bureaucratic practice highlighted by Arendt and Bauman. Occupational professionalism, which might, seems increasingly out of reach.

Stop and think box 5

Does your agency foster organisational or occupational professionalism? Think about allegiance to the agency (as opposed to service users, values, knowledge and the occupation) and how it is manifested.

If you were to try to become more of an occupational professional, how would that look? Are there things you might try?

As a social work educator, when I ask students what they think characterises social work as a profession, they often reply that our Codes of Practice and regulatory body are defining features. They might, therefore, be worth exploring.

Regulatory codes – at the heart of the profession?

In relation to the Welsh, Scottish, and Northern Irish codes of practice, Reamer and Shardlow (2009) point out that the clue to their essence is in the titles – they are codes of *practice*. The authors describe them as narrow managerial tools, which have as their main purpose the regulation and control of social workers' behaviour. This disregards the ethical impulse and ethical character of social work and means that following the rules of behaviour has become the priority task, replacing the previous central guidance of applying values. An ethical dilemma in the past might have been addressed by thinking through the competing value tensions, whereas now the thinking though might be in terms of 'how best to comply with the rules'. Whitaker and Reimer (2017, p. 11) found that when social work students, for example, pondered and reflected on an ethical dilemma, they were 'reflecting to comply' with professional and agency rules and guidelines. Their responses prioritised what the codified, standard response should be and they deprioritised their own personal feelings. Remember the Bauman (1989, p. 21) quote presented earlier, that suggested that when 'devotion to the welfare of the agency' took priority over all other influences, 'personal views and preferences' were the influences most likely to be suppressed? That seems to be exactly what Whitaker and Reimer found which is extremely concerning because those personal feelings might have indicated a value tension inherent in what they were doing or being asked to do. This 'reflecting to comply' response is entirely at odds with the suggestion by Fenton (2016) that students and social workers should be positively encouraged to use feelings of ethical stress as an impetus towards ethical action. Ethical stress is the discomfort experienced when one's values are in conflict with practice expectations (Fenton, 2015). So, for example, when faced with a dilemma and following the 'rules' or procedure produces a feeling of ethical stress, workers should interrogate and reflect on that feeling – what is it about? Why am I feeling like that? Do I need to question the instruction/procedure/advice and actually have a discussion/argument with my manager? It seems that, instead, those feelings of ethical stress are being suppressed and ignored.

PRACTICE EXAMPLE 2

Ahmed

Imagine you are a relatively new social worker in a mental health team. A service user, Ahmed, does not want to keep taking his medication because of the side-effects, and wants to try to live with the symptoms and manage them. You know there is a recovery network operating in the area and could link Ahmed to that. Your team leader, however, says that this has been tried before and Ahmed became a 'nightmare' – barricading himself in his flat and talking about suicide. When questioned, your team leader reluctantly admits that he has never been assessed as being a potential risk of harm to anyone else but, nevertheless, tells you to tell him he *must* keep taking his medication or will end up as an involuntary patient in the local psychiatric hospital.

You feel ethical stress about this: you have a good relationship with Ahmed, you know he trusts you and you think that he should be allowed to try a recovery approach. However, you want your manager to think well of you and are tempted to follow her instructions. You know you are sometimes considered too 'soft' by the team and don't want to have that reputation.

What do you do? The choices are:

1. Reflect to comply – to rationalise following the instructions and to draw on *practice* codes about 'minimising risk' and 'preventing harm to the service user and others' whilst supressing the real experience of ethical stress that this generates. OR

2. Reflect and interrogate the feeling of ethical stress. You feel that the instruction is actually *wrong*. You try to find out why and to think it through. Ahmed has the *right* to have a say, and take charge of his treatment. Service user choice, the right to take risks, working in partnership, respect for persons, social justice, not abusing power etc. are all elements of *ethical* codes that would support you helping Ahmed to fulfil his wishes. Legally, and in policy terms, you also have support. What about knowledge? You know the importance of relationship-based practice, of trust and of the myriad of factors that impact on mental health. You think that, although it might lead to a difficult journey, you should support Ahmed on that journey and help him with an alternative treatment.

I hope you have chosen option 2! This would, of course, mean a return to your team leader to have a discussion and to persuade her that supporting Ahmed is an option. This is the experience of ethical stress leading to ethical action (Fenton, 2016). You would go armed with your values and knowledge (theoretical, legal, ethical and policy). You would win the argument!! You at least have a chance of doing so. So what if your team leader says you are just 'too soft/nice/naive'? You are also *right!*

The practice example above can also been seen through an organisational/occupational lens. Reflecting to ignore the feeling of ethical stress, and to find a way to comply with the manager's instructions, is an example of 'organisational professionalism'. Perhaps you know that the team do not 'rate' the local recovery network. Perhaps the team has a very medical model bias and make decisions on that basis. You are fitting in well as an organisational professional by going along with your manager. And, regulatory codes can be drawn on to justify your actions. However, you know deep down, that you don't really agree. Allowing that feeling to burgeon and to be able to *use* it can transform you into an occupational professional. Turn to codes of ethics (rather than practice), for example, that apply to the occupation:

> Respecting the right to self determination: Social workers should respect, promote and support people's dignity and right to make their own choices and decisions, irrespective of their values and life choices, provided this does not threaten the rights, safety and legitimate interests of others (BASW, 2014b, p. 8).

Having even a general social work ethical awareness should make a social worker feel uncomfortable about the manager's instructions. And, really, at the start of a social work career, having a general ethical awareness is fine – as long as the feeling is followed up and *not* supressed. It is clear at this point that codes of practice can be utilised in reflections to comply with instructions or procedures. That notwithstanding, surely regulation is a good thing? It helps workers be clear about what they should be doing, doesn't it?

Perhaps the situation is not quite as simple as that. Van Heugten (2011, p. 175) appraises developments in western countries which amount to 'deprofessionalisation' in terms of eroding the contribution of sociology and social science to the social work knowledge base and the prioritisation of competency-based employer requirements. The author points out that in the UK, this was a perfect fit with the neoliberal project in that it removed critical thinking and scepticism from the social work task. The author states:

> Educators who are familiar with theorising about practice continue to assume that the capacity to analyse and reflectively amend or build practice theory is a core requirement for social work. However, employers increasingly seek graduates who are willing to *simply follow guidelines* and apply their assigned piecemeal part of 'evidence based practice' (ibid. Emphasis added).

Verhaeghe (2012, p. 134) makes the link between regulation and neo-liberalism very clear when he discusses the 'Big Brother feeling' which is characterised by demoralising and constant regulation, counting and audits. This causes people to adapt their behaviour and put more effort into the things that can be, and are, counted and measured. He states that things that cannot be counted, such as care, begin to disappear. Note recent investigations into poor care in hospitals, care homes and from professional carers at home (e.g., *Telegraph*, 2017). As well as tightening budgets and high staffing ratios (in the name of profit – another sign of neoliberalism), might the decreasing focus on the work itself and the increased focus on the measurement and regulation of that work also be a contributory feature? The suggestion is congruent with van Heugten's further point that neoliberalism has caused a significant increase in managerialist processes and rules which include the fragmentation of roles as follows:

> The fragmentation of roles, for example into those of needs assessors and service deliverers, may enable cost saving. It also enables tasks to be completed by a more technologically oriented workforce, who are not required or encouraged to draw on an educated capacity to reason across complex systems and contexts (van Heugten, 2011, p. 183).

Essentially, as discussed earlier, this idea is at the heart of Bauman's writing about the holocaust. The division of labour into more and more discrete tasks means that workers carrying out each individual 'bit' of the process are more distant from the eventual outcome and are protected from having to overcome pangs of conscience or ethical stress. They just do their 'bit' very well (and without discriminatory interpersonal behaviour), with little cognisance of the bigger picture (as mentioned in relation to Eichmann earlier). McLaughlin (2008, p. 56) offers a good example of this in his description of social workers demonstrating 'their anti-oppressive credentials by admonishing the asylum seeker for his sexist language whilst at the same time refusing them services, or taking their children from them, because they are not considered "one of us"'.

McLaughlin, Leigh and Worsley (2016) also point out that regulatory codes run the risk of holding individual social workers responsible for problems that are actually organisational and systemic such as budget cuts, low staff levels and excessive caseloads. Also, they suggest that employers, who may be risk averse and wary of media attention, might tend to formalise investigatory procedures and responses to social workers when they do make mistakes, which inevitably does happen. Said codes, therefore, may work directly against the kind of learning-from-mistakes culture that Munro (2011, p. 61) had in mind when she said:

> Safety management moved to the view that blaming individuals for errors and mistakes is rarely helpful or productive. It produces inadequate learning and, in some cases, creates new obstacles to improving performance. Instead errors and mistakes should be accepted as to some degree inevitable and to be expected, given the complexity of the task and work environment. In place of a blame culture, where people try to conceal difficulties, it is better for people to discuss problems so that they can be managed or minimised.

Regulation is, of course, a significant characteristic of managerialism or 'new public management' which was introduced as part of the neoliberal project, and was imported from the private, business sector to stop waste and inefficiencies within public services (Ferguson, 2008). Managerialism is characterised by contracted-out services, increases in procedures and prescriptive processes, consequent reduced autonomy for workers, leading to micro-management, an emphasis on performance management, targets and key performance indicators and, of course, increased regulation. A significant body of research has found that this increase in regulation, inspection and performance management has led to a real impact on morale and practice, because of the tensions between these managerial demands and social workers' desire and ability to exercise their professional judgement towards outcomes that are often difficult to measure or quantify. (McKendrick and Webb, 2014)

McKendrick and Webb also point out an example of managerialism and its acceptance by describing a local authority setting where workers were only allowed to decorate their workspace in the corporate colours of the local authority. More surprisingly, there was little objection to this! The authors then go on to describe more broadly, social work and other public services where there is 'branding' and logos for all communication, corporate dress codes, identity badges and corporate cars. Sitting alongside an external regime concerned with regulation, discipline, inspection and control, it is easy to see a picture emerging that reflects the essence of loyalty, acceptance and rule following as described by both Bauman and Arendt. As Smith (2011, p. 3) states:

> Regulatory systems have become entrenched to a point where, through a process of governmentality ... they assume a taken for granted status in the minds of practitioners. While generally internalising this perceived need for regulation, practitioners know, nevertheless, that there is something rotten at the heart of much current-day social work; the technicist, rule-bound and administrative grind of daily practice rarely accords with what most of them came into the job to do.

Conclusion

So far, then, we can clearly see the dangers in distant, bureaucratic practice, in organisational professionalism and managerialism, in regulation
and behavioural codes. We can also see how this can be accepted and
assimilated into social work agencies despite working against the social
justice and service-user focused aims of the social work profession.
Professionalism, per se, and codes *do not* guard against this kind of practice; highlighted by Arendt and Bauman as potentially dangerous and
oppressive:

> No wonder that social workers ... have been trained to believe that the secret
> of success over defeat in their work should be sought and could be found in
> the letter of procedural rules and in the proper interpretation of their spirit.
> When 'procedural execution' takes over from 'moral assessment' as the guide
> to job-performance, one of the most conspicuous and seminal consequences
> is the urge to make the rules more precise and less ambiguous than they
> are, to taper the range of their possible interpretations, to make the deci-
> sions in each case fully determined and predictable 'by the book'; and the
> expectation that all this can be done, and that if it has not been done it is
> the sloppiness, neglect, or short-sightedness of the social workers and their
> bosses which are to blame ..., if only we, the social workers, could design
> and write down in the statute books a clear inventory of the clients' enti-
> tlements and an eindeutig (unambiguous) code of our conduct. I put it to
> you that the beliefs and expectations in question are illusions; and that just
> how illusory they are becomes clear the moment we recall that social work,
> whatever else it may be, is also the ethical gesture of taking responsibility for
> our ineradicable responsibility for the fate and the well-being of the Other;
> and that the weaker and less able to demand, to litigate and to sue the Other
> is, the greater is our responsibility. We are all our brothers' keepers (Bauman,
> 2000b, p. 10).

So, this chapter, depressingly, comes to an end having explored the
problem without offering any solutions. Are there any solutions? Well,
it could be suggested that this is the very arena where radical practice
comes into its own. If you want to be a lazy radical social worker, you
won't fall into the kind of unthinking, rule-following, narrow-task-doing
practice discussed in this chapter, and you will be able to be an occupational professional social worker. Take heart and move onto the next
chapters which consider steps on the way to becoming a lazy radical
practitioner.

Summary of main points

➤ Bureaucracy can distance workers from the consequences of their behaviour.

➤ A rule or procedure-following approach is dangerous because people can practice without engaging in the moral and ethical substance of the situation, or without seeing the bigger picture.

➤ Organisational professionalism, which appears to increasingly characterise social work, lends itself to unthinking procedure or instruction-following practice.

➤ Regulatory codes can also foster such behaviour, especially if workers 'reflect to comply'.

➤ This type of practice is congruent with a neoliberal context and so is difficult to change, as can be seen in the muted impact of the Munro report.

4

Lazy Radical Social Work Step 1: Relationship Building, Trust and Emotional Engagement

Around the time of the Enlightenment, and the dawning of modern society, 'modernity (or at least its dominant guises) impose(d) a divide between reason and emotion' and 'co-opted [social work] to its consuming and unifying logic of human progress through the advance of science and reason' (Smith, 2011, p. 7). Smith describes social work as 'a child of modernity' and suggests that a consequence of this is that social work struggles with its 'rational/emotional dualism' (ibid.):

> Thus, social work quickly became a narrow, municipal, bureaucratic activity obsessed with classification, categorising, assessing and labelling, seeking legitimacy through claims to 'evidence', 'best practice', and increasingly to codified rules of practice and behaviour. More than anything, the task became de-personalised (ibid.).

We saw in the last chapter how this can have the effect of distancing social work from its original ethical impulse and distancing social workers from feeling emotionally engaged with the people they are working with. This can make it easy for practitioners to unintentionally collude with oppressive and unfair procedures, processes and decisions.

More recently, however, the suggestion that social work should embrace its relational and emotional character has been apparent; for example, Munro (2011) as discussed in the last chapter. Ingram, Fenton, Hodson and Jindal-Snape (2014) encourage social workers and students to embrace the 'soft features' of social work. The authors draw a distinction between 'hard features' such as legislation, policy and theory and 'soft features' of values, emotions, relationship building and reflection. Managerialism, evidence-based practice and procedural, rational-technical practice are all concerned with the hard features of social work and are congruent with the distant, bureaucratic practice described in the last chapter.

This chapter will, therefore, consider relationship building and emotional engagement as the first step in radical practice. Ferguson (2013, p. 201), as mentioned in Chapter 1, suggests that 'One view, then, is that value-based work prioritising a worker-client relationship, once regarded as traditional – mainstream – practice, has now become radical in contemporary, managerial environments'. This idea will be analysed and promoted as the beginning of a social work practice that can withstand the problems and tensions illustrated earlier.

Relationship based practice

What is relationship-based practice? Fenton (2016) draws on Hennessey's (2011) concepts of 'inner' and 'outer' worlds to suggest that it should be purposeful and describes the characteristics of purposeful relationship based practice as:

➤ Hearing the service user's voice, getting to know him or her and his or her views and feelings, demonstrating empathy for his or her 'inner world'.

➤ Providing care in manner and actions.

➤ Promoting social justice.

➤ *Intervening*: models of social work, risk assessment, practical help, etc.

➤ *Applying rules and restrictions*: as an exception and only for as long as and to the extent required … attention to the 'outer world'. (Fenton, 2016, p. 136)

In the above, Fenton accepts that there are certain 'tasks' a social worker must undertake, such as filling in a risk assessment form; and that some models of intervention might be useful, such as task centred work or whatever. She also accepts that social work sometimes must apply rules and restrictions, but recommends that this still be undertaken within an ethics of care approach and without excess (Held, 2010). In other words, the 'outer world' cannot be neglected. However, the service user's 'inner world' must receive as much attention, even though statutory practice can often be content with a sole focus on behaviour or 'outer world'. Lazy radical practice begins, then, with equal attention to the service user's 'inner world' and, as such, purposeful relationship based practice is a useful starting point.

Factors that influence relationship-based practice

'Underclass' thinking

What might get in the way of engagement with a service user's inner world? We know that time is scarce for busy social workers, but in on-going contact with families, for example, there is time to be *the kind of social worker* who wants to get to know the service users, even whilst having to undertake certain prescribed duties. There are ways to do the tasks that begin and end with relationship-based practice. This section will explore something that can go on in social work activity that is alto-gether more sinister and damaging than shortness of time, and absolutely kills relationship-based practice stone dead. The concept in question is an, often concealed but nonetheless existing, belief in an 'underclass' as introduced in Chapter 1.

Charles Murray (1990) wrote about the British 'underclass' – a class of unemployed drop-outs who were predominantly single parents or the product of single parent households. He painted a repellent picture of peo-ple whose behaviour was at the heart of social problems in this country. The connection between this way of understanding social problems fits exactly, of course, with neoliberal framing of social problems as behav-ioural not structural. Jones (2011) describes how notions of the traditional working class, that included unemployed people, older adults and other people who were in poor circumstances, have been supplanted by a carica-ture of an 'underclass', exemplified by the word 'chav' (or 'gadgie' in north east Scotland, or 'schemie' or 'tinky' or many others). He claims that even people who would never think about using racist or sexist language, do use these kinds of words and do poke fun and look down on the 'underclass'. This may well be a sign of the neoliberal discourse playing out, ethnicity, gender and disability are not the responsibility of the person, whereas belonging to the 'underclass' is – you are unsuccessful, thick, smelly, amoral and rough, and your behaviour is the reason for all of that. You, therefore, are deserving of our derision and condemnation and a behav-ioural, correctional form of social work practice is all that is required.

Jones describes how the media prop up and perpetuate stereotypes of the underclass in tabloid stories and narratives. He also notes that this does have an effect on people, citing the fact that, as mentioned in Chap-ter 1, over 70% of people working in British television thought that Vicky Pollard (the *Little Britain* character depicting a young single mother who swaps one of her children for a Westlife CD!) was an accurate representa-tion of the British working class. JRF (2014) also found that attitudes to people in poverty had hardened over previous decades and a survey pub-lished in the *Independent* (2013) also reported that the public had bought into the stereotypes portrayed in the media. They believed, for example, that benefit fraud was 34 times higher than it actually is. Interestingly, the latest British Attitudes Survey states that:

> After 7 years of government austerity, public opinion shows signs of moving back in favour of wanting more tax and spend and greater redistribution of income. We also find that attitudes to benefit recipients are starting to soften and people particularly favour prioritising spending on disabled people ... [however] there is little support for more spending on benefits for the unemployed, perhaps because half of people think the unemployed could find a job if they wanted to (British Social Attitudes, 2017).

Although attitudes may be softening a little (perhaps because of the plethora of evidence of poverty, such as increasing numbers of homeless people and the presence of foodbanks; and the numerous stories of disabled people being assessed unfairly as 'fit for work'), they are softening towards the *deserving* among us, such as people on low wages (demonstrated by the urge for fairer distribution of income) and people with disabilities. In regards to unemployed people, however, stereotypes and neoliberal self-sufficiency discourses are still robust – the 'underclass' is still, conceptually, in use. Garrett (2017) has, in fact, pointed out that the term 'underclass' is increasingly being used uncritically, even in some social work literature. This is a key point, because it moves the concept from one that is used, as in this book, to encapsulate a way of thinking about people to something that actually and objectively exists. So, the 'underclass' is a real thing, with its attendant negative features, rather than a construct created by narrative that supports ideas of neoliberal failure. This is concerning and adds weight to the importance of teaching students explicitly about it.

Another explicit feature of this type of 'underclass' thinking, tied to the moralising self-sufficiency discourse, is that structural factors such as poverty, inequality and deprivation are absolutely considered to be excuses. Wills, Whittaker, Rickard and Felix (2017, p. 991), for example, describe how recent governments have defined families with problems as anti-social. After the riots of 2011:

> Structural factors such as poverty or racial inequality were eschewed as explanations for the riots, as were ill health, poverty and poor housing. This gave way to a pathologising of 'at risk' families alongside a narrative of personal responsibility and choice that holds individuals to blame for their problems.

Garrett (2017) discusses the point that 'underclass' is not a new term, and was used by a Scottish Marxist, John Mclean, in the very early 20th century, and by a Swedish economist, Gunnar Myrdal, in 1963, to explain how class in society evolves and how certain structural and economic changes impact most severely on the most disadvantaged groups. In their analysis, however, and this is of utmost importance, they were not concerned with *problematic behaviour* of the 'underclass'. Poor people were not seen as responsible for creating the 'underclass', the fault lay fairly and squarely with structures that benefitted the rich. The moralising self-sufficiency discourse illustrates a real shift, then, to behavioural explanations for poverty and a pejorative use of the word 'underclass'.

So, what might 'underclass' thinking mean for social work practice? Smithson and Gibson (2017) undertook a qualitative study with parents involved with the child protection system in England, and found that the system was unsupportive of parents, and did not pay heed to the emotional impact it had on families (attention to their 'inner worlds'?). Specifically in terms of relationships with social workers, half of the families described positive experiences which included social workers who 'treated the family in a human way: taking an interest in the parent, making an effort to build links and spend time with the family, and demonstrating empathy and an understanding of the parents' circumstance' (Smithson and Gibson, 2017, p. 568). On the other hand, poor social worker relationships were described as prejudging (before meeting the families), 'not getting to know the family and not taking time to find out about that family's situation' (ibid.) and a lack of compassion and empathy. The parents valued the relationship when they felt the social worker *cared* about them and when they understood the emotional toll the child protection system takes. Parents also talked about the increasingly authoritarian approach adopted by neoliberal agencies (as described by Rogowski in Chapter 1), summed up by one parent as, 'I felt that we have been blackmailed … if you don't do this, this will happen, so do it' (ibid., p. 569). This has the result of silencing parents, in case they are seen as uncooperative. Ultimately, the parents felt that they were treated as 'less than human' (ibid., p. 572). This is the consequence of thinking, and acting, in an 'underclass'-informed way, where people are absolutely responsible for their own situations of poverty and deprivation and the belief that these things should not influence parenting in any case: 'Even in those circumstances, *I* wouldn't neglect or mistreat my children'. Oh yes? And how do you know that? Even if that is the case, can you have some compassion and empathy for how difficult parenting in those circumstances might be?

Higgins (2016, p. 523) argues for a more humane form of social work practice with children and families but suggests that a 'rigid and antagonistic approach to service users' is in evidence. The author draws on a study that found that 'social workers tended to express little empathy … and, instead, evidenced a considerable degree of confrontation combined with a low level of listening' (ibid.). Once again, this is at odds with the type of social work practice this chapter promotes; one which does not limit the humanity of the families we work with and one which is underpinned by the principle that, as Higgins cogently sums up: 'making children safe is compatible with treating parents and carers as colleagues and co-partners' (ibid., p. 525), in other words, making a human-to-human connection.

Hingley-Jones and Ruch (2016, p. 238) shed further light on this self-sufficiency, less-than-human discourse. We might call it the 'rational actor' construct:

> This construction sees parents ... as 'liberal subjects' who could change if they wished to (they are seen as having agency); the fact that they have not changed then legitimates the ruling government's view that certain controlling and disciplining social policies should be put in place ... social workers can be caught up in this punishing attitude, seen to be accepting of such constructions of 'family' and not always ethically or with a full view of the social factors actually impacting on them.

How congruent is that with the prevailing British belief mentioned earlier that people could simply get a job if they wanted one? And with Gove's construction of people who need to be told to stand on their own two feet? And with the form of social work uncovered by several authors above? And with how parents experience their social workers in the Smithson and Gibson paper? The scale of the task of changing the paradigm or promoting a more radical, humane practice where the belief is that social factors *have an impact* should not be underestimated!

A worker in a study by Hyslop (2016, p. 30) said: 'I think to survive in social work, you've got to be able to just see the client and not the circumstances around them'. Commenting on this, Hyslop states that 'Just seeing the client implies perceiving the person as she/he potentially (and innately) "is" rather that as she/he is in the current context. Social context needs to be understood in order to be differentiated from the latent potential in the individual client'. In order to do this, Hennessey (2011) would suggest that workers need to engage with service users' 'inner worlds'. There is so much focus on 'outer worlds' that is, behaviour, that inner worlds can be completely overlooked. For example, visiting a family and giving them goals and targets to work on for next time, or doing a questionnaire to 'measure' suicidal intent, or asking a young person if they had been in trouble that week, are all signs of an 'outer world' focus. This is at odds with seeing the client as she/he potentially is, and is completely bound up in the current context. An 'inner world' is characterised by a person's thoughts, feelings, opinions, values, hopes, dreams, memories etc. None of this can be accessed by a superficial, managerial practice which looks to service users for compliance more than anything else. Of course, if you see the parents or family as 'less' than you or 'less than human', as explored earlier, then you will have little interest in their inner worlds and little recognition, even, that hopes and dreams exist for that person. Think back to Bauman's 'dehumanisation' condition that made the Holocaust possible (Bauman, 2000b, p. 21), introduced in Chapter 3. Dehumanisation occurred through 'ideological definitions and indoctrinations' (ibid.) which fits with everything that has been said so far in this chapter. Relationship-based practice, and finding out about a person's inner world, leads to their 'humanising' and causes the less-than-human, underclass stereotype to be broken down. In turn, this allows access to Arendt's 'animal pity' or, less dramatically, simple compassion and empathy. It should be even clearer now how Bauman's work has absolute relevance for social work in the current climate.

It is hoped that by this point the principle that relationship-based practice is absolutely essential in good social work practice, has been well established. However, as Ferguson (2013) contends, practising in a relationship-based way is radical in the current social work context, so, if you want to practise in this way, expect some criticism!!

Building trust

Whincup (2017) studied the social work activity between children and their social workers and found that relationship-based practice was a fundamental part of the work done. Most of the relationships were characterised by talking, and 'getting to know' each other was absolutely foundational. Trust also featured within this and the time taken for trust to develop is acknowledged. Whincup concludes by challenging the view 'that social workers cannot and/or do not engage in meaningful and sensitive direct work as it is evident that, despite calls on their time, some very clearly can and do' (Whincup, 2017, p. 979).

On the other hand, Reimer (2013) offers an important cautionary note from her study of engaging with parents where child neglect was an issue. The author notes that parents in this situation have been found to be more difficult to engage with, even compared to families involved in other types of child maltreatment. She also notes that practitioners involved in this work report more feelings of hopelessness and burnout. Reimer studied the relationships between workers and parents in Australia and found that trust emerged as the key factor involved in building a relationship. Trust featured in Whincup's study also, although it seems that it becomes, perhaps, more difficult when the relationship building is with the parents rather than the child. Parents drew on previous negative experiences, did not want to engage with yet another professional and yet were under pressure to do so due to fear of repercussions from statutory agencies, all of which reflects Smithson and Gibson's (2017) findings.

Identifying with the worker was something that emerged from Reimer's study that seemed to really make a difference in terms of trust. Both being smokers, for example could make a huge difference (and I recognise this from my own social work practice). Although the suggestion is not that people take up smoking (though…), there is something to be said for status or 'power shedding' (Turbett, 2014, p. 52). Social workers who choose to exaggerate material, economic and status differences between themselves and service users who may by living in poverty, can do so by drawing up to the house in an expensive car, dressing in expensive clothes and ostentatiously using expensive phones and other devices, refusing to sit down or accept offers of tea and other hospitality and, essentially, behaving in a 'superior manner'. A superior manner was indeed something that families in a study by Gupta (2015) said they had experienced. Beresford, Croft, and Adshead (2008, p. 1403), in their study of service users' opinions about their social workers, state:

> One of the characteristics of practice that emerged from what service users said was the lack of professional trappings that accompanied the social work role. Service users, in our study, welcomed this and saw it as a real strength.

Something else to think about here is McKendrick and Webb's (2014) observation discussed in Chapter 3 that social work agencies are becoming more corporate and, thus, do display the trappings of managerialism which may well involve company cars, phones, dress code expectations etc. In essence, elements of a distancing and 'differencing' type of social work.

Stop and think box 6

Think about what might be meant by the signs of status. Think about yourself and friends and colleagues. How do people 'display' their success and, thus, their position on the social hierarchy? By what they wear? What they have? Telling others about material success by way of expensive holidays, a new car or whatever? Why do you think people do this? Is it natural? Do you see children of school age beginning to do this? How do you feel about that?

Challenge your thinking about this by reading *The Spirit Level* (Wilkinson and Pickett, 2010) and, in particular how very unequal societies put pressure on people to display success in this way. The steeper the hierarchy, the more important it is to show your high status position on it.

Returning to Reimer's study then, the author identifies the following as attributes a worker needs to begin to build trust:

> Workers providing a first impression that they were genuine/authentic, active in their attention to the parent, willing to help, focused on capacities, empathic, non-judgemental, flexible, collaborative and confident....Underpinning all of this was a perception of worker respect for the parents (Reimer, 2013, p. 464).

It is easy to see how finding out about the parent's 'inner world' is completely congruent with the above. The author actually pinpoints that the worker needs to 'gain parents' perspective' (ibid.) which requires so much more than a behaviour-focused, 'outer-world' compliance approach. Parents described 'testing' the workers to see if they were judgemental, trustworthy and if the parents could find a connection. This is a very important point that workers should be aware of and alert to. Recognising when they are being 'tested' gives an importance to what might be seen as intrusive or flippant questions. Parents asking 'do you have children' for example, might not best be answered by extolling the virtues of your grade 8, cello-playing star, but might involve an eye-rolling, slightly exasperated comment about having teenagers. This is in no way to suggest being unauthentic, but unless you are Mary Poppins, you will have some troublesome experiences to draw on. If you don't have children, you might need to think of points of recognition between yourself and the families you are working with and how you might frame responses to questions that may be designed to 'test you out'. 'No I don't have children, but I was a terrible handful myself when I was younger' or 'no but I have worked with loads of children and families who were struggling a bit. It's hard going being a parent!' You must, however, always remain properly authentic in your responses. I remember being asked if I had ever 'gone to the berries' (usual summer, casual employment in the north east of Scotland where I grew up and worked as a social worker). It was a very equalising and human experience to discuss and laugh about our days at 'the berries'. Connected to this, in Reimer's study, was parents' point that 'an integral aspect of trust development involved workers themselves providing some level of personal disclosure' (ibid., p. 466).

Personal-disclosure is a very difficult and contested area, and one which students can often worry about. They often talk of 'professional boundaries' without interrogating what that actually means, just vaguely understanding that they must not be too friendly. Here, again, the notion of a *purposeful* relationship is a useful way of differentiating between a social work relationship and a friendship. There has to be reason and a shared aim, or work on making changes or whatever in a social work relationship; mutual benefit is not the goal. Trevithick (2012) supports self-disclosure in that it can help people feel less alone or 'different', and can bring a great sense of relief to a person who might feel very isolated in their suffering. Trevithick also notes that it can help service users see us as ordinary people, a point which links very clearly to Reimer's finding that identifying a point of connection is important for people to trust their workers. However, Trevithick is emphatic in her statement that, 'self-disclosure should not occur unless it is in the interest of the individual seeking help' (Trevithick, 2012, p. 217). She cautions against using self-disclosure for our own aims of unburdening ourselves or wanting to talk about ourselves. I have known social workers who have done this and it is a very concerning use of our powerful position to hold an audience captive. Trevithick suggests that there are no hard and fast rules about disclosure, but in the light of the findings from Reimer, it is important that practitioners do reflect and understand how useful it can be (and how sensitively it should be done).

Supporting the notion that self-disclosure is a tricky area, Knight (2014) found that students, although the majority said they were comfortable with self-disclosure, actually did not do it. Amongst the sample of students, 80% did not self-disclose, or did so infrequently. The author also found that educational preparation did influence whether students understood and were willing to engage in self-disclosure. Whilst these findings are heartening in that it seems clear that students are not using self-disclosure indiscriminately, the question is raised as to whether self-disclosure is under-used. The benefits from the Reimer study suggests that further attention might be paid to the usefulness and necessity of self-disclosure when attempting to relationship-build with parents who might have good cause to feel caution in terms of trust and engagement.

A final point from Reimer, and echoed by Featherstone, Morris and White (2014), is that parents not trusting or engaging with social workers is a very understandable and natural reaction to a situation that engenders fear, apprehension and suspicion. It is therefore down to workers to *understand* this rather than simply blaming the families and labelling them as difficult or avoidant.

Risk

Hingley-Jones and Ruch (2016, p. 236), also writing about parents in the child protection system, highlight risk as another complicating feature. They describe the risk-anxiety combination as 'toxic' and suggest that the situation has been made even more difficult by governmental austerity policies which have led to cut-backs in agencies, shortages of staff and tightening budgets. This, in turn, has led to more emphasis on accountability, efficiency and performance management. This situation, they suggest, makes relationship-based practice extremely challenging due to producing a practice that is 'increasingly authoritarian rather than authoritative and combative rather than compassionate' as described in Chapter 3. This type of bureaucratic, distant and managerial practice is actually very compatible with the current neoliberal context and thus, hard to shift: hence the muted impact of Munro's recommendations as already discussed (see Chapter 3). Many academics have written about the emphasis on risk in social work practice and especially the links between risk and neoliberalism (Webb, 2006; Fenton, 2015). Risk aversion abounds and makes the kind of responsive practice required for relationship based practice very difficult. Fenton (2015) found that social workers experienced significant ethical stress, or value conflicts when they experienced their agencies as risk averse, such were the constraints on their practice.

Hingley-Jones and Ruch (2016) give an example of risk averse practice, when they describe a worker doing a routine visit on behalf of a family's usual worker with the police and, when finding no one at home, went along with the police in breaking down the door. There were no new concerns about this family and such an extreme reaction can only be down to a priority concern about 'but what would happen if something *was* wrong'. It is the classic consideration of agency safety as priority. Similarly, a report by the Prison's Commission in Scotland (Scottish Government, 2008) found that parole recalls to prison had increased in a decade by 1000%! The authors speculate that this is down to more risk averse reporting to the parole board, rather than decisions being made and action being taken internally by the agency. Now, an automatic referral to the parole board removes any risk for the agency. The danger of risk averse practice is that agency 'devotion' comes first and what is the right reaction in terms of the service user, albeit with a sensible weighing up of risk, is expendable.

A context where this kind of authoritarian practice and concentration on risk can burgeon, is in work with offenders as in the parole example above. So, for example, Goldhill (2017) investigated the supervision activity between probation workers and women service users and found evidence of practice that is entirely at odds with the kind of relationship-based practice this chapter promotes. Goldhill exemplifies this practice by using the example of an interview between Steph (worker) and Bimla (service user) which, she states, is unlikely to facilitate any change in Bimla's life:

> By showing her disapproval of Bimla's behaviour the previous week and ensuring she checks the current state of her alcohol intake, Steph is carrying out a tick-box exercise; she neither listens to Bimla's concerns nor engages with Bimla's feelings. After the first exchange ... Steph initiates all conversation,

disallowing any displays of emotion … . It appears that as a result of Steph's attitude towards her, Bimla stops trying to say anything about herself, responds with monosyllabic words and gestures and sinks deeper into hopelessness (Goldhill, 2017, pp. 288–289).

The author draws on further research which suggests that this kind of interaction between a worker and service user can lead to a 'toxic environment … whereby self-destructive behaviours are more likely and probationers lose faith, not only in the officer seeing them but in the agency as a whole' (ibid.). This absolutely resonates with a study by Trotter, Evans and Baidawi (2017, p. 400) who studied interviews between social workers and young offenders and concluded:

> The limited research undertaken in corrections and other fields suggests that challenging is more likely to be effective when it is *exploratory*, non-blaming, empathic, encouraging, respectful, firm but fair, and focused on positive ways of dealing with situations. The limited research also suggests that forceful or critical challenging is likely to be associated with poor client engagement, and negatively correlated with achieving therapeutic goals.

The authors found that workers who were critical and authoritarian (like Steph) created withdrawal and disengagement on the part of the service user, which was exactly how Bimla reacted.

PRACTICE EXAMPLE 3

The Thomson family

Imagine you are about to start working with a family where the father, James Thomson, has been prosecuted for domestic abuse, but has returned to live with the mother and their two children. You are supervising the children who are deemed to be in need of safeguarding.

The mother, Sandra Thomson, is very reticent and suspicious of you, and you know that she had told her previous worker about her relationship with James which led to worries about domestic abuse being escalated. She feels that there has been a far too heavy-handed response to what was, she says, a one-off incident.

Imagine that the previous worker is handing the case over to you, and says the following during the handover:

Underclass thinking

➤ I would *never* put a man above the safety of my children. How can she?

➤ They are just a bit different to us – different values, morals and priorities.

Lack of trust

➤ She won't tell me anything at all. She must have stuff to hide.

➤ She doesn't like me anyway, I've seen the way she looks at me and she sometimes asks me personal stuff in a challenging way.

Risk

➤ The main thing in this case is the risk assessment in relation to the kids. You just need to make sure you document every instruction you give the family and, basically, they need to start showing you they're making progress or else....

Look back through this chapter so far and think about some of the ideas in relation to these three factors that can really get in the way of relationship building. Can you understand them in a different way to the previous worker? What will you *do* differently?

Emotional engagement

Another of Ingram et al.'s (2014) 'soft' features of practice is emotional engagement. The authors consider this to be a fundamental part of relationship building. Without re-hashing all the arguments covered so far about Bauman's bureaucratic distancing of practice from the original ethical impulse and Arendt's danger in distancing people from 'animal pity' it is worth reflecting on just how central emotion is to heeding their warnings.

Empathy is usually the way that emotional engagement is framed in social work. This idea of empathy in social work is drawn from Carl Roger's core conditions of counselling (Rogers, 1966) and is often cited as essential in relationship-based practice (Trevithick, 2012; Ingram, 2015). Empathy is about understanding how a person feels, usually by engagement with their 'inner world' and by getting to know them. As Ingram and Smith (2018, n.p.) state:

> An example of use of self in practice can be found if we think about the use of empathy within social work relationships. Empathetic social work requires the worker to tune into the emotional world of another and be able to communicate this understanding within the relationship. This requires a social worker to be able to develop a relationship that has a level of trust which facilitates the sharing of emotions, and in turn the social worker must also be willing to emotionally engage with this information in order to understand it.

Encapsulated in the above passage, the importance of empathy, trust and self-disclosure to relationship-building is evident.

Although the above might sound relatively straightforward, empathy is something of a contested concept. A study by Grant (2014) found that social work students in the UK self-assessed themselves as being empathetic, so they *feel* empathic. However, anecdotally, some students will say things like 'because I don't know anyone like him/her (a young man, with a poor educational history unemployed and in trouble with the police, for example), I just have to *guess* what it's like for them'. Gair (2013, p. 144) found that only limited empathy was demonstrated by students for indigenous people and states that, 'compassion or empathy for marginalized and scapegoated groups will mitigate against their further scapegoating, whereas a lack of empathy may perpetuate it' but found that some students 'could not feel empathy because they had not experienced the situation'. In effect, this is what students in my class sometimes allude to.

Bloom (2016) makes a strong case 'against empathy' for the reasons given above. Bloom states that empathy is like a spotlight – highlighting those near to us and like us, and keeping those further away and more different in darkness. He states that empathy is *meant* to do this and is a mechanism that ensures we look after 'our own' with more care and attention than we do others. Instead of empathy, Bloom suggests that we should be trying to encourage a 'rational compassion', wherein principles of moral behaviour and kindness would lead to a more just response than a gut-reaction like empathy. Compassion and empathy both feature in the BASW (2014b, p. 11) code of ethics: 'Social workers should ... act with integrity and treat people with compassion, empathy and care'. However, it would be fair to say that in social work education and practice, empathy, rather than compassion, is the usual rhetoric. It is worth considering, then, whether students in my class and the subjects of Gair's study, might have felt more for the service users in the end had the classes aimed to evoke simple compassion and kindness.

Stop and think box 7

Try to think of a person in your own community who you think is very different from yourself. This might be a member of a different ethnic or religious group, a homeless person on the street or a very disabled person. Be honest with yourself once again – these are your own, private thoughts.

Now try to feel empathy for them in an imaginary situation. Can you do it? Are you guessing? It would, of course, be much easier if you were working with that person because you could ask, listen and tune-in. However, do you think it would be more

▶

◄

difficult than with, say, somebody you know with less difference to yourself? Is Bloom right?

Now imagine the same, different from you, person in a sad and difficult situation. Can you feel compassion? Is that easier with somebody more like yourself, or is there less disparity between the two?

None of these questions have right or wrong answers – the only requirement is that you engage and grapple, honestly, with them.

Stickle (2016, p. 121) differentiates between compassion and empathy as follows:

> Compassion is a sympathetic consciousness of others' distress together with a desire to alleviate it ... inherited from the Judeo-Christian roots of the profession ... empathy [is] a more cognitive process that focuses on understanding the emotions experienced by another.

The author further suggests that the recent decades of self-interest, economic prioritisation and individual autonomy (in other words the neoliberal hegemonic doctrine) have eroded our capacity and desire to genuinely care for each other, hence, for example, the hardening of attitudes towards poor people (JRF, 2014). Maybe empathy is congruent with that world view in that you can understand others' emotions but still feel disinclined, or ambivalent, about wanting to help, even though some authors suggest that empathising *should* lead to an impetus for moral action (Fenton, 2016). Within the definition of compassion, however, there is no *should* or room for ambivalence, a desire to alleviate the other's distress is essential to compassion. A worker needs to be 'moved to help' (Stickle, 2016, p. 123). Stickle suggests that people can be trained to be kind and compassionate, but I would suggest that people drawn to social work usually have an initial ethical impulse (Bauman, 2000b) to help, but that the context of neoliberal social work degrades and disallows that. As Verhaeghe (2012) states, we can be extremely compassionate and caring beings, but also have the capacity for egotistical, selfish and cruel behaviour – and which aspect of our humanity triumphs, depends on the environment. If the limited world of social work encourages, rewards and promotes the type of neoliberal practice described earlier then the uncaring, distant and managerial social work that we are all capable of will prevail. Having said that, structural changes can be brought about by enough individual behaviour change, so knowing this, and resisting it through social work education, could be extremely influential.

Another aspect of compassion, according to Wilkinson (2017) who draws on the work of Martha Nussbaum to illustrate it, is that it is an intelligent emotion; that we must understand its moral context and understand and deconstruct who is responsible for the suffering of the person in question. These cognitive aspects of compassion should, Nussbaum contends, lead to action and to the conceptualisation of social justice.

So, empathy or compassion? At this point, it is debatable. Segal (2011, p. 266) suggests a concept of 'social empathy' which he defines as 'the ability to more deeply understand people by perceiving or experiencing their life situations and as a result gain insight into structural inequalities and disparities'. This is congruent with the discussion of Nussbaum outlined by Wilkinson, above, when people are required to use cognitive ability to *understand* the context of another's suffering. To interrogate why it is happening. In the case of service users of social work, and absolutely in keeping with a radical position, the context and responsibility is often comprised of structural inequalities and injustices. In this respect, whether 'social empathy' or 'compassion' is utilised is somewhat immaterial – the feeling, emotion and desire to understand and help are the important components.

Frank and Rice (2017) build on the work of Segal and suggest that, in order to evoke social empathy, social work educators should use fictional novels and literature, poetry, art and music to allow students access to the feelings of people in poverty or other difficult circumstances. Nussbaum also suggests this, in particular using stories about people's compassionate responses to the plight of others – to invoke debate and thinking in students about compassion and what it means. Beddoe and Keddell (2016) suggest unpicking complex case studies for the same reasons. Newham (2016), in a study of nursing practice, found that compassion was more likely to be expressed *in action* if suffering was witnessed by the nurse. This was exacerbated if the suffering was perceived as undeserved and as serious enough. The perception of suffering is influenced by how the worker constructs the reality of the service user, and if they view the situation as of the service user's making (i.e., they are entirely responsible due to poor choices and bad behaviour), then suffering will be perceived as deserved and, possibly, not serious – the service user could change it and get a job/stop neglecting their children/stop using substances. A neoliberal construct of the problem can lead directly to a reduction in perceived suffering which in turn can lead to a reduction in compassion.

The neoliberal construct of the problem, as already discussed, is easy to grasp and can seem like common sense. Such a reductionist, and 'dumbed-down' understanding of problems is extolled by neoliberals as can be seen in John Major's quote that, in regards to crime, society needs to 'condemn a little more and understand a little less' (*Independent*, 1993) and in Narey's report on social work education calling for less attention to structural and sociological issues. Providing an alternative way to understand the problems of service users is the subject of the next chapter, but in order to evoke compassion or empathy, there is one facet of understanding which needs some attention now. When faced with a service user who seems to be making bad choices, how do we, who have perhaps never been in that situation, understand those choices and, perhaps, 'see' the suffering that might be masked by those choices.

Poverty and pleasure

It might be useful here to think about George Orwell's *Down and Out in Paris and London,* his famous book written about his experiences of being in absolute poverty. There is an interesting theme that plays out in the book which concerns pleasure. When absolutely at rock bottom, Orwell and his friend come unexpectedly into money which they spend as follows, 'We ran out, brought bread and wine, a piece of meat and alcohol for the stove, and gorged' (Orwell, 1933, p. 43). They also ended up going out for dinner and, thus, spending nearly all of their money, which might have with responsible budgeting, lasted some time. They also already had a plentiful supply of tobacco, about which Orwell states, 'it was tobacco that made everything tolerable' (ibid., p. 34). Tirado (2014, p. 82), who describes her experiences of poverty in contemporary America also talks about moments of pleasure, and how finding them is wonderful. She also describes cigarettes as the thing that provides some pleasurable moments and, thus, makes life tolerable:

> Unless you're prepared to convince me that smoking and smoking alone keeps me poor, then, please, spare me the lecture. I know it's bad for me. I'm addicted, not addled. There are reasons that I smoke and they are reasonable ones. They keep me awake, they keep me going. Do they poison my lungs and increase my chances of getting cancer? Obviously. Does that stop me? No. Because the cost-benefit isn't as simple as *I like it* vs *I'll possibly live longer.* It's *I will be able to tolerate more* vs *I will perpetually sort of want to punch something.*

Tirado expands her thinking on this to include many other small pleasures, and reveals the humanness of wanting to find pleasure in life, 'Junk food is a pleasure that we are allowed to have; why would we give that up? We have very few of them' (Tirado, 2014, p. xv) and 'It is not worth it to me to live a bleak life, devoid of small pleasures so that one day I can make a single large purchase' (ibid., p. xviii). These remarks really call into question the judgements that some social workers level at people in poverty about not budgeting or saving for something. It is so easy to sit in judgement without understanding, or even trying to understand by listening and tuning into people's inner worlds.

Weinberg (2016) researched workers' discourses and understandings of the young mothers they worked with in a residential establishment. One point of note was that when the young women sought pleasure, especially sexual pleasure, they were judged harshly. Desire was missing from the workers' discourses. Tirado also talks about seeking connection and feeling pleasure and worth through sexual encounters and, again, this is not understood from the service user's perspective and is, as a consequence, judged and taken as evidence of irresponsible behaviour. An associated issue is the middle class privilege of lack of surveillance or *privacy* (Weinberg, 2016). Constant surveillance, unreasonably high, ideal standards (which the middle classes can lower once behind their closed doors) and disapproval of normal, pleasure-seeking behaviour can be a toxic mixture for people already in difficult material circumstances. Social workers who understand this are essential for lazy radical practice – those who do not, might well judge and oppress.

The other aspect of poverty that Orwell and Tirado share is that it 'annihilates the future' (Orwell, 1933, p. 17). Tirado states: 'It does not matter what happens in a month ... none of it matters. We don't plan long-term because if we do we'll just get our hearts broken. It's best not to hope. You just take what you can get as you spot it' (Tirado, 2014, p. xviii). Again, social workers will often discuss the lack of planning from some service users and the day to day scrabble to just manage. And again, *trying to understand* this from service users' point of view is absolutely essential, or other explanations – such as they are just irresponsible – will fill the comprehension gap (and is supported by the media and hegemony, as discussed previously).

Finally, both authors talk about keeping up the appearances of not being poor. Trying to avoid the shame that comes with poverty (Gupta, 2015). Wilkinson and Pickett (2010) also shed light on this in their seminal study which demonstrated that increasing inequality is significantly correlated with increased social problems, including lack of trust and anxiety. Demonstrating your place on the social hierarchy becomes very important, so the display of material wealth becomes the norm, and having low status on the hierarchy becomes damaging for people – hence borrowing money and spending on items that can 'prove' one's worth. JRF (2010) demonstrated, however, that UK household debt was increasing due to inadequate income (e.g., people moving in and out of poorly paid work, or family breakdown) rather than over-consumption, but it is important that the pressure to display material success is understood rather than, again, taken as evidence of irresponsibility.

PRACTICE EXAMPLE 4

Shanice and her two children

Imagine you are having a conversation with a social worker who believes in a neo-liberal construct of society, and thinks that people make their own choices and, ultimately, *that's* the problem. The problem isn't poverty, it's the poor – their behaviour underpins and causes the situation. She is discussing Shanice, a black woman, and her two children, a family she is not enjoying working with. She makes the following statements:

➢ Shanice just doesn't budget. When she gets her dole money, she takes the kids out to Pizza Hut. For heaven's sake, that money could last them a good few days!

➢ She would have more money if she didn't buy fags and booze.

➢ She always has people back to her flat and has parties and has one night stands!

➢ Shanice spends money on brand name trainers for the kids and she has an iphone and stuff – then gets into debt. That's just stupid!

➢ I just don't know why she doesn't plan better.

Can you offer an argument against this view? Can you bring some understanding to this view of Shanice by referring to Wacquant's stereotype of the 'Welfare Queen' (Chapter 2)? Is it just a symptom of the thick, useless 'underclass' or might George Orwell and Linda Tirado have some light to shed?

The point here is that although social workers might see behaviour that looks like, and often is in fact, underpinned by poor choices, it would be better to understand that a little more, and to condemn less (so there, Mr Major!). Choices are not made in a vacuum and the surrounding context *has an effect*. Suffering can be masked by that behaviour, but understanding what is going on, rather than relying on observation of behaviour and stereotypes such as the 'Welfare Queen', should allow social workers to still witness that there may well be suffering and, thus, be more likely to feel compassion and to want to help.

Care

Returning once again to the BASW (2014b, p. 11) code of ethics mentioned earlier, remember, 'social workers should … act with integrity and treat people with compassion, empathy and care'. Where does care fit into the previous discussion? Well, care is, again, an active concept.

It is not enough just to be 'caring', the expression of care is what counts. Within relationship building this might mean listening, of course, attending and *helping*. Taking Tronto's (1993) ethics of care model as a starting point, there are five elements of the ethics of care as follows: attentiveness (listening), responsibility (actually taking responsibility – the opposite of 'that's not my job'), competence (skills and knowledge to do what is necessary), responsiveness (staying attuned to the needs of the service user) and integrity of care (understanding the bigger picture in terms of socio-political context and the reality of the service user's life). This provides a picture of how care can look in practice and is absolutely congruent with social work values. The ethics of care will be discussed further in Chapter 6.

Conclusion

Building a relationship, then, in Hannah Arendt's terms means that a social worker can get close to, and experience, the 'animal pity' that a person will feel for another in distress. Getting close to a person provides protection against distant, bureaucratic and oppressive practice. *Feeling* something for the other person comes from building a relationship with them, getting to know them and getting to know their inner world. Dehumanising another is very difficult indeed when you have access to their hopes, dreams, fears, loves and thoughts. The human to human connections are all too easily seen. This is, arguably, even more important when working with a person who is unlike yourself and different culturally, ably, sexually, ethnically, socially or in any other way. A real relationship fills the space which might otherwise be occupied by prejudice, stereotyping and assumption.

In conclusion, it's worth considering the final common feature of social empathy, compassion and care: taking action. Hearing and debating people's responses to suffering – should one take action? And do what? What is the right thing to do in what circumstances? – means that *responding* is on the agenda, as per the ethics of care. Frank and Rice suggest that evoking empathy by hearing about the plights and suffering of people, and locating that within a wider structural context should be enough to create an impetus to action, and Stickle claims that understanding another's suffering should lead to compassion which, in turn, should also lead to action. Perhaps hearing about different responses to suffering reinforces that taking ethical action is a necessary part of social work practice. This will be explored in much more depth in Chapter 6. Understanding, especially of the structurally unjust circumstances of many people, will be discussed much further in the next chapter. As can be seen, the three steps of lazy radical social work: relationship building, understanding and knowledge, and moral action are inextricably enmeshed.

Summary of main points

➤ Notions of the 'underclass' must be challenged by getting to know people and hearing their stories, rather than jumping to dehumanising conclusions about behaviour.

➤ Social workers need to understand how poverty feels for people and how it creates a context within which poor choices are often a rational and understandable response, especially in relation to pleasure seeking.

➤ Trust is central to relationships and might involve self-disclosure and finding commonalities.

➤ Risk can inhibit responsive, relationship-based practice.

➤ Emotional engagement is very important – although empathy can be difficult, compassion and kindness are always possible.

➤ Care, social empathy and compassion all have an *action* element – discussed further in Chapter 6.

5
Lazy Radical Practice Step 2: Knowledge and Critical Thinking

This chapter will explore how the second step to resisting managerial, technical-rational practice involves knowledge, understanding and critical analysis; a type of thinking-practice that is the opposite of the dangerous, 'dulling' and unthinking practice that can be understood by reference to Bauman and Arendt. Do you remember in Chapter 3, Arendt was quoted as saying that Eichmann's inability to speak in any meaningful or original way, and his reliance on clichés and jargon was 'closely connected to an inability to think' (Arendt, 1965, p. 49)? I hope the danger and unethical potential of a social worker behaving as a blind rule-follower in the manner of Eichmann has already been established, and so, as the inability to *think* is a factor in that behaviour, thinking in social work *must* be promoted.

A good starting point for this very important chapter might be reference to another influential thinker: John Stuart Mill (1806–1873). Mill (1859), most famous for his work *On Liberty*, might seem an unlikely candidate for inclusion in this book as his work is most closely associated with libertarian ideas of freedom (remember the key word of the political right being 'freedom'? see Chapter 2), which often means free market economics and freedom from governmental interference, in other words neoliberalism. His ideas 'make best sense from a liberal individualist standpoint' (Skorupski, 2011, n.p.). Having said that, Mill had radical ideas about redistribution in terms of unearned, inherited wealth (not earnings, which he viewed as being deserved), which were more progressive than anything that exists today (ibid.). That aside, there is a theme in his work which is extremely pertinent to this chapter: 'the liberty of thought and discussion' (Mill, 1859, p. 28). Mill's idea was that freedom of thought is absolute as it is entirely 'self-regarding' and that freedom of expression is 'almost' absolute, the caveat being if expression (which is not entirely self-regarding as it has an explicit connection to others) leads to the harming of non-consenting others (Riley, 2015, p. 75). Furthermore, and perhaps even more relevant to this chapter is that:

> On Liberty is about something quite different, for which Mill felt more deeply than anything else – the threat of tyranny inherent in democracy of a mediocre conformism, capable of 'enslaving the soul itself'. It is precisely here, I would suggest, that social democratic thinking has something important to learn from Mill (Skorupski, 2011, n.p.).

Mill's blistering attack on conformism in thought and speech, persuaded into reality by legal action and by social stigma where the dissenting person is shunned, resonates strongly with Arendt and Bauman's pleas for people to be thinkers. Without these dissenting voices, there is no protection against 'majoritarian despotism' (ibid.). Although Mill was often concerned with speaking out against Christian dogma, and Bauman and Arendt against the majoritarian despotism of Nazi Germany, there is a lesson to be learned about speaking out against ideas and beliefs that are promoted and perpetuated with often little recourse to argument or evidence, due to the power and support that they have. For example, just consider the 'hate speech' legislation which can be used against someone who has been offensive as opposed to inciting harm. For example, Paul Gascoigne faced criminal charges for telling a tasteless joke about a security guard's skin colour, which did not go down well with the audience and was a stupid and offensive thing to do (*Telegraph*, 2016). However we must also interrogate the *criminality* in the action and the fact that the state response to Gascoigne's words was more authoritarian than Mill was promoting in 1859! Without thinking critically about this, we might well think 'well that's good, people shouldn't be racist … .'

So, the case has been made by Bauman, Arendt, and Mill that people in general should strive to be critical thinkers. Whether we agree with that is really immaterial, but the notion that it is absolutely essential for social workers to be critical thinkers has been quite well demonstrated in this book so far. In terms of lazy radical social work, critical thinking is a key component because, without it, workers will simply follow the procedure, do as they are told (without understanding why), feel little solidarity with the 'underclass' and, ultimately, perpetuate the neoliberal, oppressive hegemony.

The problem(s) with critical thinking

So, are we producing social workers who are critical thinkers? Van Heugten (2011, p. 181), writing about the situation in New Zealand, which resonates with the situation in the UK, suggests that there is a fundamental tension between what academic institutions attempt to provide in educational terms, and the technical competencies required for registration and employment:

> Regulatory bodies, whether professional or statutory, tend to have shorter term goals requiring job readiness for the way in which work is structured and carried out currently, whilst educational institutions take a longer view. Higher educational institutions expect professional degree programmes to concentrate on fundamental intellectual knowledge, and to foster critical thinking and reasoning to enable graduates to apply that knowledge in a complex world. Points of tension occur when educational institutions are asked to provide courses that appear to devalue research and scholarship.

The author also suggests that some social work education providers do indeed capitulate to the market demands of employing agencies that, in a neoliberal regulated public sector, want social workers who will unquestioningly carry out the managerially defined task: 'In an effort to produce employees, knowledge is modulated and fragmented for technical use' (ibid., p. 182). This modulation and fragmented use of knowledge might be seen, for example, in risk assessments carried out on offenders. A body of research looking at shared characteristics and features of repeat offenders (e.g., age at first offence, whether the person has been to prison before, gender etc.) is distilled into a scoresheet which leads to a prediction of 'risk of reoffending'. The underpinning knowledge base is often redundant, unavailable, unknown, seen as irrelevant and therefore cognitively out of reach of any critical analysis.

So, there is a definite tension outlined above about what is desirable in a social worker in a neoliberal/managerial agency and what social work education holds as the aim. Perhaps critical thinking is not high on the 'desirable or essential' qualities list of some employers. Social work programmes and the standards attached to them, however, do state that critical thinking is essential for students to pass their programmes as do various standards for the profession. The required social work 'proficiencies' as laid down by the Health and Care Professions Council (HCPC, 2017) require social workers to:

> be able to assess a situation, determine the nature and severity of the problem and call upon the required knowledge and experience to deal with it

> be able to make informed judgements on complex issues using the information available

> be able to gather, analyse, critically evaluate and use information and knowledge to make recommendations or modify their practice

➤ be able to prepare, implement, review, evaluate, revise and conclude plans to meet needs and circumstances in conjunction with service users and carers.

➤ be able to use research, reasoning and problem solving skills to determine appropriate actions

The theme of critical thinking is also threaded through many of the other proficiencies. In Scotland, the requirement to think critically and analytically features heavily throughout the Standards in Social Work Education, for example the requirement to 'apply ethical principles and practices critically when planning problem-solving activities' (Scottish Government, 2003, n.p.).

A study by Sheppard and Charles (2017) looked at whether critical thinking skills were predictive of degree success within four social work programmes in England: two undergraduate and two masters level programmes. The results demonstrated that critical thinking skills were predictive on the masters programmes (congruent with academic expectations at masters level), but not on the undergraduate programmes. This, in essence, means that critical thinking skills on the undergraduate programmes, were irrelevant to the student doing well, or otherwise, on their course. An element of the critical thinking skills under investigation was the ability to recognise and deconstruct assumptions. Applying this to the issues in this book, an essential element of lazy radical practice is recognising and deconstructing the hegemony and its impact on the people social work works with. This is extremely concerning in that critical thinking skills, on these undergraduate programmes, were not important. Predictive skills were found to be interpersonal ones, such as empathy and compassion, which, as outlined extensively in Chapter 3, are extremely important but simply *not sufficient* on their own.

Sheppard, Charles, Rees, Wheeler and Williams (2018) undertook a more extensive, twelve cohort study, comprising six undergraduate and six masters social work programmes. One aim of the study was to 'identify inter-personal and critical thinking capabilities in social work graduands' in other words, students at the point of graduation and about to enter the social work workforce (Sheppard et al., 2018, p. 4). Hearteningly, the students scored significantly higher than the UK normative mean on compassion and significantly but less profoundly on insight and altruism, and were quite a homogenous group on those measures. Very interestingly, however, the social work students scored highly significantly lower on assertiveness than the UK normative mean. This is something that will be explored much more fully in the next chapter, *Moral Courage*.

Meanwhile, the main focus of interest for this chapter is the finding on critical thinking abilities. The researchers found that social work graduands scored *highly significantly lower* (and with large effect size) in critical thinking ability than either the normative UK sample or the law/business sample (chosen for similarities in the professional/occupation nature of their jobs). This is shocking! New social workers in this comprehensive study of twelve programmes and six universities are significantly poorer at critical thinking than the average UK population, albeit that we explicitly aim to produce critical thinkers and analysers. Also of note is that there was a highly significant difference in critical thinking scores between masters and undergraduate students, with the masters doing significantly better. Having said that, the masters mean score was still less than both the UK mean and the law/business mean. The undergraduate mean on its own was enormously below the UK and law/business means and roughly the same as a score attained by chance, that is, had the respondents simply guessed the answers. In fact, a quarter of the sample scored less than this chance mean.

In making some suggestions about the implications of the findings of this extremely important study, the authors consider strengthening entry requirements for social work, as discussed in Chapter 1. They also suggest that social work education should focus more on critical thinking, close examination and deconstruction of problems and arguments, including recognising and analysing assumptions. The 'logic requirement' (ibid., p. 16) in thinking about practice is, according to the authors, the gap. If the answer does not simply lie in students pre-dispositions (if it does, we return to entry requirements) then social work education needs a stronger focus on this requirement. The authors conclude by emphasising that social work education needs to provide for students 'a framework to enable the enhancement of reasoning capabilities' (ibid.).

A framework for reasoning

In the light of the above, we can conclude that there is a problem with critical thinking in social work. Providing some kind of theoretical framework or model for this is probably doomed to fail, as the imposition of a top-down method of *thinking* within such a strongly dominant neoliberal paradigm for practice, with its attendant non-thinking, procedural, surface-explanation approach (Ferguson, 2008), will make little impact. Much akin to how the Munro recommendations have had little impact, such is the dominance of the paradigm (see Chapter 3).

Barak (2016, p. 1777), for example, states that social workers often 'prioritise individual therapy and individualistic solutions to social problems over interventions that link the individual to a broader socio-political context' and notes that critical social work has often been criticised for the difficulty in its implementation on an individual level. Barak states that mass media, conformist social values and anxiety around critical thinking have created a situation where people *want* to conform to the prevailing structure because there is a lack of understanding about an alternative. The neoliberal paradigm is just too overwhelming.

However, rather than giving up and giving in to the neoliberal hegemony (and thus abandoning any attempt at lazy radical practice) there is another way to approach this, starting with what actually happens now, in real practice, with real social workers. To augment, or enhance *that*, might be a way of encouraging critical thinking in practice that is realistic and possible.

Whittaker (2018, p. 2) undertook a study into how social workers in child protection make decisions. He suggests that their decision making is congruent with a 'dual process' model that consists of two systems: intuitive reasoning (system 1) and analytical thinking (system 2). Our concern with the lack of critical thinking, then, could be described as a concern with the under-usage of system 2. Whittaker sums up the model as follows:

> Intuitive thinking (system 1) operates rapidly and automatically and with little sense of voluntary choice or effort. For example, during a telephone call with a loved one, we are often quickly aware of their mood. By contrast, analytical thinking (system 2) is controlled, effortful and able to undertake complex mental operations that require considerable effort, such as mathematical calculations (ibid., p. 4).

So, our intuitive thinking provides rapid, often emotional, answers to whatever situation we are trying to make sense of (system 1). This is then followed by a quality assurance and monitoring facility which is part of deduction, reasoning, logic, knowledge and rule application (system 2). This system may generate alternative explanations, will weigh evidence and knowledge and might then endorse or override the system 1 conclusions/feelings. Interestingly, the author suggests that when the intuitive decision is accepted with little or no revision (after scrutiny) by the analytical system, the person attributes credit to the intuitive system ... 'I just knew... .' Whittaker, in his study, is drawing on the work of Kahneman (2011) who developed the dual process model. To understand some more how the different systems work Kahneman's work on both will be explored a little further.

Intuition (system 1)

In terms of intuition, Kahneman describes two main ways of understanding what is going on. One is the recognition of patterns and information, and therefore increases with experience. In social work this might be known as practice wisdom. Whittaker found that one of the main differences between newer and more experienced social workers lay in the ability to understand and recognise patterns, whilst also understanding that each family is unique. The other way that intuition operates is via heuristics, or mental shortcuts that serve to help a person deal with significant amounts of information. Heuristics, which might involve recognition, might also be based on stereotypes, readily available information (e.g., the stories the media chooses to emphasise) and erroneous rules-of-thumb. Clearly, then, system 1 is fallible.

Analysis (system 2)

This systems takes effort, knowledge and deliberation and is much more difficult. Kahneman describes a very familiar situation which all students of social work or any other discipline will recognise. To sustain a concerted mental effort over a period of time is very difficult; think of sitting down to write an essay and being constantly distracted by checking facebook or emails or rummaging in the fridge or, even, cleaning the sink! So, system 2 requires self-control, effort and application to the task that might not be completely pleasant to experience. Kahneman points to evidence that suggests that after taking part in a system 2 task, people are averse to undertaking another one. System 2 is depleted.

Stop and think box 8

This example is taken from Kahneman's book *Thinking fast and slow* (Kahneman, 2011, p. 44).

A bat and ball cost $1.10
The bat costs one dollar more than the ball
How much does the ball cost?

A number came to your mind. The number, of course, is 10: 10c. The distinctive mark of this easy puzzle is that it evokes an answer that is intuitive, appealing and wrong. Do the math and you will see. If the ball costs 10c, the total cost will be $1.20.

▶

◀

Kahneman, above, is demonstrating here how fallible (and yet confident!) system 1 can be. You were probably aware of the effort required to work out the correct answer. As Kahneman says, 'The bat and ball problem is our first encounter with an observation that will be a recurrent theme of this book: many people are overconfident, prone to place too much faith in their intuitions. They apparently find cognitive effort at least mildly unpleasant and avoid it as much as possible' (ibid., p. 45).

Kahneman's work may have some light to shed on the quarter of the sample of students in the Sheppard et al. (2018) study who would have scored more highly had they guessed the answers. Anecdotally, reflecting on my own experience as a social work educator, I do recognise the type of student who relies (often very confidently) on system 1 and seems unable to employ system 2 – the manifestation of that being opinionated assignments, with little reference to literature (again, reading and, more to the point, *understanding and applying* the reading, takes sustained and proper use of system 2) and minimal, or no, analysis. Kahneman talks about the 'troubling' finding that a group of students were quite quickly satisfied to accept an intuitive, system 1 answer to a problem. He states:

> 'Lazy' is a harsh judgement about the self-monitoring of these young people and their system 2, but it does not seem to be unfair. Those who avoid the sin of intellectual sloth could be called 'engaged'. They are more alert, more intellectually active, less willing to be satisfied with superficially attractive answers, more sceptical about their intuitions (ibid., p. 46).

If social work needs people who can think critically, a clearer and more targeted approach is perhaps required to assess students and weed out the very poor critical thinkers, *even when* their interpersonal skills are good. As Sheppard and Charles (2017) found, as mentioned earlier, interpersonal skills were predictive of success on a social work programme while critical thinking was not.

PRACTICE EXAMPLE 5

Dan

Dan Newman is a single father about whom you have received a referral. The school is concerned that his daughter, Lorna (6), seems quite dirty and unkempt, is often tired and sometimes hungry. You visit Dan and his daughter and discover that he is unemployed, drinking too much (you see evidence of empty bottles) and quite low.

Your system 1 kicks in as you confront this situation – Dan needs a job and to stop drinking – he's a bit of a waster (system 1 is referencing the school's view, other people you have come across like Dan, media stereotypes of unemployed layabouts drinking all day and an emotional reaction to Lorna who is a very appealing child). Ok, you take quite firm and authoritative action on that basis. Imagine an even stronger system 1 response had your team leader said to you on the way out 'I know Dan's type, he'll need a kick up the backside'.

Now, rewind and imagine the situation again with the same system 1 reaction. This time however, you actively employ system 2 and you *slow down* the formulation of your conclusion/response. You employ knowledge about poverty and the job situation. What is there in the area? Mostly temporary, insecure and poorly paid work? You think about knowledge you have around why people drink too much or use substances, about attachment between father and daughter, and about other possible explanations for the situation rather than just Dan being uncaring and useless. You want to get to know Dan and what he says about the situation so that system 2 can really do its work properly. You take time to do that, properly listening to him, caring and trying your best to practice in a relationship-based way as per Chapter 4.

Is it obvious how this kind of system 2, thinking-practice is exactly congruent with lazy radical practice step 1 – relationship based practice? A framework for practice is indeed emerging.

Brown and Rutter (2008, p. 6) suggest that 'it is too easy to limit thinking about practice to thinking only of practice – that is, we get wrapped up in the detail and specifics of particular cases ... rather than dealing with general underlying issues'. The authors give an example of what they mean by describing the situation of a worker reading case notes and uncritically following the 'team view' (which might be biased) rather than thinking for herself about the case more broadly. This could just as easily apply to following the team leader's view of Dan. They also suggest that managerialist pressure can reduce our time and capacity for critical thinking, a suggestion which chimes with the thinking in this book thus far. It would also appear that the authors are describing an 'anecdotal' form of practice where people tend to discuss the descriptive detail of cases on an anecdotal level, without connection to conceptual thinking. This way of thinking about practice is certainly recognisable to me and students (and practitioners) can become very stuck at the anecdotal level. I would suggest that these are the students who would score poorly on critical thinking measures. Connecting thoughts and ideas in a conceptual way is missing.

Kahneman also draws attention to other features of system 1 thinking that should be particularly cautionary for emerging social workers. For example, there is an appeal in knowing very little, or making any knowledge base acquired, redundant. Kahneman demonstrates that what feels important to people when they make sense of a situation is the coherence of the information. So, constructing a story that is coherent with the neoliberal hegemony, such as 'Dan should just get a job – work is the way out of poverty' is extremely persuasive as it is congruent with the neoliberal messages you have had all of your life. Even knowing the statistics about the reality of in-work poverty, applying them to Dan (and applying the abstract to the concrete is another difficult system 2 process) is less appealing than constructing a story around what you see and your underpinning, neoliberal assumptions. According to Kahneman, coherence can cause over-confidence and, as mentioned previously, I have indeed witnessed that. The author also discusses how system 1 is adept at substituting one question for another. So, we ask a difficult question, but actually answer an easier one. For example, in the Dan scenario, we are asking 'what is the situation with Dan and Lorna', for which system 1 might readily substitute 'how much do I like/dislike Dan'. These mental short cuts are called 'heuristics' and system 1 is expert in their utility.

The final feature about which social workers should be cautionary (although there are many more in the book) concerns the application of statistical facts and knowledge. Because much of lazy radical knowledge involves applying statistical facts to challenge the neoliberal hegemony, the concept explored by Kahneman is extremely important. The central idea is that:

> System 1 is highly adept at one form of thinking – it automatically and effortlessly identifies causal connections between events, sometimes even when the connection is spurious....As we shall see, however, system 1 is inept when faced with 'merely statistical' facts, which change the probability of outcomes but do not cause them to happen (Kahneman, 2011, p. 110).

Think back to the introduction of *The Spirit Level* (Chapters 1 and 4). This is a text that I use prolifically with students, and one with which they significantly struggle. In the past I have wracked my brains about this – *why* is it so difficult to grasp the central messages in the book – from reading and also from rigourous exploration in the classroom. Some students just seemed unable to 'get it'. They could understand what the book says in an abstract way, that social problems are greater in unequal, developed countries, but then absolutely fail to consider the idea of inequality or apply the thinking to a young man who experiences many social problems, even when that was the point of an assignment. I can see now that, again, these were the students who were relying on system 1 thinking – the students needed *causal* connections so resorted to 'his family didn't help him' and 'his behaviour is the sole problem'. Economic inequality is not directly causal to, for example, the fact that the young man disengaged from school and became embroiled in violence and substance misuse, so some students found it almost impossible to hold the relevant, *indirect* connections in their minds. In other words, system 2 thinking was, once again, very weak.

Although this sounds dispiriting, and the evidence from Sheppard et al. adds to that sense of despondency, some hope can be brought to the discussion by Bloom (2016). Bloom cites several examples which demonstrate people's inclination to rely on system 1 and to, therefore, think irrationally or, as in the example above, to *not* see things as relevant if not directly causal. However, he goes on to point out that when mistakes *are* explored with the person (e.g., the bat and ball calculation) they do then 'get it'. He also notes that when widely held errors are exposed, we shake our heads 'at how dumb people can be' (ibid., p. 229). When we reflect, therefore, we can employ system 2 thinking to really understand the problem. As Bloom says:

> It turns out that every demonstration of our irrationality is also a demonstration of how smart we are, because, without our smarts we wouldn't be able to appreciate that it's a demonstration of irrationality (Bloom, 2016, p. 229).

Concerns, then, about social work students' lack of critical thinking, might be better investigated by finding out which students, when offered the 'real' answer to a calculation or further explanations about relevant information and connections, still cannot see how their thinking has been irrational or system 1 dominated. Maybe the after-the-fact realisation is the real indicator of a good enough system 2. If this is the case, then the next question concerning those 'good enough' students must be about how to encourage them to make the effort to engage and employ system 2 far more frequently.

Bloom (2016) has an explanation for the underuse of system 2, which resonates with my experience of teaching undergraduate social work students about politics, policy, poverty and inequality. He describes how a vast number of people, when questioned about their political affiliations, don't really understand why they support the party they do (don't understand tax, for example). He draws a comparison between this loyalty to a party and loyalty to a sports team and the conclusion that he comes to (reluctantly) is that these views 'don't really matter' (ibid., p. 237). Again, he is making the point that causation is of utmost importance to people. Views about tax, nuclear disarmament and global warning have no direct causal connection to my daily life – in much the same way as concepts such as poverty and inequality have no direct causal connection to a young person from a poor and deprived neighbourhood who drops out of school and starts offending with peers. Moreover, the hugely important, relevant but indirect, or more distant, connections are difficult for people to hold in their minds, attend to and apply in a system 2 deliberation. Bloom goes on to say that this is not about people's lack of capacity for reasoning and that to judge that capacity we should not look to examples where the truth or right answer doesn't matter. He turns to examples where the right answer and truth matters enormously and directly and uses the examples of adults having discussions about whether to buy a house or what to do about an elderly parent. Or, in terms of politics, the engagement of people in local issues such as where to build something or speed limits in local streets. He sums up by saying that when the decision making, knowledge and thinking feels directly relevant,

> ... the level of rational discourse here is high. People know that they are involved in real decision processes so they work to exercise their rational capacities: they make arguments, express ideas, and are receptive to the ideas of others. They sometimes even change their minds (Bloom, 2016, p. 238).

So, social workers and students need to feel that the knowledge they draw on is absolutely relevant and connected to the situation they are facing and that their aim to come to a well thought out resolution is possible. They also need to know that they have agency, that they can make decisions and have opinions, rather than just gather information. This is made more difficult by decision making being pulled upwards (so decisions made by meetings or senior figures rather than by autonomous social workers) and the resultant abdication of responsibility for decisions. This theme will be explored further in the next chapter.

In conclusion, if social workers are making decisions which can be readily understood by reference to the dual-process model (Whittaker, 2018) then social work education should, perhaps, explicitly teach and *use* that model as a framework for reasoning. Students need to know in an explicit and upfront way that good system 2 thinking is an absolute requirement for social work practice.

The use of this dual-process model is, it could be suggested, foregrounded by how a practitioner approaches the situation in the first place. Sheedy (2013, p. 5) calls this a 'world view' and suggests that students need to develop this in order to be able to practice coherently. Having knowledge readily available, and congruent with a world view means, of course, that thinking conceptually and critically about the situation will be facilitated – the conceptual framework is at hand through which to analyse and consider our intuitive reaction to the situation and system 2 is operationalised.

Foregrounded knowledge leading to a world view

In lazy radical practice, knowledge is significantly concerned with the effect structures, policies and politics have on the lived realities of people. The next section will outline the kinds of knowledge social workers should become familiar with before 'doing' social work. The various bodies of knowledge can be thought of as relevant foreground information where connections to the presenting problem might be more indirect but very *influential* on the situation, rather than directly causal. System 2 thinking is essential. Each topic below is not in any way exhaustive and should be considered a brief introduction and pointer.

Inequality and poverty

Remember the quote from Allan Weaver in Chapter 1? The fundamental view that people are shaped by their circumstances and therefore it being unsurprising that people can become hardened by growing up in deprivation, is one that is a key political principle of social democratic, or left wing thinking (Garner et al., 2009). It is also very much at odds with the 'underclass' theory promoted by Charles Murray (1990) where the causation idea was flipped and the notion was that social problems exist because people 'like that' cause them. People are innately incorrigible, especially single mothers and their children. Apart from this thesis feeling instinctively wrong, apart from it being at odds with all of the values of social work, apart from it being wrong in terms of what most social workers who practice relationship-based practice know about the potential and characters of the service users they work with, it is also absolutely wrong when you follow the logic to its conclusion. For example, if useless people or the 'underclass' cause themselves to be in deprivation and cause all the trouble in society, then it follows that the 'overclass' or those who hold power in society have also caused themselves to get into that position, yes? And yet, although only 7% of the population attend fee paying schools, 71% of top military officers, 74% of top judges, 51% of leading print journalists and 32% of politicians (more in the conservative party) are privately educated (*Guardian*, 2016a). So the attribute that people who end up in those position of 'overclass' power have in common, is: very significant economic privilege. We do not know whether they are just cleverer and better anyway – although I would, of course, question that in the same way that I would question whether poor people are more stupid – but we do know *for a fact* that they are wealthier and have vast benefits that come with that. Not only the private education but the attendant social and employment networks. So, for example, unpaid political internships can only be taken up by those with real economic comfort – who else can afford it? And such a path is the one often taken by our politicians. Trade union activism, which might have been an alternative route into politics for working class people, has been drastically weakened and is therefore less available (Jones, 2014).

OK, so we need to think about this myth of meritocracy. The *Guardian* (2016a, n.p.) quotes an author, James Bloodworth, who writes about the sham of meritocracy as saying: 'Yes, it is about the choices an individual makes. But those choices don't occur in a vacuum – they are enabled, usually by money or contacts'. The article goes on to say,

> Over the past half century, the ideal embraced by all British governments has been a meritocracy achieved by equality of opportunity. But, for Bloodworth, this is a sham. 'You have to have cognitive dissonance to talk about a meritocracy while doing nothing about the gaps between the rich and poor, or while not closing down the private school system. Unless you're talking about that, you're not really serious about meritocracy or equality of opportunity'.

If we can grasp that 'making it' in life, or, alternatively, failing, is not only about a person or family's own individual character and abilities, but that the absence of privilege or, indeed, harsh under-privilege, can make life much more difficult and can shape a person's behaviour, then we are on our way to lazy radical social work. Also, an area of understanding we need is how poverty and inequality actually affect people. Everyone is different and, as Weaver said, some (exceptional, perhaps?) people can escape from grim, poor and violent beginnings, but not all. And those with whom social workers work and who remain in those circumstances need social workers who understand the backdrop to their lives rather than condemn them for it.

To return to *The Spirit Level* (Wilkinson and Pickett, 2010) introduced in Chapter 1, we can sum up that vast levels on economic inequality within a country are correlated with most social problems. The authors dig into why that might be and it's this understanding that students of social work really need, and it does take system 2 thinking, so get ready!

The social hierarchy is arranged by status, and that status is usually economic, because in our western capitalist democracies, more often than not, success is measured by economic achievement. Immediately, therefore, the wealthy, privately educated individuals discussed earlier have a place very high up on the hierarchy, leaving the rest of us struggling to climb higher and to prove that we are not a 'loser' and not languishing at the bottom. How do we 'prove' that? Well, think of the emphasis on having the right house, car, phone, TV, internet provision, trainers, jacket, holiday, make-up, perfumes etc. etc. On the surface it might just seem that we 'like nice things' but it is hard to ignore the boasting, display, brand names, competition and other behaviours that we witness in relation to these acquisitions. So, how is this relevant? Wilkinson and Pickett claim that the constant pressure to status-display leads to anxiety (think about debt, for example), stress from working and buying and wanting to 'keep up with the Joneses' or having your children pester you for the right brand of things so they do not get teased at school. This anxiety, especially when you are on the lower end of the hierarchy, can be experienced as constant pressure. How do you show you are 'good enough' when you simply do not have the money?

Wilkinson and Pickett (2018, p. 35) draw on many examples of studies where people were asked to complete problems or undertake tasks, and where cortisol (the stress hormone) was measured. The studies of most interest to the authors were ones where doing tests in front *of others* were examined. Without fail, the thought of being evaluated by others significantly increased levels of stress. In other words, social-evaluation was consistently the biggest contributor to stress. The authors state that:

> What is at stake is your social (as distinct from your physical) self-preservation, which … is a matter of your social value, esteem and status, based largely on other people's perception of your worth.

The authors contend, and indeed demonstrate, that the above increase in stress grows with increasing inequality and contributes to rising levels of anxiety and mental illness.

So, families under this kind of pressure, on top of real worries about making ends meet financially, and actually having enough for a child's birthday present are subject to significant strain. Social workers need to understand that. JRF (2017a, p. 76) states, 'The stress of living on a low income can be linked to relationship breakdowns in couples, and between parents and children'. The report goes on to show that UK children between 10 and 15 report poorer relationships with parents when family income is within the poorest fifth of the population, compared to the two richest fifths. Likewise, relationship distress within couples also varies according to income. This is persuasive evidence, and completely understandable, that stresses and strains of living in poverty makes family relationships more difficult.

Another point made by both Wilkinson and Pickett and by Darren McGarvey, the Scottish rapper also known as Loki, is that when you cannot compete on the social hierarchy with the usual capital of money or status, then you find other ways to do so. Young men especially will use violence and peer group standing to gain respect and status, when they have little else at their disposal (see Chapter 1 and the critique of Cohen's analysis). So many assaults perpetrated by young men are in response to a real or imaginary slight, or a challenge to their status (Wilkinson and Pickett, 2010). I recognise this from the many interviews I had with young men convicted of assaults when I worked in criminal justice services as a social worker. McGarvey (2017, p. 33) states in relation to people he became involved in fights with:

> Their biggest fear was losing face in front of other people in the community and this gave them an edge. If people were honest, they'd admit that fighting is extremely unpleasant. Sadly, backing down from a confrontation or admitting that you don't want to fight can leave you vulnerable to humiliation as well as more aggression. It's this fear of being ridiculed, cast out or attacked that subtly directs your thinking in violent communities.

In essence, status *really* matters, and the steeper the hierarchy, the more it matters. Status seeking can take many forms and being a 'hard man' or 'top dog' is one way to achieve it when few alternative means are available. It is little wonder that violence is greater in more unequal societies (Wilkinson and Pickett, 2010).

It is important that you read more about poverty and inequality and that you use your system 2 thinking skills to really digest the connections between these issues and families' lives. Do not get drawn into easy system 1 thinking that looks for behavioural causal connections – poverty and inequality *affect* people and we must not forget that or we do the people we work with a real disservice. We also will most likely employ the 'moralising self-sufficiency discourse' (Marston, 2013, p. 132) as discussed in Chapter 2, exacerbating a simplified, blame and coercion based type of social work. Such an approach is absolutely at odds with our social work value base.

Economics

In order to understand the connection between politics – policy choices – poverty and inequality, social work students need a basic knowledge of economics. If we believe that poverty and inequality have an effect on the lives of those we work with, we need to properly understand that they do not happen 'unfortunately' or 'inevitably' but that they are consequences of deliberate and strategic political choices. As Yanis Varoufakis (2017, p. 10) said to his daughter, 'To have any say in humanity's future, you cannot afford to roll your eyes and switch off the moment words like "economy" and "market" are mentioned'. Varoufakis, cogently and accessibly, explains how global economy has evolved and how we have come to be driven by the needs of the market – a market economy rather than an economy that has markets. This includes economic worth becoming the *only* worth that is understood as having any value. Other values are very much degraded. Varoufakis gives examples of other 'goods' which have another kind of value by using examples such as doing something for altruistic purposes and feeling good about that – the offer of money or payment completely tarnishing that feeling.

Varoufakis also urges us to understand how economic 'crises' and 'crashes' happen – the ones where the neoliberal common sense states that we have to cut back on welfare and public spending and implement other 'austerity' measures. In a (simple) nutshell, businesses borrow money to invest in, say, the latest technology. They are, in effect, borrowing from the future – future profits they expect to make which will allow them to pay back the loan with interest. The bank benefits from that interest, so unscrupulous bankers can lend money irresponsibly in order to make as much as possible from the interest. Anyway, as automation increases significantly, goods are produced much more cheaply (lower wages, for example), but ruthless competition does not allow businesses to keep their prices high – they must reduce them to compete. Then, those businesses do not make enough profit to pay back the loan (that maybe should not have been given in the first place), they call their banker and say they cannot pay up, the business, and many of them, go bust, then banks are out of pocket and, thus, an economic crash has happened! Rather than the banks paying (and interestingly, bankers usually keep their huge salaries and bonuses!), the public bails out the banks and recoups the money from austerity measures – the ones that hit the people who reply on that public money.

The above picture illustrates what happens in a ruthless, neoliberal economy. In the past, post World War 2, western democracies based their policies on Keynesian economics (after the economist John Maynard Keynes). The difference here was that the government accepted a mixed economy (rather than a purely market economy) where some industries were publicly owned and some privately. The government would intervene to stop the above 'crashes' happening, (by borrowing to invest in business) and would recoup the money when the economy had recovered and was performing well (Fenton, 2016). This was at the same time as the NHS and welfare system were created, within the philosophy that the government had a role in ensuring a reasonable standard of living for everyone (Turbett, 2014). With the move to a neoliberal market economy, that role disappeared, markets were created in every sphere (care, utilities, education, postal services, prisons, social work, health, etc.), and the 'caring' role of the state vanished, to be replaced by a strengthened law and order function. When the state withdraws, businesses and corporations are free to do what they can to keep profit high, and this often means poor wages, zero-hour contracts (no holiday or sick pay), insecure, part-time employment and far fewer workers' rights. Think of the legislation that limited the power of the trade unions, for example.

The conclusion to all of that, then, is welfare benefits curtailed and the poorest, disabled and vulnerable in society really suffering economic hardship and insecurity *and* a new group of workers who are termed the 'working poor' because even though they work hard, they are working in such poor conditions that their full-time wages are not sufficient to keep them out of poverty. Inequality and poverty have resulted from neoliberalism working *in the way it is intended to*. These are not 'unfortunate' consequences, these are the results of deliberate economic policy. So, when you hear of prisons being overcrowded (think lack of public money), care services being very poor (ask if they have been privatised, and that company putting profit before anything else), the NHS in trouble (again, public money curtailments), a friend whose father can't get a care package even though he is suffering from Parkinson's disease (think lack of public money and resultant high thresholds for services), the increase in homelessness (think cuts to housing benefit, the lack of social housing and the increase in private landlords with less regulation, etc.). Are you getting the picture? As Ferguson, Ioakimidis and Lavalette (2018, p. 9) state:

> Unless social work practitioners and academics seek to critically engage with these dominant analyses, there is a danger that they will also be persuaded to accept – and collude with – policies that are profoundly harmful to some of the most disadvantaged sections of society, including users of social work services, but that, in reality, are neither theoretically nor morally justifiable.

To understand more about this, an excellent starting point is Varoufakis's (2017) book *Talking to My Daughter About the Economy*.

Hegemonic neoliberal narratives

For this knowledge section, a few 'common sense' neoliberal hegemonic discourses will be considered as examples of the kind of narrative that absolutely dominates and is so very hard to critique. First of all, however, a metaphor used by Bloom (2016) is worth considering. 'The megaphone man' is a wonderful illustration of how hard it is to resist hegemonic ideas and how easily they are absorbed. The megaphone man is a person at a party with a megaphone and a plethora of stupid and unthinking opinions, who constantly blasts out those opinions and drowns out others' conversations. This situation means that more sophisticated understanding and debate is completely hampered. Now to a few ideas that are blasted out to all in society in much the same way the megaphone man blasts out his inanities to everyone at the party:

People could easily work if they wanted to

The main reason for people not working is that they are sick or disabled (JRF, 2017b). This has been the picture for many years now and dispels the stereotype that lazy scroungers are the ones relying on tax-payers' hard earned money. Tax-payers might have less punitive attitudes towards benefit claimants if they understood this fact.

JRF (2017b) demonstrates that the main reason for claiming benefit is sickness or disability and JRF (2015) shows how certain groups are redefined in a neoliberal, free market economy to be among the 'able but not wanting to work' group:

> The benefit cap aims to prevent certain households (such as those who are working-age, workless, not in receipt of DLA [Disability Living Allowance]) from making high value benefit claims that outstrip median earnings. In practice 11,000 lone parents with a young child aged under 5 are having their benefit capped. If the expectation is that these claimants will respond to the cap by moving into work, the cap is effectively extending conditionality to a group of claimants that would not normally be expected to actively seek work.

Even though 'the UK is among the least generous countries in Europe when it comes to paid leave and unemployment benefits' (*International Business Times*, 2016, n.p.), the stereotype of the lazy scrounger languishing on generous benefits abounds. The question also must be asked about the inordinate attention paid to the very small group of people who are, indeed, benefit cheating but who do not cost the country anything like the amount lost through tax evasion. Media attention to the former is so significant that Britons believe benefit cheating to be 34 times the amount it actually is (The Week, 2016). Reflecting the priorities of neoliberalism, the tax evaders (the richest people in the country) are not attended to or punished in anything like the way the benefit cheats (the poorest) are.

> In any case, at £1.3bn to £1.6bn, it appears outright benefit fraud accounts for less of a burden on the taxpayer than the £4.4bn officially assumed to be lost by evaders [with another 2.7bn lost through 'legal but dubious' tax practices]. So why, the government was asked this week, does it devote more resources to the former?

The Guardian says as many as 3,600 people work in the DWP investigating abuses of the benefit system, while 700 work in the two units at HMRC that deal with the richest taxpayers....The government also rejected the figures (ibid.).

Work is the way out of poverty

Poverty started to rise for some groups in 2011/12, and has been rising more steeply since 2013/14. This rise is taking place in particular among those groups for whom poverty fell most over the last 20 years – lone parents, families with three or more children and families with young children. The rise in poverty is striking among lone parents in work, particularly in full-time work, and among couples where parents work but where there is not at least one full-time and one part-time worker. Projections suggest that these poverty rates are likely to continue to rise sharply over the next few years (JRF, 2017a).

Currently, poverty is quite equally split between workless and in work households, which is quite a shift from 20 years ago (ibid.). The JRF report gives the three main reasons for this as:

➢ The labour market (many more zero hour contracts, poorly paid work and temporary, insecure, casualised, part-time employment. Remember, in a free market economy, markets are indeed 'free' to more or less design their own terms of employment, and profit can really be maximised by squeezing wages, no sick or holiday pay, for example).

➢ State support (in work benefits have been cut).

➢ The cost of living (continues to grow).

Thinking about the introduction of a national minimum wage, many of the gains made have been offset by changes to tax credits and in work benefits:

The net effect of wage increases, tax cuts and reduction in working-age tax credits varies across different types of families. This is illustrated by research analysing the impact of policy changes on incomes in 2022 compared with 2010. For example, focusing on families with two children where adults are earning the national minimum wage:

➢ families where two parents work full-time benefit more from better pay and tax cuts than they lose from benefit cuts; their net income increases by £8 a week

➢ families where one parent works part-time and the other full-time lose £2 a week

➤ single earner couples lose £11 a week

➤ lone parents working full-time lose £16 a week

➤ lone parents working part-time lose £26 a week (JRF, 2017a, p. 25).

We can easily see, then, that work is definitely not the way out of poverty any longer. This very unfair situation should move even those who believe that people 'on the dole' are lazy scroungers to feel some disquiet about hard working families who cannot get themselves out of poverty despite their graft. Think back, also, to Wilkinson and Pickett's central idea about the psychological effects of inequality and the work that has been done on the shame of poverty (Gupta, 2015) and consider whether a future among the 'working poor' would fill anyone with hope, optimism and motivation to work hard at school...?

People are not really poor – look at the things they have

This is something that is frequently raised by students – if people are poor, how come they have flat screen TVs, iPhones, brand named trainers for their kids, and money for fags and booze? This is not only inexplicable to many students, but also attracts a moral judgement about how parents could be spending their money more wisely, on providing for their children, on good food (I mean, vegetables are cheap – yes?) and on more sensible budget plans. This has already been covered in Chapter 4, but is worth a short revisit. Fenton (2016) points out three factors that are worth considering:

1. The pressure to display one's status, so as to fend off feelings of shame (Wilkinson and Pickett, 2010). This is a really powerful phenomenon, especially in an unequal and materialistic country like ours. Think of how young people in schools might exclude and ridicule someone who doesn't own the 'right things' or who lives in the 'wrong' estate. Think about how adults compare and judge themselves against others in terms of house, car, holidays etc. It is *hard* to not care about those judgements.

2. The easy access to credit which makes buying things so easy. Household debt has increased significantly over the last decade, with deregulated banks being able to lend indiscriminately and make huge profits. Money lenders and 'pay day' loans are also readily available, and charge huge amounts of interest. Fenton points out, however, that the main reason for debt is people moving in and out of poorly paid work (JRF, 2010).

3. Thirdly, writers such as Linda Tirado, have explained very clearly, from a poor person's perspective, that smoking and drinking – pleasure and relief-seeking behaviour in effect – is necessary in the grim day-to-day grind of living in poverty (see Chapter 4). Planning ahead seems futile within that struggle.

The other lens through which to view this is, what do we mean by living in poverty. Because someone has a home, food and a TV, does this mean they are not living in poverty? Is relative poverty a bit of a con?

There is no 'real' poverty in this country

Absolute poverty is a state of poverty which means a person does not have the means for the basics of life, including shelter, food and warmth. Relative poverty is when a person has less than 60% of the median income of the country (JRF, n.d.). Margaret Thatcher famously said there was no 'primary poverty' in this country (see Chapter 2) and thus, in effect made an appeal to a return to absolute measures of poverty. Other right wing MPs have made similar appeals, because of course absolute poverty has indeed decreased, and neoliberalism could be held up as a success (and, let's face it, that would be a very good thing for right wing politicians!).

Is relative poverty, then, a fair way to measure poverty? Many measures have been included in the 60% measure, including what the population judge to be necessary for a reasonable life in this country. As Lansley and Mack (2015, p. 10) state, relative poverty is 'one that reflect(s) the standards of today' rather than a past measure of absolute poverty where people might need to be starving on the streets to be considered poor (as in Victorian Britain, but getting more likely all the time). They give the following example, and many others:

> Jennie lives in temporary accommodation in Redbridge, north London. She is a single mother with three sons over the age of 10, all of whom have disabilities. While she tries to make sure her sons are fed properly, she struggles....She sometimes gets offered food by friends and neighbours but in order to ensure her sons are properly fed, she regularly goes without herself....Jennie worked as a hairdresser when she left school, but her middle son ... contracted meningitis as a baby leaving him visually impaired. Jennie, now 41, left work to care for him, having separated from her husband when the children were young, she moved to a woman's refuge and has lived in a variety of temporary accommodation for the last ten years.

> Most of the family's benefit income goes on food, fuel, school clothes and local travel, with rent being paid by housing benefit. They rarely socialise and

have never had a holiday. They do have a television set, a fridge and a washing machine. Jennie often runs out of money: 'But I have to stay strong for myself and for my children, and I hate being in the situation that I'm in now' (Lansely and Mack, 2015, pp. 1–2).

So, is Jennie and her family poor? I think most people would agree that she is. Talking in absolute poverty terms she would not be considered poor, as she has the basics for the survival of her and her children. However, to consider this as acceptable, is to believe that 'those on low incomes (do not) have a right to participate in growing prosperity' (ibid., p. 11). Can you see how relative measures are the only fair way to judge poverty, especially in such a rich country as ours? Taken alongside the vast inequalities in our country, relative poverty measures highlight the moral problem by exposing the grim lived reality for very many, and growing numbers of, families.

Lansley and Mack also point out that twice as many people lived in relative poverty in 2012 as did in 1983; the number of people who cannot afford to heat their homes properly has trebled since the 1990s; one in ten people live in a damp home; and the number of people skimping on meals has doubled since 1983. A BBC report in May 2018, exposed teachers' shock and concern about the numbers of children they are now seeing who are hungry, dirty and obviously living in stark poverty (BBC, 2018b). Suffice to say, poverty is very much a problem in contemporary UK, and understanding of it must result in interventions that are about more than simple individual level behavioural change.

Tying things together

The bodies of knowledge covered above must be considered as introductions only. It is important that social workers read about these topics and keep up to date with changing knowledge and changes to the sociopolitical context within which we all live. Understanding this type of knowledge leads to a consistent and social-justice informed world view and makes it possible to understand why resisting neoliberal hegemonic practice is important.

Becoming immersed in the discussion and analysis of the above bodies of knowledge, in itself leads to practising critical thinking skills. Anecdotally, and from assessing a vast amount of students' work over the years, I can see that conceptual thinking and the application of concepts to ordinary day-to-day human behaviour is very challenging. As mentioned previously, a small scale study also suggested that it may be significantly harder for younger students than for their older counterparts (Fenton, 2018).

So, we need to understand the 'dual-process' system of thinking and reasoning and understand that this is how social workers often make decisions. Starting from this realistic understanding, we should try to enhance our use of the 'dual-process' model, specifically enhancing the use of system 2.

In order to develop system 2 thinking, we can employ Sheedy's idea of developing a 'world view' as mentioned earlier. Sheedy states that a '"world view" is comprised of paradigms or "frameworks of thinking"' (Sheedy, 2013, p. 15). A paradigm is a framework comprised of beliefs, values, theories and rules that one uses to understand the situation one is faced with. Within a world view, different paradigms will exist for thinking about different things, and in this case, we are concerned with a paradigm for critical, system 2 thinking in relation to social work situations. System 2 would utilise such a paradigm in order to make sense of, or analyse, the incoming information. If a worker's social work paradigm is constructed from neoliberal assumptions and beliefs, a moralising self-sufficiency discourse, a diminished understanding of social work values, especially in relation to social justice, and a preoccupation with rules and procedures, then analysis will be informed by this which in turn will lead to oppressive, hegemonic understandings and actions. A lazy radical paradigm, on the other hand, would provide a framework for critical, system 2 thinking based on social work values of redistribution of resources, understanding the effects of, and objecting to, inequality and poverty, rejecting of moralising self-sufficiency discourse and an understanding of structural barriers, rejection of reductionist neoliberal assumptions, real knowledge of the individual or family, compassion and care.

So, system 2 requires foregrounded knowledge which is well understood and therefore easily accessible *and* uses a paradigm, based on anti-neoliberal understanding and real belief in social work values, through which to analyse and critically think about the situation we are faced with. The study by Whittaker and Reimer (2017), discussed in Chapter 3, suggested that students, when they considered and reflected on an ethical dilemma were reflecting to comply with rules. This means that the paradigm used prioritised rules and procedures, especially if the reflector was essentially concerned about 'doing things right' rather than 'doing the right thing' (Munro, 2011, p. 6). This might mean that a lazy radical paradigm should also include rules and procedures, as an acknowledgement that, of course, we cannot ignore these things, but that the paradigm requires augmentation with the elements covered above. A drive towards overall *coherence* in terms of the knowledge bases above, lazy radical thinking *and* acknowledgement of rules and procedures should then be possible, with any jarring element (more often than not, the 'rules' element) leading to ethical stress and possible moral action (see next chapter). Remember Kahneman's conclusion that when things are coherent in a person's mind, they are even more firmly held and more powerful? It might well be that this is an extremely useful mechanism for promoting lazy radical practice and for producing the desired thinking-practice.

Conclusion

Arendt (1964) adds weight to the idea of the coherence of information being so important. She states:

> We see ... how unwilling the human mind is to face realities ... which contradict ... its frame of reference. Unfortunately it seems much easier to condition human behaviour and make people conduct themselves in the most unexpected and outrageous manner than it is to persuade anybody to learn from experience ... that is, to start thinking and judging instead of applying categories and formulas which are deeply ingrained in our mind, but whose basis of experience has long been forgotten and whose plausibility resides in their intellectual *consistency* rather than in their adequacy to actual events (ibid., p. 37, emphasis added).

Given everything in this chapter, then, social work education must endeavour to expect, encourage and assess critical thinking ability; must work very hard to deconstruct consistent, coherent, unquestioned neoliberal world-views and make available a lazy radical conceptual framework including the relevant bodies of knowledge (and to understand how difficult a task that actually is); and to challenge mediocre conformism in the shape of sound bites of superficial knowledge or uncritical acceptance of ideology over evidence.

Summary of main points

➢ It is essential that social workers are critical thinkers, uncritical conformism is dangerous.

➢ Technical competencies, often valued by employers, can dominate and supplant 'thinking-practice'.

➤ There is worrying evidence for very poor critical thinking skills in some social work graduates.

➤ Kahneman's dual-processing system is a useful way to understand the kind of thinking required. Understanding more than simple behavioural explanations for social problems takes system 2 thinking.

➤ Foregrounded knowledge is essential for critical thinking and social workers must keep abreast of that.

6

Lazy Radical Social Work Step 3: Moral Courage

Moral courage refers to the virtue of having *the strength to do what is right in the face of opposition* (Barsky, 2009, n.p.). Barsky asks the following:

> The question is not simply, 'Should we provide education to foster moral courage?' but 'What should moral courage education include?' What knowledge and information should we provide, and what types of learning experiences should be used to promote moral courage? How can we ensure that social workers not only know what is the right thing to do, but that they have the moral strength to put that knowledge into action?

This chapter will attempt to explore and address Barsky's questions and to shed some light on what is, in essence, a call for moral courage within social work which simultaneously recognises the necessity and difficulty of enacting that particular virtue.

Having spent quite some time focusing on the Sheppard et al. (2018) findings that significant numbers of social work granduands are very poor at critical thinking (Chapter 5), this chapter will now turn to the finding from the same study that the graduands also scored significantly lower on 'assertiveness' than the normative public sample. The study showed that the spread of scores related to assertiveness was variable, similar to the spread of critical thinking. Again, there was a very poor group who dragged down the mean scores of the entire cohort. Sheppard et al. recognise that the subjects of this study were at the very beginning of their careers, which might affect assertiveness, but nevertheless, many of the group were reasonably assertive whilst, as in the critical thinking measures, a number of students scored very poorly. Thinking about moral courage, it can be safely assumed that in order to take action one needs to be assertive. Many examples of 'action' are about having the difficult argument or advocating or objecting and, therefore, assertiveness is crucial.

Sheppard et al.'s findings are concerning because moral courage is so central to the kind of practice that social workers should aspire to; again, the opposite of the Eichman-esque unthinking rule following approach. Quinlan, in a study of the character requirements of different degree courses, analysed through the Quality Assurance Agency (QAA) benchmark statements, found that, in social work, courage featured *implicitly* but was not named. She makes the point that asking students to, for example, challenge others, stand up for social justice and respond to prejudice requires significant amounts of courage and concludes: 'the statement paints a picture of social workers negotiating interpersonal and intrapersonal minefields in the service of ideals' (Quinlan, 2016, p. 1046). This cogently captures the enormity of the task we ask of social workers. It is difficult to negotiate that minefield, but it is necessary to do so if social work is about 'ideals' or values in practice. And, of course, every-thing in this book is about the promotion of values and the importance of keeping them central to everything we do. Students and social work-ers reading this book might be now thinking that morally courageous practice is going to be too difficult. Read on, however, because it really is do-able.

Quinlan (2016, p. 1041) also asserts that a traditional purpose of the university was 'character development of its students' and an assumption that it would contribute to the public good through its students' char-acter, moral development and their consequent contribution to society. This is congruent with the traditional definition of the 'professions' as having an altruistic orientation, concerned with public good or public service (see for example, Millerson, 1964, cited in Cunningham, 2008; Sullivan, 2005). Of course, this definition or purpose of the social work profession could easily be viewed through a neoliberal lens, that for the 'public good' service users need to be controlled, coerced and 'made' to pull their socks up. To counteract this, we once again need to be able to refute neoliberal assumptions (see Chapter 5), and to understand social work values in a progressive and radical way (see Chapter 1). A social work 'public good' means understanding that poor public conditions have detrimental effects on people and that individual change alone is not enough to improve the situation.

Organisational, as opposed to occupational professionalism was dis-cussed in Chapter 3 and the suggestion was made that social workers need to identify more with the social work *occupation* as opposed to the *organisation* they find themselves in, in order to be a proper professional. Doing so guards against neoliberal framing of both the social work task and the 'public good'. Occupational professionalism also means using a real social work knowledge base, of the type described in Chapter 5. Parton (2008, p. 159), for example, illuminates this point by suggesting that the knowledge base of social work has changed (in line with the neoliberal evolution of social work). It has moved from one primarily concerned with representing the service user as a social and redeemable person, and working with them on the premise that people are capable of change and worthy of care, regardless of deservedness, to one where:

> No longer was the focus on trying to understand or explain behaviour, for social workers were less concerned with why clients behaved as they did than with what they did. It was behaviour rather than action which was the focus. Depth explanations drawing on psychological and sociological theories were superseded by surface considerations (ibid.).

This is congruent with Ferguson (2008, p. 131) who states that neoliberalism has led to a 'preference for a "social work of surfaces" over deeper explanations of behaviour'. This culminates in a 'professional' practice where the behaviour of service users (their 'outer worlds'; Hennesey, 2011) is the primary focus, and 'organisational' imperatives ensuring that said behaviour has been monitored properly, is the task. Once again, in this portrayal of practice, moral courage is unnecessary.

However, in critical social work terms, this prioritising of 'hard', surface knowledge (observations, reports of behaviour, medical knowledge, etc.) over more subjective forms of knowledge can be challenged (Fook, 2012). Knowledge gained by social workers through their work with service users in getting to understand their 'inner worlds' (Hennessey, 2011): witnessing the consequences of poverty and austerity, for example, can take its place alongside 'factual information' about service users' behaviour. Service users' knowledge about what it is like to *be* in the circumstances they are in and *how* those circumstances are affecting them can also be held to be of equal, if not greater, importance. Acting on those forms of knowledge; advocating, expressing opinion in intimidating decision making fora etc. is the job of a social worker, *but* it takes moral courage to do so.

So both university and the social work profession demand that social workers contribute to the public good and that they stand up for the core values of the profession. The social justice value principle as covered at length earlier in the book is congruent with an anti-neoliberal standpoint and with an anti-self-sufficiency discourse, and therefore social workers, to do real social work, must courageously stand up for an anti-neoliberal understanding of the individuals and families they work with – including critiquing their agency's practice, debating for a more compassionate and understanding practice and advocating on behalf of service users.

Is there hope for the above kind of practice? Returning to the Sheppard et al. (2018) study, and to the Whitaker and Reimer (2017) study, we might conclude that many of the new generation of social workers lack critical thinking skills, lack assertiveness (courage) and reflect and think to *comply* with the rules rather than negotiate an ethical dilemma any other way. Although it is dispiriting to write this, that description would fit Adolf Eichmann very well indeed. This is very worrying and, as a reader of this book, the hope is that you will undertake to be a very different kind of social worker – one who wants and strives to do real social work, with values at the heart of practice and courage to stand up for, and implement, them.

Morally courageous social work?

So, on the assumption that there *is* hope for a different kind of practice, and that the qualities required can be learned or encouraged (back to the debate about pre-disposition or education...), this chapter will now consider what is required from education. May, Luth and Schwoerer (2014) give an overview of a number of studies that demonstrate the positive impact of ethics education on ethical reasoning in business, and are very clear in their belief that courage is indeed malleable and can therefore be learned/encouraged. They also undertook a study with business students which looked at whether moral efficacy (ability to handle moral dilemmas), moral meaningfulness (the importance of ethics in practice) and moral courage (standing up for what is right even in the face of possible adverse personal effects) could be enhanced by attendance at a course on ethical decision-making.

The study was interesting in several ways. The idea of the three dimensions of ethical behaviour is important in that they are all very relevant to how a social worker might respond to a situation. So, for example, there needs to be a belief that the worker does have agency to make a difference and *can* act – much more than being a 'cog' for example (see Chapter 3) – moral efficacy in other words. Moral meaningfulness also encapsulates the ability to see ethical meaning in situations – ethics is only important in a situation if the situation/dilemma is considered to have a moral dimension. A study of criminal justice social workers, for example, found that workers tended to see the downgrading of helping and welfare-based work, and the promotion of managerial techniques, as problematic, but only in a practical, not an ethical sense (Fenton, 2015). So, being unable to 'help' a family with welfare issues or to assist them with what was really required, even though social work values and education would say that helping was central, was not seen as a value conflict, just a practical problem (usually one of resources).

So, actually identifying moral meaningfulness in the first place is important. This is so closely linked to being able to deconstruct the neoliberal hegemony and to think critically about assumptions, that without that ability, moral meaningfulness might indeed be missed. Social workers might still feel compassion or whatever towards families they see struggling and with whom they have built relationships, but without critical understanding of that struggle, technical social work practice might simply continue unquestioned. Fronek and Chester (2016, p. 164) provide a cogent illustration of how the injustice enshrined in our societies, which significantly affects service users, should be disturbing to social workers:

> We cannot in good conscience be proud of [our societies]....Our governments are intent on the expulsion [of refugees], preventing their entry and abandoning them at sea, and politicians boast about what is nothing more than a concentration camp renaissance....The big media corporations, owned by a few, assist in this shaping of public discourse on this and many other issues. When language changes – for example from 'asylum seekers' to 'illegals', from the unemployed, people with disabilities and the aged to 'leaners' – meanings are altered to support ideological positions and political interests and these shifts objectify those people most in need and deem them less worthy.

The authors draw on the work of Hessel (2012, cited in Fronek and Chester, 2016) to suggest that the response to these injustices should be rational and knowledge-based outrage. They point out, however, that armchair outrage is insufficient, the outrage must lead to action. I would say to any reader, however, that this does not have to mean activism as already discussed in this book. It can mean 'practivism' – action within your practice as per lazy radical social work! So, herein lies a very important point. Social workers need to critically understand the injustice in the first place (Chapter 5); are more likely to feel outrage in practice when they have built relationships with the people affected (Chapter 4); and then can *use* the understanding of the situation (the moral meaningfulness) to identify the moral issues as such (not just as practical issues), to feel moral outrage or ethical stress (Chapter 3) and thus feel an impetus towards moral courage and action.

Stanford (2011, p. 1520) found that the personal moral code of a social worker, including compassion, empathy and a social justice understanding, was the deciding factor in whether they would 'control and dismiss' or 'protect and advocate' when working with service users. The 'protect and advocate' group, importantly also had a belief in the possibility of change which was missing from the other group. Herein, then, we again see moral efficacy (belief in helping towards real change) and moral meaningfulness (links from the situation to social justice, critical thinking), leading to morally courageous behaviour (advocating, for example).

Simola (2014) also defines three characteristics of moral courage: courage is something freely chosen by the actor, the purpose to be achieved is morally worthy, and there is a risk to the actor. These three elements map onto May et al.'s three dimensions very well and, in order to understand moral courage more fully, will be used in this chapter as follows:

➢ Social workers need to believe and understand that they have agency as proper social work, occupational professionals. This must take precedence over agency-loyal organisational professionalism when there is a conflict.

➢ They need to see the moral aspects to their work in every situation, not define moral problems as only practical ones and need to understand how important the ethical dimension to social work is – the *central* place of values. This understanding should help to fuel passion and, sometimes, outrage which might provide an impetus to the next dimension – action. Likewise, the experience of ethical stress (only experienced when a social worker has a well developed value base) can also be used as an impetus to action (Fenton and Kelly, 2017).

➢ They need to understand the perception of a 'blame culture', understand how to navigate that and understand that although there are personal risks in standing up for what is right, it *is* worth it.

PRACTICE EXAMPLE 6

This is a practice example drawn from a good many years ago, but which illustrates the idea of moral efficacy, meaningfulness and courage quite well.

A student was on placement in a prison social work department. She was given her first parole report to write, by gathering information from guards and others who worked with the prisoner and by getting to know him and doing her own assessment. On allocation of the report, other workers in the office said 'folk don't get parole on first application'. The student said 'oh ok', but went away and thought critically and analytically about that. First of all, she raised the question 'is this an actual prescribed, written down piece of policy?' If the answer to that had been 'yes' she may still have felt that some moral action in questioning the policy might be required. However, the student found out that this was no policy, simply a 'how we do things here' rule of thumb. Think organisational professionalism and unthinking task-doing! So, let's consider what the student did through the components of moral action:

Moral efficacy: The student was moved enough by thoughts of injustice and by her knowledge of the young man in question to believe she could do something about this or find a way to deviate from what was only a 'rule of thumb' (knowledge and relationship-based practice).

Moral meaningfulness: The student could see that this could be a real breach of human rights if the prisoner did indeed fit the criteria for early parole release, but was denied it on the basis of an untrue assessment in the name of 'looking credible' (which was the reason given by the team). This was not a practical problem of how to write the report in such a way as to lead to a logical 'no parole' recommendation, but was a moral one of not allowing the prisoner an honest and fair assessment (critical understanding and values knowledge).

Moral courage: The student spoke to her practice educator about her dilemma, having drawn on knowledge of human rights, parole policy documents, desistance theory, relationship-based practice, knowledge of the prisoner and his 'inner world' and a myriad of other knowledge sources. She was able to deconstruct the 'rule of thumb' is such a way as to expose its basic unjust foundation and its incongruence with social work values (ethical stress leading to moral action).

There were risks to taking this action in that the student made herself quite unpopular with the rest of the team. The practice was revised, because the practice educator who was also the team leader was persuaded against it. A neat and just outcome such as this does not always transpire however, but the student had at least taken action to *attempt* to do something about the injustice. Note the elements in brackets – within this type of moral social work we can clearly see the lazy radical practice steps!

To return to May et al. (2014), the authors found that ethics education had a significant impact on moral efficacy and moral courage, but not on moral meaningfulness (although it did with students who scored more poorly on this dimension at pre-test stage). The course was mainly concerned with the exploration of ethical issues and working through responses. It may have been that considering ways workers *can, should* or *are allowed to* respond increases the students' repertoire of possible behaviours and arms them with agency and courage. The authors recommend that future business courses target ethical education and outcomes and this might well be the case for social work education also. Imagine the power of hearing from real social workers and managers who operate ethically, who see moral meaning in their work and who can demonstrate real examples of moral courage. An eight week programme (as per May et al.'s study) focusing on that, could be extremely powerful. Adding weight to the idea that education can enhance moral courage, Oliver, Jones, Raynor, Penner and Jamieson (2017), in a small UK study, found that a course of study on 'having the difficult conversation' positively impacted on students' courage in being able to raise difficult issues with their practice educators whilst on placement. So, for students and readers – seek out those role modules who you can see practice ethically. Have a chat with them about this chapter or about being courageous enough to question how things are done.

Moral courage in an ethics of care framework

To bring some clarity to learning about moral courage, and very much in keeping with the ethos of this book, it might be useful to consider moral courage through an ethics of care framework (introduced in Chapter 4). Simola (2014, p. 31) points out that, in keeping with traditional research on moral courage, care ethics 'reflect a focus on speaking with authenticity and integrity, despite pressure to do otherwise, or the possibility of censure'. Simola goes on to say that moral courage is underpinned by rational, conscious deliberation and describes it as an activity that can be seen as sitting within Kahneman's system 2 thinking. Although care ethics developed as an alternative to Kolberg's ethics of justice, Simola suggests that rational, conscious reasoning is common to both. For the purposes of lazy radical practice, this highlights the irrefutable link between critical thinking and moral courage. Morally courageous acts are impossible without the preceding step of critical thinking. Having said that, Simola also suggests that automatic responsive system 1 thinking is not incompatible with the process and can be integrated into a holistic cognitive engagement.

In a thorough-going review of the literature on moral courage in business, Simola identifies features which are necessary for the enactment of morally courageous acts. The first feature is that moral courage is roused when there is a perceived threat to the 'collective vitality' (ibid., p. 33) which, in terms of care ethics, means a threat to the quality of relationships between people, especially inauthenticity, carelessness or harm. In terms of social work, this is a hugely significant idea. If a social worker views 'the collective' as the agency only, then threats to the relational quality within that collective might be *from* another worker who is morally courageous and speaks out on behalf of service users. Protecting the agency from harm and preserving the relationships within the organisation might well become the subject of an interpretation of moral courage (in an organisational professional way). So, for example, covering up for a colleague's oppressive and bullying behaviour towards service users because 'the collective' excludes service users and the only important relationships are the internal agency ones. Consider, for example, the case mentioned earlier, of a social worker who added her name to a report which had been altered by her manager, then lied about it in court (BBC, 2015). The manager was described as being quite a dominant person, and the social worker was relatively new, but, nonetheless, the actions taken were not only unethical but also illegal. This is a stark example of several things: (1) The dominance of organisational professionalism – the rules and operations within the agency are absolutely paramount – occupational knowledge, values and legal and ethical literacy are very much lacking

(Preston-Shoot, 2011). (2) Relationships *within* the agency must be preserved at all costs and some people will go to real lengths in order to do so. (3) The service user who was the subject of the report was absolutely not included in the perceived network of relationships. The internal ones mattered, and the relationship with the 'other' or service user was, in this case, excluded from that network.

In contrast to the above, if the agency is one where lazy radical practice is the norm, with its core tenet of solidarity with service users, then 'the collective vitality' will *include* those service users as part of the social work community. This, in turn, means that a perceived threat to the relational quality of the collective will *include* poor behaviour and uncaring treatment of service users. Witnessing such would feel like something very wrong and toxic, the underlying process, according to Simola, being a real threat to the norm of how we treat each other (including service users). Thinking back to Chapter 4, it is clear how relationship-based practice is the only way to make this happen – service users are only part of the collective, and social workers are only in solidarity with them, if proper relationships have been built. Any notions of service users as a separate group, such as an 'underclass' or 'not like us' or 'other', immediately makes the idea of an holistic collective highly unlikely.

Three agencies in Canada were explored by Kosny and Eakin (2008). Although these agencies included service users who had 'done wrong', the staff were absolutely committed to the mission of the agencies and perceived the service users as victims of an unjust society. The staff felt very much in solidarity with them and reported very few ethical conflicts or situations where they felt they could not act on their values. In fact, the situations that gave rise to stress for the staff were the ones where they felt they might have been kinder, or might have helped more or had themselves failed to act properly on their values. One way of understanding what was going on here, is that the 'collective vitality' very much included staff and service users on an equally important footing with relationships between them all as equally important.

Simola underscores the above with the central idea of 'a perceived connection with others through the experience of shared humanity' (2014., p. 36) and connects that to another essential feature of moral courage – caring. The idea of easier caring for others whom we perceive as like ourselves is pointed out, and reflects Bloom's (2016) thinking discussed in Chapter 4. However, Simola also notes that through shared humanity, extending care to the 'other' is possible. This can be encouraged by exposure to a range of divergent others (which social work itself facilitates – via placements and practice) as well as exposure to affecting words and images. Again, this was discussed in Chapter 4 as a way for social work education to encourage rational compassion or empathy in students. Simola (ibid., p. 38), however, extends the discussion of caring by contrasting caring habits with 'acaring' habits (practical and morally neutral skills) and 'noncaring' habits (hurtful patterns of action that harm others).The finding from Fenton (2015) mentioned earlier is interesting here, where intrinsically moral problems of not being able to help people with welfare and other needs (due to managerial imperatives) were experienced as practical and morally neutral difficulties. Does that suggest that the agency and workers within it were 'acaring'? Perhaps active 'care' is downgraded in many social work agencies?

Stop and think box 9

How much does care feature in social work education? Probably not much. Why is that do you think?

Think of what you associate 'care' with – is it with social care? Personal care? How can we increase attention to care in social work education? After all, it is central to social work ethics:

> Social workers have a responsibility to apply the professional values and principles set out above to their practice. They should act with integrity and treat people with compassion, empathy and **care** (BASW, 2014b, p. 11).

The final impetus towards moral courage from Simola's paper is that of moral identity. First of all, practising care habits can lead to consolidation of caring as a central feature of a person's moral identity and Simola is clear that practising caring habits can lead to a consolidation of caring as a moral identity. On the other hand, disregarding care leads to the erosion of the caring part of moral identity. The author also makes it clear that congruence between the moral identity of the individual and the moral identity of the agency or organisation means a high level of well-developed moral identity and the ability to 'use voice' and/or take moral action. This is akin to the agencies in Kosny and Eakin's study, but less likely to be true in contemporary statutory social work agencies. Keeping moral identity alive and, thus, raising the likelihood of moral action means finding alternative networks with congruent moral identity and purpose such as peer/colleague allies and networks such as SWAN (Social Work Action Network, 2018).

Meanwhile, to return to social work education, a clear and explicit moral identity, with care at its heart, must again be a strong feature of social work programmes. If we want to help students develop moral identity, including moral courage, then we need an environment that is conducive to that, especially in the light of identity sustainability in an eventual potentially neoliberal and oppressive setting (Nicolas, 2015; Rogowski, 2015). This is yet more reason for promoting lazy radical practice as an approach to practice.

Ethical stress leading to moral action

Fine and Teram (2012, p. 1313) undertook a study in Canada to investigate what prompted social workers to take ethical action. Their central finding can be summed up by the following quote:

> I think it's very important to know what you consider to be right and very important to speak up when you think something is not right and to explore it and to be willing to sort of be one of the few voices and not just go with the flow because everyone else is comfortable with it.

The social worker above clearly knew what he/she perceived to be the right thing. That *knowing* is key, because knowing draws on knowledge and critical thinking (Chapter 5), knowledge of and a relationship with the service user involved (Chapter 4) and then the recognition, or feeling, that something is 'not right'. The social worker also felt that 'speaking up' was possible and, perhaps, would be effective (moral efficacy) and viewed the entire situation as moral (against what he/she 'considered to be right' – moral meaningfulness). We can therefore see all of the elements already explored in this chapter, apparent in this one quote. Fine and Teram also uncovered that, for the social workers who were able to take action, they almost felt there was no alternative, such was the drive to do the right thing. They had a clear sense of what was right (moral meaningfulness) and the primacy of the welfare of the service user in common. This is exactly the kind of moral courage that lazy radical practice seeks to encourage.

Returning to the analysis of the quote above, the next section focuses on the feeling that something is 'not right'. Throughout the book so far, there have been references to the experience of ethical stress (see particularly Practice Example 2, in Chapter 3). In relation to reflection, and the temptation to reflect to comply (Whitaker and Reimer, 2017), an alternative response is advocated – reflect on the feeling that something is 'not right' and really attend to, and analyse it. The feeling that something is 'not right' is, more often than not, due to the ability to act on our values being thwarted. When we act in a way that is congruent with our values, we feel a sense of rightness, even if the action is difficult. However, if we are required to take action, by a procedure, by a manager's instruction, or by a rule of thumb (see Practice Example 6 earlier in this chapter) that is at odds with our values, we should experience ethical stress (Fenton, 2015). In Fenton's study, social workers felt ethical stress when they perceived their agencies to be restrictively risk averse and when the climate of the agency was not conducive to value-driven work. Fenton and Kelly (2017) also suggest that prolonged ethical stress can lead to 'moral injury', a more severe form of ethical stress, and again, argue strongly for social workers to use those feelings as a guide to ethical action rather than to bury or 'cope with' them.

Moral injury and resilience

Fenton and Kelly (2017) have adapted the idea of moral injury from a concept used to describe how ex-service people could be affected by witnessing real acts of cruelty, inhumanity or immorality and not being able to do anything about it. The authors fully recognise that the moral injury in social work is nothing like as severe as that which might be experienced during war times, but do draw a parallel. The authors also draw on the body of literature that suggests ex-soldiers should do more than try to cope with or recover from their moral injury, but should use the experience as an impetus to question the 'rightness' of the practice of war or of the more specific actions taken in the name of war. It is herein that the usefulness for social work can be seen. Social workers suffering from ethical stress or moral injury (and only those with a well-developed sense of values and moral identity will do so, that is only those workers will see moral meaningfulness in the situation) should be encouraged to reflect on and recognise what these feelings mean, and to reflect on *why* they feel like that, and then on *what* might be done. Learning about all of this during social work education, and learning that the right thing is to *act* in a morally courageous way, is central to encouraging this kind of morally courageous practice once a student qualifies. Instead, however, there is often a neoliberal-congruent strand of social work education concerned with coping with these feelings, as if they were negative emotional hindrances, rather than positive impetuses to action – in other words, a focus on individual resilience.

Ferguson (2018, p. 15) illuminates that social workers indeed do not tune into the feelings of ethical stress, but do in fact often simply 'cope with' them. Consider the quote from one of the social workers:

> No, and you just turn the music up loud in the car and you forget about it, and then you focus on the next visit. But it's like if you have a lot [of difficult visits] together, then it would be draining. And that's what I was saying about,

> I think, like when I went, before I went on the visit today, I was sort of ranting to [colleague] about it like 'Oh God, you should have seen her the other day what was she like with me, and now I've got to go'. I think it's, I really draw on that, you know, being able to offload a little bit, just briefly and her being like, 'Oh yeah', do you see what I mean?

Ferguson discusses the limits to reflection and the, sometimes, 'defended' self which allows social workers to cope with high levels of anxiety. This is understandable and, as a practitioner, I can relate to the limits on reflection-in-action when one is simply trying to cope and survive. However, there is a paucity of thought in the above example. 'Oh God you should have seen her the other day' is actually in reference to a mother who was terrified of losing her daughter. The worker did not seem to think about that as a reason for the sustained shouting she was on the end of (and that would be traumatic, I understand that), and actually tried not to think about anything by turning her music up. It also seems to me that the social workers were using reflection in a very self-regarding way – 'how things impact on me'. *What about reflecting about the service users?* Ferguson makes a cogent case for the limits on reflection-in-action that will be recognisable to any practitioner, but evidence of more thought for service users would not be an unreasonable expectation, even if this was expected only after the fact when fear and tension were no longer features. Ferguson (2018, p. 21) notes that although some non-reflection can be healthy (in these very emotionally charged situations), 'any kind of non-reflection should only be a temporary state and needs to end with supervisors providing containment, and enabling critical thinking on what has been experienced'. Ferguson is also clear in his conclusion that critical reflection *on* action is crucial, and it can be suggested that this should not require a reliance on supervisors and supervision, but should be part of (lazy radical) practice at its best – analysing, employing system 2 thinking and bringing knowledge to bear on the situation. How, otherwise, can 'difficult' and sometimes frightening service users be understood and connected with (see Chapter 4)?

Garrett's (2016) critique of resilience theory within social work has some utility in understanding the above situation of social workers. Discussing how resilience is criticised due to being very individual actor-centred and, thus, downplaying the part structural issues play in a person's well-being or 'success', Garrett suggests:

> For example, the structurally generated scale of poverty in the USA and the enormous disparities in wealth are not the focus of research interest. Instead, and despite 'growing recognition of the importance of analysing contexts, "resilience" research remains principally preoccupied with the individual and assumes

the individualized nature of adaptation' (Bottrell, 2009, p. 336). This criticism is related to the charge that it 'can depoliticise efforts such as poverty reduction and emphasise self-help in line with a neo-conservative agenda instead of stimulating state responsibility' (Mohaupt, 2009, p. 67) (Garrett, 2016, p. 1918).

This idea, the promotion of self-help for service users and adaptation to circumstances which should be the target of state intervention, mirrors an emphasis on self-help for social workers in neoliberal practice contexts that should be the target of resistance and critique. In other words, in relation to social workers, resilience can become concerned with positive adaptation *to* neoliberal, oppressive contexts rather than with positive adaptation *in spite of* neoliberal, oppressive contexts. The former might well look like the unthinking task-doing already explored in this book so far, whilst the latter might be increasing resistance behaviour, increasing advocacy and working *more* in solidarity with the service user against a punitive regime.

Interestingly, van Breda (2018) responds to Garrett's resilience critique with an appeal to recognise that people do have agency and that the person-in-environment construct has always been at the root of social work. In essence, van Breda wants a discussion that goes beyond the 'agency-structure binary' (ibid., p. 2). Garrett and van Breda both accept that resilience theorising *can* be co-opted by the neoliberal agenda but van Breda's point is that it need not be so, and that there is a rich body of literature in relation to this, especially focused on social ecological theory. Van Breda concludes that agency *and* structure are important for good outcomes for service users. Applying this to the social worker parallel drawn previously, it can be suggested that social work contexts do need to change in order that social worker ethical stress or moral injury reduce, *but* that resilience and agency of social workers to adapt *in spite* of that continuing context can also reduce ethical stress – by social workers allowing the resultant ethical stress to lead to action. This is adaptive practice that might not have been required in a more welfare-focused practice environment. The other important point from both authors is that practitioners need to understand how resilience theory can be used in a neoliberal fashion, to reinforce the discourse of individualism, and must be alert to that rather than collusive.

Decision abdication: lack of courage?

As introduced in Chapter 3, Whittaker (2011) undertook a very interesting research study looking at social workers' defences against anxiety. As a foundation for his research study, Whittaker considered Menzies

Lyth's famous 1950s study on how nurses in a hospital setting coped with anxiety. Several features of that study resonate with the thinking in this book – for example, relationships were discouraged, by breaking down the nursing role into repetition of the same task for many patients, rather than performing all of the required care tasks for one patient. Relationships were therefore undermined, patients were dehumanised, and 'doing the task' became the primary objective. Remembering the work of Arendt in relation to Eichmann, we can see how dangerous and oppressive this way of working is. Also, there was an abdication of decision-making which in practice led to always asking the manager to make the ultimate decisions and therefore taking no responsibility for the outcomes of the decisions (and therefore not risking any blame).

Whittaker's study considered these anxiety-defence strategies in relation to child protection teams in North London and found that the upward-delegation of decision-making was one of the most common strategies and was often subtle in its enactment. For example:

> The team manager asked a social worker 'What is happening with the [X] case?' The social worker said that she had spoken to the school and the teacher had been concerned about the child. The team manager asked, 'So what do you think we should be doing?' The social worker responded by describing the information in more detail. After several minutes the team manager said, 'So what do you think we should be doing?' The social worker appeared tense but went back to describing the information received. After a few minutes, the team manager stated what the social worker should do and whom she should contact. The social worker seemed relieved and strode off to start the tasks (Whittaker, 2011, p. 487).

Whittaker found that this strategy was used far less frequently by experienced staff. For them, following their own judgement reduced anxiety.

Mirroring another finding from the Menzies Lyth study, Whittaker found that social workers used many checks and counter checks when they had to make a decision – even a small decision such as being 'allowed' to contact another professional. Likewise, Menzies Lyth's finding that the proceduralisation of tasks and doing things the 'correct' way dominated, and this was also similar in child protection. Practitioners could closely follow procedure and, again, enjoy 'not being required to make a choice and therefore incur the burden of decision-making' (ibid., p. 489). Social workers also prized this type of procedural knowledge above traditional social work knowledge which, once again lends itself to organisational, as opposed to occupational, professionalism (see Chapter 3), and to an Eichmann-esque procedure following form of practice.

Considering all of the above, Whittaker questions whether social workers really would welcome reduced bureaucracy and increased autonomy (as per the Munro recommendations, for example). Fenton (2015) also found that only 30% of the respondents in her study of criminal justice social workers agreed with the statement 'I would like more autonomy'. It seems that practitioners welcome the safety and security afforded by procedures and upward delegation of decision-making. Is this a lack of moral courage? How can lazy radical practice be in any way reconciled with Whittaker and others' findings? Whittaker sums up the problem:

> This may result in the paradoxical position that the social work profession largely supports the Munro Review's analysis of the problems [too many dense procedures, not enough autonomy] while resisting the implementation of solutions (Whittaker, 2011, p. 492).

What is to be done? One positive finding from Whittaker's study is that more experienced social workers were far less likely to resort to social defences against anxiety. It might be tentatively suggested that, in keeping with some of the other ideas in this book in relation to the younger, newer generation of social workers, it is not only experience that contributes to this difference, but also that more experienced, older workers are more likely to have a different, welfare and anti-neoliberal approach (Fenton, 2014). It might be that having an alternative framework for practice which produces ethical stress recognition, moral outrage and therefore an impetus to action, as opposed to an unquestioned neoliberal/managerial framework makes a difference in how social workers view and respond to these procedural and decision-making restrictions. Once again, we return to the importance of social work education providing such a framework, and to the importance of students reading books like this one that also provide an alternative framework for practice.

Social work education

Morley and Macfarlane (2014) studied 80 social work students who undertook a critical social work programme and found that their ability to identify ethical issues, to understand the lives of marginalised people and, most crucially for this chapter, to take moral action increased after the programme. For example, students said:

> Linking critical theory to practice has been the most important learning for me.... Practising social work from a critical perspective in the future gives me the ability to locate all these points of resistance; to challenge the dominant discourses ... (p. 344).

I have been able not only to assist clients but also to challenge unhelpful dominant discourses within my own organisation ... (p. 349).

[I've become] more conscious of listening; really listening to what people say, to the difference in their response [from mine] rather than interpreting their experience through mine or privileging my experience (p. 345).

Encapsulated within those quotes from students, we can identify: the deconstruction and understanding of the neoliberal hegemony (knowledge and critical thinking); the desire to help service users and getting to know them (relationship based practice); and challenging dominant discourses (moral courage). The three steps of lazy radical practice in fact. We can also see, in relation to moral courage specifically, moral efficacy (the belief that challenge is worthwhile); moral meaningfulness (that there is a moral dimension to the practice situation which can be at odds with the dominant discourse); and moral identity formation ('practising in the future').

This is a hopeful study, with an example of one type of social work education having an impact on students in the way that this book suggests is absolutely necessary. Once again, we return to the idea that a more robust form of social work education that does not leave an empty space that neoliberal, procedural and distant practice can easily fill, is key to changing the practice of the next generation of social workers. Students entering practice should have a robust framework for lazy radical practice, which means they will be equipped to do real social work, based on real social work values.

Conclusion

To conclude this chapter, it is worth thinking about Hannah Arendt's (1964) essay 'Personal Responsibility Under Dictatorship'. Can the bureaucracy, procedures, rules and managerialism of some statutory social work services be considered as 'dictatorship'? As Arendt (1964, p. 31) says 'bureaucracy is the most cruel of rulership' and when social workers are having to ask 'can I make a phone call?' (Whittaker, 2011), we can see just that 'dictatorship' is maybe not too far a stretch.

Arendt's essay was written in response to the controversy initiated by her book on Eichmann. Much of the criticism centred round that idea that Eichmann could not, or should not, be judged by people who were not there at the time (Eichmann's own defence as it happens). Also, Arendt stated that much of the criticism was based on the idea that none of us is a free agent and therefore not really responsible for what we do. This resonates with discussions I have had with colleagues in relation to this book, and moral courage in particular. Colleagues have criticised my thinking, by postulating that it *is too difficult* for social workers to be morally courageous. Of course they would just do the tasks, and not consider wider moral or ethical issues, or would subsume them beneath the requirement to do things properly and follow the rules (Whitaker and Reimer, 2017), because they do not want to get into trouble, they have a mortgage to pay and want to be seen to do a good job by managers. It doesn't seem enough for me to say 'but, surely, they have to try to do what's right?'

Anyway, to return to Arendt. The 'personal responsibility' part of her thesis has already been discussed in Chapter 3, in terms of her construct of 'cog-theory', and the ultimate question of choosing to be that kind of cog, or continuing as a cog whilst knowing how morally wrong things are. Moving to the 'under dictatorship' part, we need to understand this as under bureaucratic and managerial dictatorship in social work. Even under the most extreme dictatorship in Nazi Germany, some people refused to participate in the new order. Arendt says that these people did not have a better system of values than those who willingly took part (often it was the more respected in the community who did, willingly, take part), but what set them apart is that they *thought about* what they were doing (Chapter 5). Also, they allowed the dissonance between what they were being asked to do (participate in killing people) and their conscience to cause them to feel troubled and to, then, act on that feeling (ethical stress leading to moral action). Arendt states that values and moral codes can easily be changed overnight and thus, those that hold firmly to codes and rules are not reliable in every case. What is required is *thinking* – not technically or theoretically – but doubting, questioning and, ultimately, making up their own minds. The people in Arendt's examples sometimes died for failing to obey, whereas in the world of social work with its bureaucratic dictatorship we are probably more likely talking about disapproval from a manager or team, or having to debate your own stance. Consequences that, although unpleasant, are really quite unimportant. Arendt makes the final point that obeying superiors or procedures implies support for them, so, in social work, if ethical stress is generated because a worker feels the action is wrong, then they *must* question it or they are, in effect, supporting it.

Just to conclude this section, then, it is absolutely clear that the link between critical thinking (Chapter 5) and moral courage is undeniable. To doubt, question and, sometimes, resist after a personal and ethical analysis of the situation is the only way that morally courageous action can be triggered. If this does not happen, if there is, as Mill warned against, a mediocre conformism to how things are done around here, or to the instruction or procedure, then unthinking Eichmann-esque, oppressive and value-poor practice will prevail.

'The only thing necessary for the triumph of evil is for good men to do nothing' (Edmund Burke 1729–1797).

Summary of main points

> Demonstrating moral courage is not easy and involves risks to oneself.

> The university and the profession demand that people contribute to the public good and uphold the values of social work. This takes courage.

> Ethical education is important and can have a significant impact on students.

> Social workers need to see the ethical content in their work and must have a belief in their own agency.

> An ethics of care is a useful framework within which to situate moral courage.

> Ethical stress can be an impetus to moral courage and action.

> Social workers need to be brave enough to make, and articulate, decisions rather than simply wait to be told what to do.

7

Doing Lazy Radical Social Work: Getting Beyond the Individual

This chapter will begin with a thinking exercise based on a real assignment case-study. It will then explore how students, who have struggled with thinking conceptually about poverty, inequality, neoliberalism and other socio-political influences, tend to approach and interpret the scenario. The chapter will then deconstruct how a lazy radical approach might look.

Stop and think box 10

The allure of the individual level of understanding.

I teach a module focusing on the deconstruction of the neoliberal hegemony. The assignment is an analysis of a Scottish case study as follows:

Kyle is 18 years old and has been charged with Breach of the Peace for the third time. He has appeared in court for all three offences, although was also dealt with for similar acts by the children's hearing system when he was younger. The Sheriff has requested a court report and you are the criminal justice social worker responsible for compiling it.

Kyle's schooling did not go well. He truanted and caused trouble, seemingly not interested in applying himself at all. He then engaged with a project worker for some time after being excluded from school, and made some improvement, but then began to spend time with an older peer group and drank alcohol regularly. He then disengaged from the project.

Kyle had been living with his dad, his dad's girlfriend and his grandmother. He used to stay some of the time with his great grandmother to whom he was close, and when she died, his drinking escalated. His grandmother could not cope with his high level of drinking and resultant aggressive and disruptive behaviour and had to ask him to leave the house. His dad reluctantly agreed. He occasionally returns for a night or two, but is mainly sofa-surfing with friends and sleeping rough.

▶

Even if Kyle's behaviour did improve, he says he does not want to return to the family home. There is very little space (his dad and girlfriend have just had a baby) and he does not really get on with his dad's girlfriend. His dad has not worked since being made redundant five years ago from his job as a welder when the factory closed down, and the family survive on benefits. They are poor and struggle to make ends meet.

The aim of this assignment is to identify and explore the wider political and societal issues which are impacting on Kyle (and, where appropriate, his family).

Students should discuss, in their essays, the influence of inequality (*The Spirit Level*, for example), and poverty on the family, including how neoliberal policy choices might have made things more difficult. But, do you see the temptation to stick to an individual level of understanding? From my experience, these individual level understandings take three broad forms: punitive, identity/discrimination and therapeutic. Have a think about your initial reaction to, and understanding of, the case study. Then read on!

The punitive, individual level of understanding

Louise Casey was commissioned to undertake a study with families with complex and multiple problems, focusing on those who caused the most difficulty in their communities. Her summation of the study resonates very closely with the understanding that I see some students bring, and sometimes adhere to, in the course of their social work studies:

> What came from these families' stories were that they had entrenched, longterm cycles of suffering problems and causing problems. Their problems were cumulative and had gathered together over a long period of time – perhaps over generations. Listening to the families there was a strong sense of them having problems and causing problems for years. The longevity of their relationship with services was also striking. In many cases their problems began with their own parents and their parents' parents, in cycles of childhood abuse, violence and care which are then replayed in their own lives (Casey, 2012, p. 1).

Students talk quite glibly about the 'cycle of deprivation' and, if asked to explain, they paint the same picture as painted by Casey – difficult and troublesome families, where substance misuse, abuse, neglect, unemployment, criminality and harshness prevails and is 'handed down' intergenerationally as children learn to live, and parent, in the same way. Even if students genuinely wish to engage and 'help' families (especially the children), the backdrop is one of behavioural and value problems exhibited by bad family units. It is little wonder, then, that they recognise and sometimes agree with portrayals of families such as:

> Of course, nothing can ever excuse the unspeakable cruelty of Baby P's mother. But this harrowing Mail investigation lays bare how society's amoral and bru-talised underclass breeds such monsters (*Daily Mail*, 2009). Or

> When a truly abhorrent crime happens, you can be sure of one thing: it'll have taken place in a welfare ghetto. (*News of the World*, cited by Warner, 2015, p. 225)

In my role as a social work educator I do see the above beliefs held by students who have not known people who live in poverty and, thus, have internalised the frightening and disturbing picture painted by the tabloid media. They might also have spent time on social media 'liking' and signalling their own moral character by agreeing that people should be 'thrown in jail' or worse (like if you agree!) or 'not allowed to have children' (like if you agree!) or whatever. It is easy and popular to join in and 'like' simple statements about moral positioning such as feeling anger towards child abusers.

Thinking about Kyle, this narrative can be directed at him in terms of 'he should have "stuck in" at school' and 'he should get a job'. If, through teaching and discussion in lectures, students grasp that the 'right' answer is that Kyle's poor decision making is made in a context where good decision making is difficult, they then tend to limit their understanding to the family-as-context level. Good families can overcome poverty and deprivation (they will be working, providing role models and prioritising homework), whereas bad families (as per Casey's 'troublesome' narrative) will produce children like Kyle who, through no fault of their own, are set on a bad path. This returns their thinking to the so-called 'cycle of deprivation'. On a very basic level, and erroneously, students might believe that children born into the most deprived, 'underclass' families – as depicted by Casey, the *Daily Mail* and the *News of the World* – are probably less intelligent than kids from better families. This would reflect a social Darwinism type of belief rooted in the far right wing idea that a 'natural' hierarchy has formed with those 'fittest' families at the top and the worst of them at the bottom. A meritocracy, in other words. However, a 2014 report from the Social Mobility and Child Poverty Commission demonstrated that:

> Kids born rich and poor start out more or less equally 'smart'. Or, more specifically, the high-attaining poor kids are achieving roughly on a par with the high-attaining rich kids at the age of five. Pre-school achievement is evenly distributed across class divisions (Calder, 2016).

Attainment divisions increase as children age, but the idea that children are born equal needs to be something that students and social workers understand from the outset. It is worth dwelling on the idea of meritocracy a bit further at this point. Wilkinson and Pickett (2018, p. 151) draw on the words of Boris Johnson to illustrate how he, and many others in society, articulate their deeply held belief in a meritocracy:

> He articulated the view that economic equality will never be possible because some people are simply too stupid to catch up with the rest of society: 'Whatever you may think of the value of IQ tests it is surely relevant to a conversation about equality that as many as 16 per cent of our species have an IQ below 85'. Comparing society to a box of cornflakes, he praised inequality for creating the conditions under which the brightest triumph: 'the harder you shake the pack, the easier it will be for some cornflakes to get to the top'. Inequality 'is essential for the spirit of envy and keeping up with Joneses that is, like greed, a valuable spur to economic activity'.

Also

> Boris Johnson's crediting differences in intelligence to biology, and his belief that people have a 'natural' endowment of talent, mainly determined by the genes they inherit from their parents, are not new. At least since classical times there has been a tendency for the rich and powerful to believe – and encourage others to believe – that members of each class in society are made of different stuff (Wilkinson and Picket, 2018, p. 155).

The authors then go on to deconstruct this view and it is important that students understand the challenge to it. Firstly, they look at the evidence of significant gains in IQ over time. We are all, it would seem, more intelligent that our grandparents (which immediately calls into question genetic causes of this). This is due to changes in how we view knowledge and what is important – and more recent changes result in societies adopting a more scientifically based view at different times. The industrial revolution was probably the biggest change, and more formal schooling, more cognitively demanding jobs and leisure pursuits, more interaction between a larger adult and smaller child population, more availability of books and reading as well as other *sociological* changes contributed significantly. In other words, these changes were social and political, not genetic.

Next they look at how small developmental advantages are amplified by environmental factors. So, for example, a child who might show a slight aptitude for playing a musical instrument, through practice and lessons will build on that aptitudinal advantage and, thus, it will grow.

Many studies show that small developmental advantages conferred by age that a child starts school, for example, will deliver substantial differences in outcomes years later. Other studies looking at sporting and other talents show similar findings. This plasticity in brain development leads to actual physiological differences in brain construction. Taxi drivers, for example, have physical differences in brain make-up after learning 'the knowledge' (extensive knowledge of London streets). The authors conclude that it is training and practice that makes the difference to what we are good at.

One way to interpret the above, which students often articulate, is that even if children start out equal, the gap widens due to families who 'don't prioritise education' or 'are not committed to/motivated by/seeing the worth in education', therefore do not give their children the opportunities of encouragement for training and practice. There is a moral judgement within that understanding which, once again, boils down to 'only selfish and uncaring families are in this position. If they cared about their children, it would make all the difference'. Lansley and Mack (2015), point out that, despite significant evidence to the contrary, the idea that poverty is handed down from parents to children due to poor role models, poor parenting or whatever – parental behaviour in effect – has real traction in the public imagination. Lansley and Mack (2015, p. 74) refute the idea as follows:

> There is, of course, a link between parenting and outcomes for children: children who are abused or maltreated are at long term risk: strong parent/child relationships are associated with higher cognitive abilities, and academic outcomes and social competencies. Positive parenting ... contributes to a child's school achievement regardless of any family disadvantage. But it is not the case that poverty and wealth do not matter independently of parenting. Kathleen Kiernan, professor of social policy and demography at the University of York, and colleagues have examined the extent to which positive parenting mediated the effects of poverty and disadvantage. She concludes: 'Children's achievements can be adversely affected by poor parenting; it can also be affected by poverty ... despite the best efforts of their parents, children in poverty and relatively disadvantaged circumstances still remain behind their wealthier, well-parented peers'.

This is, again, explained by the added 'cultural capital' wealthier parents have. Books, language, activities outwith school etc. are all features of middle-class childhoods, and will be discussed further below.

These poor families, where students believe that parenting is poor and *that's* the problem, are the same families where employment is not prioritised, and worklessness is handed down from generation to generation. Headlines and media reports stating, as a fact, that there are families where three generations have never worked (MacDonald, 2015), for example, fuel this narrative and it can be understood as a 'truth' underpinning many students' beliefs about families in poverty. In fact, as previously mentioned in Chapter 1, the claims about 'three generations' were investigated, there were no examples to be found, and it turned out that one of the exponents of this 'fact', Iain Duncan-Smith, had only been relying on 'personal observations' (MacDonald, 2015, n.p.). The caricature, however, is extremely powerful and congruent with neoliberal 'common sense' ideas about people as poor due to their own behaviour and choices.

So, what do students really need to understand about the above neo-liberal narrative? Calder (2016, p. 43) uses 'class fate' as 'a shorthand term for intergenerational inequality, or social immobility'. He considers class fate and education, pointing out that the UK governments are immensely concerned about the attainment gap between those entitled to free school meals (parents on benefit or poorly paid wages) and the rest. Students also often default to thinking of education as the universal panacea for poverty. If only Kyle had worked hard, stayed on at school and secured a place at university (like them) he wouldn't be in this situation. He should have just tried harder – success is open to anyone if they work hard at school. What they don't consider are the 'soft' advantages that better-off children (often including themselves) have:

> Those who arrive in state schools best equipped to exploit them – for example those whose parents have university degrees – will profit most from any general advances. Parents' (and indeed grandparents') capital will allow better-off state educated kids to live in higher-priced housing near better schools, to get extra tuition, to pay postgraduate fees and simply (in terms of cultural capital) to embolden their children to feel that the educational road is one down which they are expected and entitled to travel – a road for *them*. And in case that journey doesn't work out, better off parents are more able to fund a safety-net, or a plan B (Calder, 2016, p. 54).

Fair enough, a student might think, but even poor parents can encourage and help their children to do well in school. Calder (2016) points out, however, that poorer parents are up against it from the start. Poorer, unhealthier housing and nutrition, air pollution and exposure to chemicals all vary with income and where a family can afford to stay. Better-off families can afford child-rearing manuals, books, planning days out and activities and reading bed-time stories. Vocabulary is different with poorer families using far fewer words and having shorter conversations. All of this, according to Calder, mounts up. And, of course, it does.

As does not having to worry about money, benefit sanctions or where the next meal is coming from. All of these cultural-capital disparities are hugely influential. Calder also cites Lareau (2011) who theorised that middle class child-rearing methods pave the way for entry into institutions and middle class employment. So, organising children's diaries, encouraging them to take up hobbies, learn skills (musical instruments, for example) and filling their time produces young adults who are used to this type of formalised use of time. Children from poorer backgrounds are more likely to have been left to their own devices, to be autonomous, to explore and take risks. Both childhoods may be equally happy, but the point is that one *prepares* children and emboldens them for life in a neoliberal outside world. Also, Wilkinson and Pickett (2018) draw on research to convincingly demonstrate that the effects of poverty are mediated through stress and mental stimulation. That is why Labour government initiatives such as Sure Start in the UK were so important, although have been dismantled by subsequent governments.

The take-home message for students reading this section then is this: if position on the social hierarchy is *not* determined by innate characteristics of the human beings on that hierarchy, but is instead the result of *the position on the hierarchy* in the first place (i.e., it is a self-fulfilling prophecy which results in very little social mobility, regardless of how clever or talented a young child might be), then the 'cycle of deprivation' seems to make sense. However, students must realise that glib and reductionist understanding about a cycle of *behaviour* is not the complete picture. Stress and anxiety and other consequences of poverty and inequality amplify already set differences in bricks and mortar environments. The effects of this, exacerbated by greater inequality and relative poverty, are extremely damaging in terms of children from deprived backgrounds keeping up with their better-off peers, even when they are as clever or even cleverer.

To sum up, Lareau's analysis rests on the idea that family differences exacerbate income inequalities that already exist. Against a background of significant inequality, the stakes of family autonomy are high. The differences discussed above might always have been thus, but society over the last few decades has become one in which those differences matter far more. 'We are all middle class now' (*Telegraph*, 2010) resonates with this picture, because it feels almost true in that 'we are all trying to be middle class now, as it is the only acceptable way. Those of us who are not, are left behind'.

So, to return to the neoliberal view, where the 'moralising self-sufficiency' discourse (Marston, 2013, p. 132) or 'moralising underclass discourse' (Levitas 2005, p. 14), means that people in difficulty due to poverty are there as a result of their own behaviour or uselessness and undesirability. In this scenario, parents who do not prepare their children for middle class life are completely to blame. This narrative props up and justifies the neoliberal upward distribution of wealth and preservation of the wealthy elite via policies designed to increase wealth and thus increase inequality. As Jones (2011, p. 137) states:

> What if you have wealth and success because it has been handed to you on a plate? What if people are poorer than you because the odds are stacked against them? To accept this would trigger a crisis of self-confidence among the well-off few. And if you were to accept it, then surely you would have to accept that it's the government's job to do something about it – namely by curtailing your own privileges. But, if you convince yourself that the less fortunate are smelly, thick, racist and rude by nature, then it is only right that they should remain at the bottom. Chav-hate justifies the preservation of the pecking order, based on the fiction that it is actually a fair reflection of people's worth.

Chav-hate also resonates with the 'cycle of deprivation' myth, and although 'hate' is perhaps too strong a word to apply to our students, they will often simply blame the behaviour and values of the 'underclass' families they will soon be working with. They find it difficult to recognise the difficulties families might have as described by Calder and to see the structural organisational inequalities as described by Jones. It is not just the economic elite who buy into the neoliberal hegemony.

In my role as a social work educator, I have experienced that most students do not, instinctively 'buy' the 'thick and smelly' neoliberal characterisation of the 'underclass'. In fact, a small scale study (Fenton, 2019) demonstrated that students naturally sit within the left-wing, libertarian quadrant of the Political Compass (Political Compass, 2017). This is not unexpected, as those values are the most in-keeping with espoused social work values. However, as already explored, students have also been affected by the neoliberal hegemony (e.g., Fenton, 2018; Woodward and MacKay, 2012). This contradiction creates a search for understanding that is not structural, but also not punitive. The following two discourses, identity politics/recognition and victim/vulnerability, appear to provide students with that understanding.

The individual recognition level of understanding

This approach is based on a simplified version of Thompson's (2001) PCS model. Thompson's theory was that discrimination could be understood on three levels: personal, cultural and societal. Students, in my experience, revert to the 'P' and, perhaps, 'C' level when they are trying to apply the model and begin to get lost and to not recognise the relevance of the 'S' level which is usually related to policy or politics. So, they may be able to say that women should not be pressurised into staying at home with children but should have the same opportunities to work as men. When faced with the question: 'well, don't they?' they usually answer along the lines of, 'well, they might get called a bad mother' or 'some people still think certain jobs can only be done by a man'. In other words, their answers are rooted in 'P' and 'C' thinking. They very rarely talk about economic policies such as the huge cost of child care (and how a change in policy here could make a massive difference to women) or how austerity measures have affected single parents (usually mothers) more than any other group (JRF, 2017a). Understanding often stops at how women are treated on an interpersonal level.

The above approach has, in recent years, gathered weight due to the increasing purchase of the movement known as 'identity politics'. McLaughlin (2012) calls this emergence a triumph of recognition over redistribution and suggests that the non-recognition of someone's identity is now viewed as more problematic than economic inequality. In turn this means that recognition or respect for a person's identity, culture and self-definition is the solution to problems, and economic inequality is obscured.

Identity politics can be considered radical by some people, emanating as it does from the left of the political spectrum. Lilla (2017) suggests that the Reagan years in the USA (1980s), mirrored to a degree by the Thatcher years in the UK, gave Americans a neoliberal vision of their future and their nation: individualism, freedom, free markets, entrepreneurship bringing rewards, hard work being recognised and people taking responsibility for their own success or failure: the neoliberalism we have been discussing in this book, in fact. This republican, right wing vision was not countered by a coherent narrative from the democrats and, instead, explains Lilla, the left 'threw themselves into the movement politics of identity, losing a sense of what we share as citizens and what binds us as a nation' (Lilla, 2017, p. 9). In this way, identity politics was not an alternative to individualism, but rather another way of expressing it. It is this point that provides the rationale for not considering identity politics as a radical framework for understanding, but recognising it as one based on individualism. Lilla concedes that identity politics, at first, was about large movements – black people or women, for example – who had been oppressed and fought for equal civil rights and equal access to civil and societal institutions. This is, of course, radical and absolutely about social justice. The most recent example might be the legalisation of gay marriage, where the battle for equal access to the institution of marriage was fought and won. These essential and powerful movements, which led to proper equality between humans, gave way, however, to 'a pseudo-politics of self-regard and increasingly narrow and exclusionary self-definition' (Lilla, 2017, p. 11).

For example:

> As the feminist authors of the Combahee River Collective put it baldly in their influential 1977 manifesto. 'The most profound and potentially most radical politics comes directly out of our own identity, as opposed to working to end someone else's oppression' (Lilla, 2017, p. 83).

The above is a clear statement that identity is the main concern and people should certainly not be concerned with anyone else. This statement very clearly illustrates the individualistic and self-oriented positioning of identity politics which is entirely at odds with the coming together of all different kinds of people to affect economic change on a large scale. Lilla (2017, p. 87) describes identity politics as affording 'an intellectual patina to radical individualism that virtually everything else in our society encourages'. It is an individual fight for your own identity group and its success within a neoliberal hegemonic hierarchy, rather than part of a movement to tackle and challenge that hierarchy. So, for example, considering the battles to allow more women, ethnic groups, LGBT+ people, disabled people to have jobs that give access to decision-making in board rooms and other positions of power, an obvious compliance with neoliberal inequality can be seen. In fact,

> within that moral economy [neoliberalism] a society in which 1% of the population controlled 90% of the resources could be just, provided that roughly 12% of the 1% were black, 12% were Latino, 50% were women, and whatever the appropriate proportions were LGBT people (Reed, cited in Norton, 2015, n.p.).

In other words, identity politics sits happily with neoliberalism – the objective is to allow everyone the same access to the neoliberal hierarchy. The economic disparity between that boardroom and the people on the factory floor does not feature. The highly publicised gender pay gap at the BBC was an excellent example of this type of thinking. If 50% of people in overpaid media jobs are women, and those women are paid as much as the overpaid men, then the problem has been solved. The issue of those very overpaid people in comparison to workers working at the BBC for almost minimum wage is simply irrelevant. In Bailey and Brake's words, this type of campaign and this type of neoliberal 'equality' quite clearly 'supports the ruling class hegemony'.

The connection between the perpetuation of neoliberal hegemony and identity politics is summed up well by Michaels (2006, p. 6) as follows:

> A world where some of us don't have enough money is a world where the differences between us present a problem: the need to get rid of inequality or justify it. A world where some of us are black and some of us are white – or biracial or Native American or transgendered – is a world where the differences between us present a solution: appreciating our diversity.

Social work trumpets 'recognising diversity' as a key ethical principle (BASW, 2014b, p. 9). From the Professional Capabilities Framework (BASW, 2018, n.p.), a social worker will, 'recognise the complexity of identity' and from the SSSC Codes of Practice 1.5 a social worker will, 'work in a way that promotes diversity' (SSSC, 2016, n.p.). As McLaughlin (2012) says, and it seems to be the case in social work, that this 'recognition' narrative has usurped the 'redistribution' one – social workers can respect, promote, not criticise and celebrate cultural and identity differences and not know the slightest thing about the influence of poverty, economic inequality or the stresses and strains that neoliberal market economies can inflict on people. Of course, this refocusing of attention means that structural or economic matters are erased from the picture a social worker has of a situation (other than, perhaps poverty as a behavioural consequence that requires an individual, behavioural solution) whilst values can be upheld by attention to identity respect and celebration. More broadly, it masks structural issues that would require structural and policy solutions that would harm the neoliberal upward distribution of wealth. How wonderful for neoliberalism that those structural problems are, therefore, obscured and social workers can be co-opted to unknowingly support the neoliberal economic hegemony which is so detrimental to the people they work with.

Stop and think box 11

Met Police 'use force more often' against black people, was a BBC headline in May 2018 (BBC, 2018c). The story went that Metropolitan police are four times more likely to use force (such as restraint) against black people than they are against white. Diane Abbott, the shadow home secretary, stated that the 'disproportionate use of force is discriminatory'.

If this news story was presented to a class of social worker students, it would be readily and easily understood as an inherent problem with the police being racist

▶

and targeting young black men. The behaviour of the police is the cause, and the critical thinking required to make sense of this stops there. This is understanding on an individual, behavioural (of the police) level, with a veneer of structural understanding (racism). Notwithstanding that there is truth in this to an extent: there is a well-documented history of institutionalised racism in the police force and there will undoubtedly be individual police officers who are racist at heart, *but* they are not all racist and there is another way to look at this situation which takes more knowledge and thinking than just 'the police are racist': the economic argument.

Levels of violence, substance misuse, anxiety, stress, lack of trust etc. are all heightened by inequality (Wilkinson and Pickett, 2010). Poverty itself causes grim circumstances that, in turn, lead to people struggling and more prone to crime and other anti-social behaviour. Poverty in London is strongly linked to ethnicity, for example, a study by JRF (2011, n.p.) found that:

> There are definite patterns of disadvantage for people from minority ethnic backgrounds which need to be acknowledged and tackled. For instance, poverty is higher among all black and minority ethnic groups than among the majority white population.

So maybe the Met *are* dealing with more violent incidents from black people (and young men in general are more prone to increased violence due to inequality, according to Wilkinson and Pickett, 2010). To consider this point, a student needs to get beyond a simple behavioural understanding based on 'discrimination' (whilst acknowledging there is something in that also), to an economic understanding of poverty, inequality and the effects of a neoliberal society. The calls for a clamp down on the discriminatory behaviour of the police leave the vast economic inequalities and injustices outwith cognitive reach and therefore beyond consideration.

In terms of Kyle, then, an identity politics or diversity approach might mean that students talk about Kyle as being discriminated against due to his offending history and 'that is not right'. Under scrutiny, however, the students do admit that they, too, might consider a criminal record as a risk factor, and that they might not be so quick to trust Kyle. In other words, they might also discriminate and judge, and saying we 'shouldn't do that' because it is against 'social work values' is just another way of nominally, and uncritically, following the social work rules. From this angle, people just being nicer to Kyle and giving him a second chance is the way to address this case study. People should just understand that Kyle did not want to go to school. In assignments I read, this level of understanding is superficial, unconvincing and, frankly, nonsense. The students themselves do not really believe this undiluted understanding and acceptance – they *do* judge Kyle, who wouldn't? What we see is a lack of understanding of the real picture of poverty and disadvantage, barely hidden behind a veneer of 'non-judgemental' attitude.

Stop and think box 12

Try to, really honestly, think about a time when you felt judgemental about another person (service user, friend, or anyone). For example, students will talk about feeling initially angry at people in poverty, who appear to be wasting money on the latest possessions. Dwell on that feeling for a while. Then think about the idea that the rules of your profession simply state 'you are not allowed to be judgemental like that, and need to respect people's choices'. How does that leave you feeling? Disingenuous? Powerless? Frustrated? Annoyed? And you would simply keep your unchanged feelings hidden – yes?

Then think about speaking *to* the person, learning more about their feelings on the matter and attaining more knowledge about the actual facts relevant to the situation. Imagine this leading you to actually *feeling* less judgemental.

An example of this was when the benefit office employed 200 extra fraud investigators to clamp down on people cheating the benefit system (Doel, 2012). The investigators were initially very judgemental, understandably, about the people they were investigating. Imagine how they would have felt had they been told they were *not allowed* to disapprove. They wouldn't stop disapproving, they would just keep it well hidden (the thin veneer of non-judgementality, again). However, when the investigators got to know people, heard their reasons for what they had done, gained knowledge and facts on how difficult their lives were etc. they *actually* became far less judgemental. They felt compassion (ibid.).

This idea of just following the social work rules is just another version of following oppressive, neoliberal agency rules. It is not as harmful but it is still of the unthinking and superficial variety and, I would bet, unconvincing. Behaviour can still be oppressive whilst the social work rhetoric is being espoused.

Another aspect to following the social work rules about being non-judgemental, whilst not understanding the pressures of poverty and economic inequality, is in the use of social work language and jargon. In Chapter 3, we looked at the language rules and discussed Eichmann's propensity to rely on the Nazi 'language rules' which Arendt suggested demonstrated an inability to think (Arendt, 1965, p. 69). We also touched on McLaughlin's (2008) example of a social worker reprimanding an asylum speaker for sexist language whilst removing his children. Students, and others, can become 'language police' where they look for transgressions in order to reprimand and correct, and at the same time have no idea of the reality of economic oppression the same people are subject to. There is probably no better approach for ruining any chance of relationship building!

So, to sum up. The recognition or 'identity politics' way of understanding things can be understood as particular groups promoting their own identity congruent with neoliberal structures and upward distribution of wealth. Students are comfortable with that, and quite easily buy into the interpersonal anti-discriminatory framework that accompanies it. Students will make sure they do not discriminate (and will not 'judge' in accordance with the social work rules), will certainly not use discriminatory language, and will look out for, and challenge, those who do. This is all quite easy to understand and students can tick the values box by absorbing this approach with no knowledge of economic disparity or poverty.

Another individual level approach adopted by students when trying to understand Kyle's, and others', situation is one which seems to gather more traction year on year. This seems to be mirrored by increasing levels of mental health and other problems among students. How many academics, for example, have seen requests for 'reasonable adjustments' go through the roof? The narrative here is one underpinned by vulnerability.

The individual victim/vulnerability level of understanding

McLaughlin (2012) explores the victim identity and vulnerability narrative that many identity groups adopt. He explains that describing oneself as a 'survivor' means that the person is forever in a position of reference to the past – and will therefore always fail to transcend the trauma or victimisation. The constant reference to an earlier trauma is especially powerful if one's employment, persona, cause, friends group and identification is bound up with it. So, people who are activists, for example, can be quite significantly invested in keeping the trauma, anger and hurt alive. This can also mean that any attempt to explore the idea that, for example, 'sexual abuse might not be as harmful as the angriest survivor might have us believe' can lead to vilification and attack by those identity groups (Dreger, 2016, p. 108).

Within the sensitive and harrowing area of child sexual abuse, an extremely powerful 'harm' orthodoxy exists. Woodiwiss (2014) argues that a 'single story' has come to dominate understandings and narratives of childhood sexual abuse. She frames her study within a 'story telling' ontology – that we make sense of the world and of events by drawing on current, circulating narratives. Thus, if one narrative completely domi-nates, then this is the only way that people are allowed to understand and make sense of experiences. Woodiwiss argues that the contemporary single story for childhood sexual abuse constructs victims as necessar-ily sexually innocent, and as inevitably damaged by their experiences. In essence, this leaves children who may be 'sexually knowing' (Woodi-wiss, 2014, p. 147) and/or undamaged by their experiences, without a voice or narrative. They are silenced. Woodiwiss (2014, p. 141) suggests that 'we need to separate "childhood"' from 'sexual innocence' and 'harm' from 'wrongfulness', and in doing so, we can be very clear about the wrongfulness of the act, regardless of consequences of harm to the child and regardless of the sexual innocence or knowingness of the child. Building on this, Smith and Woodiwiss (2016, p. 14) suggest that, drawing on evidence from the girls who were abused by Jimmy Saville, some of them 'did not regard themselves to have been harmed by it'. The authors recognise that the girls have agency and can view their expe-riences as they want to.

The above is a difficult and sensitive subject with which to get read-ers thinking about this section, so it needs to be emphasised that abus-ers are *always and completely* to blame for their actions. The message is simply that on-going, lifelong trauma and harm should not be assumed. A young person who has a different narrative – of resilience, recovery, no-harm or dismissal – should be allowed to articulate that and for that to be respected as their truth (which is always subjective!) without a disbe-lieving, cynical, better-knowing or frowning response. As Woodiwiss says, there is *no* single story.

A, perhaps easier, example of the vulnerability narrative is examined by Kipnis (2017) in her account of life on university campuses in USA, in an era of 'sexual paranoia'. At the centre of her thesis is the idea that young women are portrayed as vulnerable victims, in constant need of protection from sexually predatory men. A core part of this narrative is that women are completely without agency, especially when interperson-ally relating to a man in a more powerful position. Kipnis (2017, p. 52) suggests that believing this picture of men and women takes a willingness to buy into a fantasy:

A female student was charging that a male professor had forced her to drink, which led to her trying to kill herself ... and the story just didn't add up. The news report took for granted that it did, but going along with that required putting my intelligence on hold ... I was being asked to sign onto a fantasy pre-sented as reality ... and this demand to *stop thinking entirely* (and the implication that any right-thinking citizen would), was too much to go along with ... I ... know the limits of professorial power, and I simply don't believe in a reality in which a professor can force a student to drink ... [This] was complete melodrama, the world of dastardly men with the nefarious power to bend passive damsels to their wills.

Once again, there needs to be a cautionary note here, that real abuse of power and forcing women to engage in sexual conduct, for example, *does* happen and *does* need to be tackled, but the morphing of this into believing that women, as a rule, can be *forced* into behaviour they do not want to simply by a man's status, paints a picture of women as extremely weak, and is one I do not recognise. Kipnis also points out that the under-standing of sexual power, as completely uni-directional and based on occupational status and gender, is also reductionist and overly simplistic. Women often have power in interpersonal, sexual relationships; as well as desires, regrets, passions, jealousies and all kinds of other human and earthy feelings. A portrayal of women as pure, innocent, vulnerable and weak is not something that I, and other old feminists, battled for in the 80s. In fact, we battled for the right to express those feelings without incurring disapproval.

Another issue that feeds the broader vulnerability narrative is that people are *harmed* by words. Once again (and I'm getting boring here by reiterating this caveat) we are not talking about extreme cases of psycho-logical abuse, including name calling *nor* are we talking about words as a precursor to violence or intended to evoke violence. Even Mill (1859), as discussed earlier, drew the line at free speech which incited violence and physical harm. What we are talking about here, is the calm expression of ideas that differ from the mainstream, might be offensive, might not be in-keeping with current zeitgeist or just might be a bit shocking. Those *opinions* or *views,* when understood as being harmful, and thus people need protection from hearing them, are silenced (e.g., no-platforming in universities). As Mill put it:

> To refuse a hearing to an opinion, because they are sure that it is false, is to assume that their certainty is the same thing as *absolute certainty*. All silenc-ing of discussion is an assumption of infallibility. Its condemnation may be allowed to rest on this common argument, not the worse for being common (Mill, 1859 [2011, p. 28]).

Fox (2016) expresses concern about young people's reaction to words and ideas that they find difficult or offensive. She states that they have internalised the idea that hearing such things will cause them harm, and talks, for example, about being part of a debate in a school where she was on the side of supporting the rehabilitation of rapists. The young women listening were horrified by her views, and as Fox says 'it became obvious

that there was an accepted, and acceptable narrative here and any challenge to it led to accusations of victim-blaming or rape apologism' (Fox,
2016, p. xiv). That narrative, or single story, as Fox soon discovered, had
validity because:

> Students had already internalised the 'fact' that rape and sexual assault were
> unquestionably the most heinous thing these teenagers could imagine happen-
> ing, a crime beyond forgiveness, and that its victims would never be able to get
> over it ... I decided, perhaps rashly (quoting Germaine Greer for recognisable
> feminist cred) to tell them that rape was not necessarily the worst thing that
> could happen to an individual. Yes, it's a serious crime, but we need a sense
> of proportion. The room erupted. The audience shrieked. A teacher called out
> 'you can't say that'. Girls were hugging each other for comfort. The major-
> ity seemed shell-shocked. Even *posing* this point of view, was a step too far it
> seemed (Fox, 2016, pp. xiv–xv).

And so, the 'harmed for ever' narrative in relation to sexual 'assault' (and
the young women in Fox's example included regretted sex and unwanted
advances in their definition), had real traction in the minds of the young
women above. Also, as well as anticipating the 'harmed for ever' consequence of a 'trauma' (or what might be defined as a trauma if a person
considers themselves to be vulnerable, for example an unwanted advance
from a man), this discourse leads to a search for past 'trauma' when life
problems occur. The narrative can be future or past orientated.

The above growing vulnerability narrative and the search for trauma
to explain a person's troubles, and the resultant emphasis on therapeutic
interventions dominates many conversations with students, who reject
the punitive 'these people are just thick and have no values' narrative but
wed themselves to an 'understanding' and 'compassionate' therapeutic
view that the individual just needs *help to change* or *help to overcome harm*
(therapy/counselling or whatever).

Adding to our understanding of this quite complex area, Verhaeghe
(2012) explores psychiatric disorder classification in terms of the medical model and notes that the understanding is that illness springs from
underlying bodily processes, albeit that environmental factors might
bring the symptoms to the fore. Therefore, 'a mental disorder, is always
the same, regardless of the patient, so that the diagnosis can largely
be confined to a label. Treatment follows a set protocol' (Verhaeghe,
2012, p. 184). There is very little space to discuss the possibility of
psychological, social or environmental factors. Verhaeghe also notes
that 'new' disorders are often classified in terms of their symptoms. For
example, attention deficit and hyperactivity disorder (ADHD) is classified
as a disease when it is simply a description of the symptoms, much like

calling a man with a bad cough as having a 'bad cough' or BC. The use of acronyms disguises the circularity of the argument: a boy is attention deficient and hyperactive because he has attention deficit and hyperactivity disorder! This provides the illusion of scientific rigour and explanation and Verhaeghe also cautions that the way symptoms are classified and grouped in order to be considered as deserving of a label is very variable and arbitrary. In fact, for some diagnoses, whether you will leave the GP surgery with a label (and often, medication) or not depends on which handbook your GP is using! Further proof that social work students need to be sceptical and doubting about labels and certainties is provided by information such as:

> In the United States, at least 9 percent of school-aged children have been diagnosed with ADHD, and are taking pharmaceutical medications. In France, the percentage of kids diagnosed and medicated for ADHD is less than .5 percent (Wedge, 2012, n.p.).

Verhaeghe goes on to stress that the belief in the certainty of disorders, diagnoses and labels (or paradigms of understanding) is fastly held, and people will often come into GPs surgery looking for a label: 'I have depression' or 'my child has ADHD'. This increasing reliance on the medicalisation of problems and the medical or therapeutic response that is, therefore, required has absolutely invaded popular culture. Significant numbers of people now 'disclose' on social media that they have been suffering from 'anxiety' or 'depression' or 'stress' or whatever, and there is definitely a certain kudos or recognition and acclaim that this provokes. So disclosures of this type are often met with vast numbers of supportive and encouraging comments. Furedi (2004) notes that in a search of UK newspapers, there were no references to 'self-esteem' in 1980, 3 references in 1986, 103 in 1990 and, by 2000, a 'staggering 3,328 references to self esteem' (Furedi, 2004, p. 3). Similar patterns were found for 'trauma', 'stress', 'syndrome' and 'counselling' (ibid.).

Wilkinson and Pickett (2010) found that, on a range of measures of social problems, unequal societies do worse than more equal ones. In essence, their thesis is that 'social-evaluative stress' is much worse when the economic hierarchy is steep, and we, therefore, are under pressure to prove our status and hierarchical position. This leads to consumerism, displaying the latest status symbols (car, phone, house, holidays, laptop, clothes), debt, anxiety and pressure. The authors draw on substantial research to underpin this explanation for their extremely important findings. Competition and success become the new tenets of life, with success being considered the normal identity. This means that 'failure is a symptom of a disturbed [identity]' (Verghaehe, 2012, p. 201).

The neoliberal self-sufficiency or (material) success-as-normal discourses then feed seamlessly into the vulnerability or treatment responses. In the case for school children, for example:

> Nearly all juvenile disorders these days have to do with failure at school. That stands to reason in the case of learning disorders, but it also applies to ADHD, CD (conduct disorder), ASD (autism-spectrum disorders), ODD (oppositional-defiant disorder), and performance anxiety. These diagnoses for the other side of the coin to high-pitched social expectations, with the result that there are now two kinds of pupils in school: gifted children, and children with disorders. 'Ordinary' children are becoming an endangered species, and the old notion of average being normal is now taboo (Verhaeghe, 2012, p. 202).

Wilkinson and Pickett (2018), in their book *The Inner Level*, which builds on *The Spirit Level,* also make a very convincing case as to how inequality, in psychological terms, increases anxiety and stress in terms of how others view us. Using significant numbers of examples, research and illustrations, the case is made that the reason societies with greater levels of inequality have more social problems is because of the real, and growing, anxiety we feel about being judged, and about being low on the hierarchy. Thus, the pressure to 'succeed' and to display that success is increasingly important, and that brings real pressure. Think of cleaning up before visitors and hiding the way we really live – we just do not want to be judged and to incur disapproval! So, in effect, there may be, objectively speaking, an actual increase in vulnerability and psychological problems influenced by growing inequality and its toxic nature, *and* more of a willingness to define social problems as individual problems of anxiety and stress, without seeing inequality as the true, socio-economic root of those problems. This is very convenient for those who like the economic workings of neoliberalism to be thought of as neutral and as having no alternative. In that context, problems *must* be individually caused and individually treated.

Another way to think about this is as an emerging regeneration of the medical model in social work. Diagnosing symptoms and offering treatment seems to be what students are drawn to, and agencies who want to identify individual problems, in an atomisation of the situation, that can be referred on for treatment (and thus 'ticked off' the list) perpetuate this tendency. So, for example, in an article by Fennig and Denov (2018), the international literature on mental health and social care services for young refugees was critically examined. In essence, the authors found how:

> through the medicalisation of refugee youth's distress, social workers may not only miss the boat on appropriate methods of healing and intervention, but

may also unwittingly divert attention away from problematic social policies and structural inequalities, ultimately promoting a culture of passive conformity to problematic state refugee policies (Fennig and Denov, 2018, p. 3).

The authors also suggest that this state of affairs is affecting mental health social work more broadly and state:

> Scholars have pointed to the heavy emphasis on DSM [Diagnostic and Statistical Manual of Mental Disorders] diagnosis in social work assessment and training, and the neglect of social, environmental and economic factors that lead to emotional distress....Moreover, social work scholars have cautioned against the central role the trauma model plays when responding to refugees' complex needs (Fennig and Denov, 2018, p. 4).

This 'trauma model' it could be suggested, has broadened its reach from mental health social work, and congruent with an increasing vulnerability/victim narrative in social life more broadly, is the go-to paradigm of many student and qualified social workers. Students often prioritise counselling or therapeutic groupwork whilst social workers, in line with managerial priorities, turn to parenting classes, anger management and groupwork programmes based on cognitive behavioural therapy (CBT) principles.

In terms of Kyle, then, a vulnerability/therapeutic lens would encourage focus on several elements in his life:

➤ Bereavement – does he need counselling?

➤ Alcohol – he has a problem! Alcohol counselling?

➤ Offending – Anger management?

➤ New baby – is he suffering from rejection? Counselling?

➤ Might he have an undiagnosed disorder? ADHD for example?

Once again, the boring disclaimer – some of the above might indeed to true and necessary, *but* we should neither assume that's the case nor turn to that as first response. Even if your agency likes to bullet point the 'risk factors' and see a response ('referred to anger management group') it may be that that is *not* required. Undertake a lazy radical assessment instead, and see where that takes you.

To bring this section to a close, then, readers should be urged to think, and speak, critically about assumptions of vulnerability and trauma. It should, perhaps, not be the first explanation arrived at or theorised when a social worker is faced with a situation. If the environment is good, most people will be able to flourish, and that should be the starting point – look to the environment first. Of course, for some people, trauma, harm, vulnerability and damage *are* real and significant and, even, insurmountable without intervention. But that's not *always* the case – that's the take home message from this section.

The individual and structural lazy radical approach

The lack of attention to economic factors and the reliance on individual level 'blame' or 'therapy' is summed up very well by the following quote:

> Sociological research has shown a clear link between the current *socio-economic system* and severe psychological and social problems. The dominant neo-liberal mindset ignores this fact, and, instead of tackling the causes, focuses entirely on the consequences: namely, the deviant, disturbed and dangerous others – psychiatric paients, junkies, young people, the unemployed, and ethnic minorities (Verhaeghe, 2012, p. 207, emphasis added).

This section, then, looks at reinstating the 'current socio-economic system' in our understanding of problems. Getting at the 'causes' of problems might be reworded as getting at the 'roots' of the problem. The Latin word 'radix' means root, and hence 'radical' means pertaining to the roots of the problem. So, lazy radical social work is absolutely the way to go in getting to the roots or causes of the problems service users experience. Not only trying to deal with individual expression of the symptoms or consequences of neoliberalism, such as criminal behaviour, substance use, anxiety, stress, not-coping, violence, and so on (only focusing on those supports the hegemony), but also looking to economic and structural root causes. As the three steps to lazy radical practice unfold, you will see how such an approach does just that.

Step 1: Relationship building, trust and emotional engagement

So, referring back to Chapter 4, finding out about a person's 'inner world' (Hennessey, 2011) is of vital importance. We are not just concerned with Kyle's *behaviour* (outer world), although discussing that might be the starting point. You want to hear his voice and explore how he feels about things and what sense he makes of his life just now. What does he think the problems and solutions are?

You are not approaching Kyle with a pre-set idea of what he is like. You are not considering him a member of the useless and 'chavvy' 'underclass' and you are not buying any stereotypes of workshy young thugs. You really want to get to know him properly. This might take a bit of your time. You understand about building trust and how difficult that might be – you are prepared for intrusive questions, you might self-disclose some information and you look for levellers. To this end you drop professional trappings, jargon and displays of material wealth. Respect is central to your approach.

In terms of risk, your work might be framed as a 'risk assessment' and you are aware of the heightened emphasis your agency gives risk. So, you must complete the work your agency asks you to do, but you do not make that the focus, you fill in the paperwork as an adjunct to the job of getting to know him. As McNeill, Batchelor, Burnett and Cox (2005) suggest, risk assessment must be 'thoroughly individualised' so, even in terms of risk, relationship building is the best route. You are aware of the concept of risk aversion, however, and reflect on your own practice to make sure you are not making decisions simply to cover your back should things go wrong.

In some ways, you find it hard to empathise with Kyle. You had a middle-class upbringing and you do not really know anyone in his situation. However, you are able to feel compassion for him, and want to treat him with kindness and respect. As you get to know him, you start to *feel* something for him. You also understand Kyle's pleasure and fun seeking behaviour. He is a young man – of course he wants to get drunk and party. You are not condemning of this, although a discussion about how, when and where that leads to trouble would be necessary. Likewise, you understand how, deep down, Kyle might be status-seeking in his peer group, which can result in trying to 'prove' he isn't struggling for money or for anything else, and can erupt in violence to protect a fragile ego.

Does it seem like a lot to do? It can really be encapsulated in one word: care. You are going to actively get to know and care about Kyle. That's not to say you will forget about risky behaviour and talk and discuss that with him; nor is it to say you might disagree and challenge him, *but* your starting point is care – and how it looks is described above.

Step 2: Knowledge and critical thinking

What kind of knowledge do you need, then, for step 2? You will have noted the difficulties Kyle has had with: a possible poor attachment (and now rejection because of the new baby), bereavement, alcohol use and anger. However, and this is crucial, you are *not* going to assume that any of those things are the causes of his current situation. Because you are a lazy radical practitioner, you are going to look to his social environment first and foremost, whilst being open to the possibility that the above factors might need further exploration. You are not going to disregard your knowledge about the after effects of loss or trauma or poor attachments, for example, you are just not going to attend to them on the assumption that they are problems. Just keep alert to the possibility.

Thinking back to Chapter 5, you need to know about poverty and inequality. You need to understand the psychological impact on Kyle, as a young man trying to prove his status, of evaluative stress, shame and pressure (Wilkinson and Pickett, 2018). You understand the pressure to have material items, to not be seen to be poor and to enhance one's status by any means available. According to *The Spirit Level*, for example, the drive to protect one's status, can quite easily erupt in violence, hence higher levels of violence in more unequal countries (Wilkinson and Pickett, 2010). JRF (2017a) also reports how poverty contributes to difficult relationships between parents and children, and between couples. Kyle is from a family who have been living in some poverty and so we can consider that the stress of this might have been a factor in the relationship breakdown.

You also enter into your relationship with Kyle understanding the socio-economic background to his situation. You know that Kyle does not qualify for Housing benefit because of his age – and having a roof over his head would make the world of difference to him and other young people in similar situations. You know that this is not just 'the way things are' and are fully aware that this has come about because of neoliberal policy choices, including austerity. You feel it is unfair and feel anger on behalf of Kyle. You are aware that a succession of neoliberal governments have squeezed the public sector and redistributed wealth upwards towards the rich, leaving people like Kyle struggling for even a place to say. Let's also assume Kyle has been sanctioned by the benefits office. You know that, actually, unemployment figures are mostly affected by the availability of work (JRF, 2017b) and that trying to *force* people into work through sanctions is both illogical and extremely punitive. In fact, it just does not work as a strategy (*Guardian*, 2018). It is here that we really see lazy radical practice in action. You just do not buy into the neoliberal, hegemonic, self-sufficiency discourse. Kyle cannot secure a base from which to start to rebuild his life and make better choices. He is kept in poverty by a benefits system that does not meet his basic needs (as well as housing, after sanctions, he has nothing for food) and has work prospects that are mainly poorly paid, insecure, often part-time or comprise zero-hours contracts (Jones, 2011). Therefore, the neoliberal rhetoric 'just get a job' is impossible for someone like Kyle, in reality, to fulfil. His benefits will be stopped and it will be difficult to re-apply if he takes sporadic work, for example. Most cases of debt are caused by this kind of moving in and out of poorly paid work (JRF, 2010).

Armed with that foregrounded knowledge, you are equipped to think critically about Kyle and his situation. You have withstood the individual, punitive level of understanding that buying into the neoliberal hegemony would have led you to, and neither are you turning to individual recognition or vulnerability narratives as a first port-of-call, that is, unconvincing assertions that Kyle should just be respected as making different (offending) choices, without reference to context; or Kyle just needs different sorts of therapy. You are *critically* understanding the situation.

In order to think critically, remember you must be prepared to employ system 2 thinking (Kahneman, 2011, and see Chapter 5). System 2 thinking means really trying to apply the above knowledge to Kyle, and understanding these indirect, not directly causal influences takes real thinking-work! It is easier to understand him on an individual level (either punitive or therapeutic), so an awareness of system 1's tendency to provide short cuts, which might mean unthinkingly following rules, needs to be avoided. You might do some of this thinking work before meeting Kyle, and certainly when you reflect upon your interaction – you will be doing something different from reflecting just to comply with the rules (Whitaker and Reimer, 2017), but will be reflecting to understand.

Step 3: Moral courage

So far, you have been building a relationship with Kyle and trying to critically understand his situation. You have been doing your best caring and thinking work. Some writers might be of the view that, in reality, that is as far as any kind of radical practice can go. You cannot *change* societal, political or economic structures, for example, can you? In traditional (real?) radical practice, of course you would be attempting to do that by taking action, protesting and campaigning. However, having accepted that you might not want to do that, has your practice gone as far as it can? Is it, as Pease (2013, p. 28) describes, enough that 'minimally, social workers can avoid pathologising service users and holding them responsible for problems shaped by structural and material conditions'?

If you have read Chapter 6, you will know that lazy radical practice does go beyond understanding, to action. Action that might sometimes take moral courage. What action might entail will vary case by case, but we are sure about what it is *not*. Action is not the tick box, referring-on, managerial practice that your agency might promote (organisational professionalism). Of course you must do all of that properly, fill in the required forms etc. but you need to do that in your own way, and do *more* than that.

Wanting to do more than just the codified tasks your agency might prescribe, firstly takes a belief that you have agency to do so. You are responsible for your own practice, in line with codes of ethics which are explicit about care, for example, and thus you have agency to do more. You also need to see that the situation has moral meaning, beyond practical tasks and you then need the courage to carry out what it is you feel you need to do. So, in Kyle's case, you might want to tackle his housing situation by advocating on his behalf with the housing department to find out what can be done for a young homeless person. You might need to approach a, sometimes hostile, benefits agency (or Citizens' Advice Bureau if you come up against barriers) to argue against sanctions or look at emergency funds. Once you get to know Kyle, you might need to help him, via support or advocacy, to attend for interviews (college, for example). All of these potential actions are about challenging structural barriers to the things Kyle needs. Ultimately about challenging social structures. There might also be charities that you would wish to contact for help with housing or with donations of furniture or whatever. All of these actions are beyond any risk assessment completion or referral for alcohol counselling. In fact, and this takes courage also, you might have to argue to *not* refer Kyle for those type of interventions if your honest view is that it is actually not required. As Tony says in *The Road from Crime,* 'Quite a lot o' the boys do dae the courses ... but if they're honest they're no' getting anything oot o' it ... they dae it coz they have to' (University of Glasgow, 2012). Getting Kyle to 'do a course' might be more about fulfilling the organisational, risk-averse methods employed within the agency rather than about doing real social work that has a chance of making a difference in his life (see Chapter 3).

You might experience ethical stress if you are required to go against what you think is the right thing. For example your team manager might try to persuade you to refer Kyle for bereavement counselling 'so it looks like we've done something' when you know it is not required. It is so important that you recognise the feeling of ethical stress and *use* it to motivate you to make a good, persuasive argument with your team manager. Also, remember, you should be making decisions about what to do in this case, with Kyle's voice central. Don't wait to be told what tasks to do, use your values, skills and knowledge to decide what you think should happen and use courage to argue for that.

Conclusion

You recognise that approaching Kyle's situation from a lazy radical perspective might evoke some disdain or accusations of naivety from colleagues who think differently, but you should be assured that you are doing the right thing in terms of social work values, knowledge and fundamentals. It is important that you find sources of support for lazy radical practice (see Chapter 8). In essence, you are approaching Kyle as an ordinary young man who is struggling a bit at the moment. You are not looking down on him in a punitive way, you are not contributing all of his problems to the way others treat him, and you are not assuming he is in need of treatment and therapy for some pathology or other. You want to make his environment as conducive as possible to his flourishing – and know that this may take some time and persistence. You are optimistic and hopeful.

Summary of main points

> It is very easy to turn to individual levels of understanding for a framework through which to view problems.

> We need to be explicitly aware of that temptation – especially in terms of individual identity/recognition or trauma/vulnerability. You need to be alert to these possible elements within a situation, but do not *assume* them or give them priority over economic, structural and environmental factors.

> The application of lazy radical practice is straightforward, but takes thought!

8
Conclusion

Introduction

Thanks and well done for getting this far in the book! This final chapter will start with re-visiting some of the assumptions underpinning the book and some of the reasons why lazy radical social work is not only desirable, but essential in the contemporary social work context. After this, the book will give an overview of each chapter to remind the reader, in a succinct way, how the ideas have unfolded.

The next section will examine what gets in the way of lazy radical practice and what social workers need to be cognisant and critical of, rather than unthinkingly accepting. To help confront and resist those barriers, the 3-step model will be revisited, in relation to the final practice example. As well as providing a reminder and another example of lazy radical social work in action, the model will again, be connected to underpinning the thinking of Bauman, Mill and Arendt, and to more formal ethical codes from BASW and IFSW. This will further emphasise the essential 'rightness' of this way of working.

Assumptions underpinning the book

The premise of *Social Work for Lazy Radicals* is that neoliberalism is not good for many of the people that social work is involved with. Some of the broad neoliberal foundational ideas that have perpetuated the ideology, and have won it popular support, are now beginning to look discredited, and have led many people to look for a feasible alternative (hence the rise of Jeremy Corbyn's Labour Party in the UK or the vote for Brexit reflecting working class disillusionment). After recounting many of the failures of neoliberalism, for example, the *Guardian* (2016b) states:

> But by far the most disastrous feature of the neoliberal period has been the huge growth in inequality. Until very recently, this had been virtually ignored.

With extraordinary speed, however, it has emerged as one of, if not the most important political issue on both sides of the Atlantic, most dramatically in the US. It is, bar none, the issue that is driving the political discontent that is now engulfing the west. Given the statistical evidence, it is puzzling, shocking even, that it has been disregarded for so long; the explanation can only lie in the sheer extent of the hegemony of neoliberalism and its values.

But now reality has upset the doctrinal apple cart. In the period 1948–1972, every section of the American population experienced very similar and sizeable increases in their standard of living; between 1972 and 2013, the bottom 10% experienced falling real income while the top 10% did far better than everyone else. In the US, the median real income for full-time male workers is now lower than it was four decades ago: the income of the bottom 90% of the population has stagnated for over 30 years.

A not so dissimilar picture is true of the UK, and the problem has grown more serious since the financial crisis. On average, between 65 and 70% of households in 25 high-income economies experienced stagnant or falling real incomes between 2005 and 2014.

So, what are some of the neoliberal, hegemonic ideas that people are now beginning to reject?

1. Wealth will trickle down, if markets are free so that as much wealth as possible can be accumulated. That has not happened. Look at the above statistics and at many of the Joseph Rowntree Foundation sources cited in previous chapters. Poverty and inequality, with their toxic and destructive effects, have burgeoned. Wealth accumulation has been at the top. Also, whilst poverty has increased amongst many social work service users, support services and social work services have been cut in the name of neoliberal austerity measures. In essence, 'inequality, coupled with the fact that the neoliberal promise that wealth would "trickle down" has proved hollow for millions of people' (Ferguson et al., 2018, p. 8).

2. Everything is better and more efficient as a private enterprise (hence the selling off of social care, the Probation Service and some Children's services, not to mention the 'contracting out' of lots of social care and social work to private companies via franchises). In fact, by 2014, 'between and quarter and a half of all community services in England were run by Richard Branson's Virgin Care' (Ferguson et al., 2018, p. 18). The problem here is that success is then measured in economic or profit terms. Short home visits to older adults and less and poorly paid residential staff, for example, all increase the profit goal, so the

business is successful in those terms. But, what about quality of care terms? Just looking at news coverage on the television illuminates people's disquiet with all of this – calls to protect the NHS, care for older people etc. abound.

Education has also become a commodity in England and Wales. Paying for university education is now commonplace, and what does that say about opportunity being absolutely skewed in favour of richer people?

3. Individuals are purely responsible for their own success or failure. They could work and make a success of things if they were less lazy and *wanted* to work. This idea meant that public support for benefit cuts and sanctions was garnered as people bought into the hegemony. However, a recent report in the *Guardian* found that:

> Benefit sanctions are ineffective at getting jobless people into work and are more likely to reduce those affected to poverty, ill-health or even survival crime, the UK's most extensive study of welfare conditionality has found (*Guardian*, 2018).

When people successfully moved into work, it was personalised support rather than punitive sanctions that made the difference, although the most common work practice of advisors was concerned with enforcing rules. Sanctions were also found to effect disabled people most profoundly and JRF (2017b) also found that the most common reason for not working was disability. Furthermore, the study found that when people did move into work, it was into a series of short-term, insecure contracts with periods of unemployment (and delays in benefit) in between. This leads onto point 4:

4. Employment has increased. The types of employment need interrogating, however. Zero-hour, insecure work, as above, prevail. Hence the new category of people known as the 'working poor'. Working full time and yet still in poverty and unable to sustain a family, is a dreadful state of affairs. This comes about due to the deregulation of businesses and corporations who are not obliged to offer security or living wages.

5. The moralising self-sufficiency discourse (Marston, 2013) and its hegemonic character. It is now an unquestioned 'truth' that people should never be dependent and that everyone has an equal chance of making it. Success or failure is down to your own hard work. This has been sufficiently critiqued in previous chapters (see Chapter 2, for example), but it is worth revisiting how poverty and grim

circumstances cannot simply be airbrushed from the explanations of why people might behave in the way they do:

> When money is tight, housing poor, living conditions overcrowded, life becomes stressful and the family home becomes a pressure cooker where parents can explode into rage at their children.... The consequences are tragic, but it is the *social conditions created by poverty and inequality which provide the context for the eruption of violence.* It is also here, alongside the very poorest and most marginalised in society, that social workers spend most of their working lives (Ferguson and Lavalette, 2009, p. 20).

A neoliberal response, predicated on a behavioural understanding of the above, might be a referral to a parenting class. A lazy radical response might look to material conditions and support to relieve some of the actual economic and material stress and discomfort.

So, the central underpinning assumption of the book is that neoliberalism does not work for the majority of people and certainly has made life harder for those on low incomes – either benefits or low wages. Life has become harder for those groups of people, whilst values of materialistic accumulation and social-media success-display have amplified social evaluative stress (Wilkinson and Pickett, 2018) and exacerbated feelings of frustration, shame, anxiety and anger. Poverty and inequality, significantly aggravated by neoliberalism, is *the* problem in society today, and *the* problem that lazy radical practice recognises as a priority.

Revisiting the chapters

Chapter 1 introduced *Social work for lazy radicals,* explaining what it is and why it is important. This necessitated an understanding of neoliberalism, as lazy radical practice stands as practice that is resistant to neoliberal hegemony. It involves seeing through the 'common sense' and unquestioned assumptions. Lazy radical practice involves looking at service users' problems through a structural lens, rather than an individual-level, behavioural lens and, thus, an understanding of poverty and inequality is required. Chapter 1 then explained how the chapters would unfold, and would include a 3-step model of lazy radical practice. The suggestion is that much of social work education balks at taking an explicitly radical stance, as it can feel too political for educators to embrace. The contention of the book is that, without an explicit method of 'doing social work', which is logical, coherent and easily justifiable on value and knowledge grounds, a neoliberal type of practice, based on unthinking task-doing, managerial imperatives and often punitive, behavioural and coercive practice is all too ready to step in and fill the gap. Considering how many statutory agencies have embraced a neoliberal form of practice, it is easy to understand how social work students will also absorb such an approach, *unless* they have an alternative framework through which to critically consider the agency's methods. The chapter explicitly considers how lazy radical practice is, in effect, 'swimming against the tide' (p. 11).

Dependence, independence and values, and the interplay between all three, is considered in Chapter 2. The key issue of independence, or of people standing on their own two feet, is considered in the light of the neoliberal underpinning assumption that everyone is responsible for our own success or failure (with external influences being irrelevant). Accepting this narrative justifies attacking the welfare system, austerity measures, sanctions and punishments. It is also congruent with the idea of a lazy 'underclass' who we would definitely not want to indulge or encourage! Looking at notions of social justice that incorporate those ideas of self-sufficiency and underclass, for example, Chapter 2 discusses family causes and intergenerational patterns of worklessness, which simply do not stand up under scrutiny. The idea that social work values are, indeed, redistributive in terms of resources, and thus compatible with lazy radical practice is analysed. The fundamental value position of caring for others is also brought to bear on the consideration of dependency, and is also completely congruent with lazy radical social work. Finally, the connection between social democracy and its connection to social work's unifying principle, respect for persons is explored. Overall, Chapter 2 explicitly lays out compelling reasons for social work to be aligned with a radical, anti-neoliberal approach to practice.

Chapter 3 explores bureaucracy, regulation and professionalism, and highlights the distancing effects of bureaucracy – how systems and procedures can obscure the moral implications, assumptions and consequences of actions from the actor. Organisational professionalism, that is, the kind of professionalism associated with how things are done in the agency/organisation as opposed to how things should be done in terms of the social work, occupational profession, increasingly dominates and social workers need to be able to recognise and critique that. Recourse to social work values, skills and knowledge becomes more difficult as organisational professionalism increasingly dominates. It is concerning that there is recent research suggesting that social workers reflect in order to comply with rules and procedures, rather than to untangle dilemmas ethically. Regulatory codes exacerbate all of this.

The first step of the lazy radical social work model is introduced in Chapter 4: building relationships. The chapter looks at the importance of trust and of self-disclosure and giving something of oneself. The chapter explores how buying into 'underclass' ideas can be ruinous to value based practice, and how other features of the current neoliberal social work context are also inhibitors. Chapter 5 explores step 2, which concerns foregrounded knowledge and critical thinking. The suggestion is made that understanding economics is essential for social workers, or they are susceptible to persuasion towards neoliberal 'common sense' ideas that the current shocking levels of inequality and increasing poverty are 'inevitable' and something for which there is 'no alternative'. Students and social workers, working with people in poverty, must understand that those policy choices which create such hardship are just that: choices. Choices, moreover, which very much benefit the wealthy. Again, recent research has cast doubt on social work students' critical thinking abilities, and this is extremely concerning. Students need to learn to understand the core bodies of knowledge and learn how to bring them to bear, and analyse situations in that context. So, for example, understanding the psychological effects of inequality within a rich, materialistic society such as ours, is fundamental to understanding how people might behave in terms of seeking, or protecting, status. Kahneman's (2011) system 2 thinking is made explicit for readers and the 'dual processing system' of cognition is explained to help students understand what is required. Social work needs thinkers. Nothing else is good enough! The final stage of lazy radical practice, moral courage, is explored in Chapter 6. Using feelings of discontent or 'ethical stress' as an impetus to *taking action* is very important. Action might be small, such as disagreeing with a manager, making a case for doing something else, asking for an ethical matter to be discussed at a team meeting, or, very importantly, arguing *for* a decision you think is right, rather than wanting others to make it and to tell you what to do. The three steps of the model are revisited below, in relation to Aayisha's situation, but do follow up some of the points by re-reading the relevant chapters.

Finally, Chapter 7 might be considered the most controversial of all of the chapters. It tries to help students move from individual level explanations for problems and situations they might be dealing with. The neoliberal approach of blame, coercion and punishment is revisited and the (still individual level, but more well intentioned) tendency to appeal to 'diversity' approaches or to diagnose vulnerability and offer 'treatment' is explored. The congruence between 'identity' and 'vulnerability' approaches and neoliberalism is also deconstructed. Much of this chapter is about resisting the temptation to revert to individual level explanations/understanding as a *first* resort. It is an appeal to look to circumstances and context first, drawing on the underpinning idea that better circumstances lead to the best chance of human flourishing. Do not assume harm, vulnerability or pathology.

Threats

So, having quickly recapped on the book thus far, it is clear that lazy radical practice is ethical, do-able and will benefit of the people we work with. What could be wrong with that? Well, this section will look briefly at what gets in the way. These points have been covered elsewhere in the book but, again, bringing them together in one place makes for a coherent and succinct understanding.

Neoliberal agencies

Gove and Narey (Chapter 1) and Major (Chapter 4) all made statements or reported on how they viewed the problems in social work. Their unifying theme was that social workers are too concerned with social justice, disadvantage and too *understanding* of people. They should be making them self-sufficient, and understanding less but condemning more. That is, condemn those who get into trouble and do not manage to somehow succeed, even when they are in extremely difficult circumstances. This is clearly and explicitly in keeping with the neoliberal direction of contemporary politics, and has, of course, impacted immensely on how social work agencies are measured, regulated and inspected. Rogowski (2015), for example, outlines how behavioural methods of understanding and punitive responses in child and family social work characterises practice in England. Nicolas (2015) writing as a practitioner echoes his thinking.

This means, then, that social work students, even if they believe in lazy radical practice, might feel thwarted when on placement or getting first jobs in social work agencies. However, they *can*, by understanding what is going on, approach their work as lazy radicals, just making sure they do all of the managerial tasks required, but do not limit themselves to only that. Yes, this might lead to having to argue and, no, you will not always get your way, but, at least you will be working ethically and with integrity. Remember, use the feeling of ethical stress to 'tune in' to why something feels wrong. Use that as an impetus to action.

Dominance of the recognition, and neglect of the inequality, paradigm

Remember in Chapter 7, we explored how students can find individual level explanations much easier to understand, and can hang onto them at the expense of understanding the more difficult ideas around poverty and inequality? The congruence of the recognition paradigm, with social work's commitment to respecting and celebrating diversity, whilst well intentioned and important in its own right, can further mean there is a risk of forgetting about economics. It is simpler to understand and to 'do'. Social work students can concentrate on respecting different cultures, using the correct language and not criticising. Webb (2009, p. 307) comes down hard on the recognition way of thinking, by arguing that 'the politics of the "right to difference" and celebration of diversity in social work is a malign tendency' and that it 'runs parallel with neoliberalism'. Chapter 7 explored how this might be the case with recognition as another expression of neoliberal individualism and its congruence with the neoliberal hierarchy of economic inequality. Webb also suggests that 'diversity' centred text books often reflect a dumbing down in social work education via the 'selling' of an simplified concept to social work students. In essence, there are two main things to think critically about when considering 'celebrating diversity'. One is that there are limits to this. We do not celebrate difference or diversity when the culture is one where female genital mutilation is prevalent; where women are routinely denied the same rights as men; nor where gay people are thrown in prison. So, it is diversity within limits we celebrate? The other thing to reflect on is that maybe we should be celebrating 'sameness' not diversity. Broad based movements against injustice such as inequality or the denial of rights for certain groups of people – both expressions of our rights to sameness – require less fragmentation and more attention to that which unites us. As Badiou (2006, p. 53, cited in Webb, 2009, p. 315) states:

> Difference is in its multiplicities, as a historical fact, but Sameness is what is to become in its singularity, as a political opening. Badiou insists that only this recognition of 'the Same' can remedy the contemporary world's 'incapacity … to name and strive for a Good'.

The rise of the vulnerability paradigm

Linked to the above, and again, explored in Chapter 7 is the real threat to lazy radical practice that the vulnerability paradigm brings. Increasingly, students turn to, and are, perhaps encouraged to turn to, explanations rooted in the vulnerability of service users. Protection, as already discussed by Rogowski and Featherstone (Chapter 3), has come to dominate children's services, so that parents are considered a risk, rather than as part of a whole family unit that needs support and help. Welfare understandings have been eroded. Likewise, adult protection has burgeoned, with risk to vulnerable people as the priority (and in times of austerity, where limited money is channelled), and again, welfare is less important (so funding welfare endeavours are also less important. Also, why should we fund that, when self-sufficiency and individual endeavour are the only shows in town?).

A corollary of the above 'protection' agenda, then is the attendant vulnerability narrative. This was explored at length in Chapter 7, so there is no need to go over old ground, but there is, perhaps, one final element to think about when considering this paradigm. As discussed in Chapter 2, in the 1950s and 1960s social work concern moved from the moral inferiority of the poor (the underclass?) to the diagnosis and treatment of their 'problems' (usually psychological or psychiatric). As Baily and Brake (1975) said, 'The poor and the deviants had progressed from moral inferiority to pathology'. This mirrors the discussion of social work students today, making sense of a case study. Although some, but thankfully the minority, will see some service users as morally inferior, or lacking in values or whatever (the punitive discourse from Chapter 7) very many more are likely to view them as in need of treatment – be it counselling, educational 'courses' (such as parenting programmes), anger management or whatever. Really, things have not moved on much since 1960, apart from we now have a much wider choice of labels and diagnoses (Verhaeghe, 2012). As lazy radical practitioners, we must not jump to conclusions about pathology, vulnerability or the necessity of treatment *even if* it is attractive to make a neat referral and tick off that task list. Think critically about this and go back to Chapter 7 for more food for thought. It is so very in-keeping with neoliberalism to, again, understand situations as individual-level problems, and trying not to 'blame' can lead a well-intentioned, but uncritical social worker straight down the pathology and treatment pathway. This last point leads on very nicely to the next threat to lazy radical practice.

Lack of critical thinking

This section relates to Chapter 5. It is worth starting with a reminder of some of the recent, very worrying research that has been carried out with social work students. Firstly, Sheppard et al. (2018) found that social work graduands were significantly poorer at critical thinking than the average person on the street (i.e., poorer than a UK normative sample) and also poorer at being assertive. Secondly, Whitaker and Reimer (2017) found that social workers reflected on ethical dilemmas to comply with rules and procedures as the priority task. Thirdly, Whittaker (2011) found that social workers in child protection would actively abdicate decision-making to senior social workers and managers, using a variety of tactics. So, we *can* build up a picture of social workers who are not good at critical thinking, simply want to follow rules (easier to manage?), do not want to make decisions and are unassertive. How would it be possible for someone fitting this profile, then, to undertake lazy radical practice with its essential elements of critical thinking and moral courage? I would say it simply is not.

If social work education continues to produce graduates who fit the above description, they will continue to support the oppressive, ruling-class hegemony (i.e., practice in a reductionist, neoliberal, task-doing, unthinking way) *and* will find a good fit with many statutory agencies. This is a terrible thought. Social work education needs to counter it in some way, and I would suggest once again, that one way to do that is to *explicitly and unflinchingly* promote lazy radical practice, and its core elements, as *the* way to approach social work in the contemporary context.

With that in mind, social work education would have to be very confident that lazy radical practice and critique of the neoliberal hegemony was the *right* thing to do. The next section, therefore, will look at the three steps in the model, their basis in writing from the thinkers whose work we have drawn on throughout, *and* their compatibility with the ethical principles of the British Association of Social Workers and the International Federation of Social Work. This is a complex analysis, so a final case study will be used to help ground the discussion.

The above 'threats' to lazy radical practice can paint a grim picture. However, the real point is *not* that we should just give up and give in, *but* that lazy radical practice is more important than ever!

Aayisha, the lazy radical model, underpinning thinking, and ethical principles

PRACTICE EXAMPLE 7

Aayisha is an 18 year old, single, mixed race new mother who resides in supported accommodation for young mothers. Aayisha had a serious opiate misuse problem but has managed to remain stable on her methadone prescription for some time. Her baby was born three months ago, and she is coping reasonably well, although feels bored and frustrated at times. She talks about having no social life or boyfriend or fun. The baby, James, appears to be doing fine and there appears to be a bond between mother and baby.

Aayisha grew up in a poor, chaotic family where alcohol and drug misuse, and a partying lifestyle were the norm. She never knew her father other than he was a black African-American – her (white) mother did not talk much about him. Aayisha was sexually abused by a boyfriend of her mother's and, as a consequence, admitted into residential care when she was 15.

Lazy radical practice starts with an optimistic and hopeful view of Aayisha. She has done really well in terms of getting off heroin and remaining stable on her methadone prescription. She is coping well with her new baby, which is a difficult time for anyone, never mind people with as little support and resources as Aayisha. It must be hard-going.

Step 1: Relationship building, trust and emotional engagement (see Chapter 4)

Beginning the social work process with the above outlook means that a relationship with Aayisha is going to be easier to build. You need to build trust, and can expect some intrusive or 'testing' questions and would understand if Aayisha is less than honest with you from the outset. You are prepared for engagement with Aayisha on an emotional level – you might be able to empathise, or you might only be able to engage in compassion and care – and that is fine too.

You have been able to deconstruct the barriers to relationship building. To start with, you have learned about, questioned, critiqued and ultimately rejected notions and ways of understanding based on 'underclass' thinking. You understand the prevalent narratives around a young woman like Aayisha – irresponsible young women who get pregnant through carelessness and a desire to sponge off the state, claim welfare and secure a house.

If you did believe the 'underclass' stereotype of Aayisha, how would that affect your understanding and interpretation of the practice example? You would be drawing on what Weinberg (2016, p. 13) calls 'the reactionary discourse' where 'young, single mothers are framed as irresponsible wanton young women or "children having children" … at "high risk" … for not being "good enough" mothers'. Within this discourse, accountability is placed on the individual rather than on the state's duty to support vulnerable citizens, and the erosion of 'family values' is seen to be epitomised by these young women. So, Aayisha fits the stereotype of 'one of them' in terms of the 'underclass' and its behaviours.

After the 2011 riots, the then Prime Minister, David Cameron, pronounced that there was moral collapse in the country with fatherless children at its heart (Calder, 2016). Even although, in terms of outcomes from children, economic stability has been demonstrated to have more influence than the structure of the family (Calder, 2016), the scourge of the single mother still has purchase in the public imagination. As the group of single mothers becomes poorer and poorer (and are the group suffering disproportionately under austerity) (JRF, 2017a), outcomes will probably deteriorate further and it will be easily interpreted, in neoliberal common-sense terms, as being down to the lack of fathers, rather than down to growing economic hardship.

So, according to the neoliberal discourse, Aayisha fell pregnant and is now, unfortunately, relying on the state. The discourse would, perhaps, lead to the idea that people should not have children if they cannot afford to raise them independently. And so, any welfare safety net should be minimal so as not to encourage others to go down that path, and to encourage Aayisha back to work as soon as possible (work is the way out of poverty!). Given that the state is supporting her and bailing her out, she has a bit of a cheek to be asking for fun and going out. She should be demonstrating that she is a good mother and not being so self-indulgent.

You reject all of the above. In fact, you are critically aware of neoliberal, hegemonic framings of situations, and can clearly see the neoliberal assumptions playing out in the above interpretation. You, in fact, agree with Featherstone et al. (2014, p. 1737) who:

> argue for the moral legitimacy of support and its difference from intervention and the need to engage with and develop a family support project for the 21st century. We will argue that this should be located within a project that celebrates families' strengths as well as their vulnerabilities often in the context of considerable adversities and (re) locates workers as agents of hope and support.

So, again, it is affirmed that you should approach Aayisha with hope and optimism, recognising her strengths and offering support, help and care as primary tasks. You do not buy into a less punitive, but just as potentially harmful, vulnerability discourse either. It might be tempting to view her situation through a therapeutic lens as above. She has been sexually abused, and the 'single-story' of Woodiwiss's theory is that this means she will be harmed and damaged forever. This is not to say that that might not be true – it might. But it also might not, and it's the assumption of the former that is dangerous. If a social worker makes that assumption, and connects, for example Aayisha's drug use (and her current reliance on methadone) as a direct result of the sexual abuse, then there is, again, an obscuring of structural or economic influence on her situation – or responsibility for addressing that situation. A social worker might also interpret Aayisha's expressed desire for a boyfriend, or fun, as a result of her seeking out affection in the only way she knows, whereas she may actually be seeking out a boyfriend and fun because she is a 'normal' young woman and that said boyfriend and fun are also very 'normal'. Pleasure is often judged harshly when it is sought by someone in poverty or other difficult circumstances. Weinberg (2016) in her research on social workers working with young mothers found that recognition and acceptance of desire or sexual need was missing from workers' constructs of the young women.

So, adopting a lazy radical approach, you find out from Aayisha, via a nascent relationship, how she views the situation and what she thinks might help. You know you must complete risk assessments and other paperwork but you do not allow this to be the only jobs you do. You are aware of risk averse practice and how that can inhibit authentic relationship building, so you try to remain as reflective as possible about why you are doing the things you are doing. The care, compassion and emotional engagement that the relationship with Aayisha is facilitating all have an action element, which would be picked up in step 2 of lazy radical practice.

Underpinning thinking and ethical principles for step 1

The moral basis for relationship based practice could be attributed to many thinkers and writers, but for the purposes of this book, where only a few key thinkers feature, it would be useful to return to Bauman and his exploration of Arendt's 'animal pity'. A feature of distancing, bureaucratic practice is that it removes people from feeling the emotional context of the other person. Distant and unknowable decision makers are a feature of this type of regime, and we can see that in child protection case conferences and Multi-agency Public Protection Arrangements (MAPPA) meetings for example. The social worker then carries out tasks as a middle man, without responsibility for unpopular decisions. As Bauman (2000b, p. 26) says:

> The technical-administrative success of the Holocaust was due in part to the skilful utilization of 'moral sleeping pills' made available by modern bureaucracy and modern technology. The natural invisibility of causal connections in a complex system of interaction, and the 'distancing' of the unsightly or morally repelling outcomes of action to the point of rendering them invisible to the actor, were most prominent among them.

Chapter 3 outlined Bauman's ideas about how ordinary people can overcome 'animal pity' in order to carry out inhumane tasks. In relation to the case study, the ideas apply to actions less drastic than murder, but still lacking in humanity and that are morally empty. Summarising and applying Bauman's three conditions for overcoming 'animal pity', and therefore recognising the danger therein, we should think about the following:

➤ The actions are authorised: the agency is managerial and neoliberal, with an underpinning moralising self-sufficiency discourse. Therefore, most managers and colleagues buy into a managerial, risk pre-occupied and punitive response to troublesome people like Aayisha. Therefore, filling in the forms, being stern and 'taking no nonsense' are all very much approved of and authorised. Management instructions are never questioned or critiqued. Loyalty to the agency is paramount.

➤ The actions are routinised: heavy caseloads and lots of similar problems allow for formulaic and codified responses to Aayisha to prevail. No time (or inclination) to try to get to know people. Refer her to a parenting class.

➤ Service users are dehumanised: you buy the 'underclass' narrative and deep down view people as somehow less than the people you know and love.

Bauman and Arendt's work on bureaucracy, then, gives substance to the importance of building relationships with, and really getting to know the services users we work with. We *must* engage our emotions in real social work, as this is a vital part of our moral compass and can guide us when things do not feel right or fair (ethical stress) and allow us to feel for the other. Through building a relationship we are far more likely to care and to feel compassion.

As far as more formal ethical principles are concerned both BASW and IFSW also have something to say about relationship based practice, care and compassion – *emotional* social work. Here are just a few examples:

BASW (2014b):

1.1 Social work grew out of humanitarian and democratic ideals, and its values are based on respect for the equality, worth, and dignity of all people.

2.1 4 Treating each person as a whole Social workers should be concerned with the whole person, within the family, community, societal and natural environments, and should seek to recognise all aspects of a person's life.

2.2 5 Working in solidarity.

3 Social workers have a responsibility to apply the professional values and principles set out above to their practice. They should act with integrity and treat people with *compassion, empathy and care.*

Principle 1 Social workers should build and sustain professional relationships based on people's right to control their own lives and make their own choices and decisions. Social work relationships should be based on people's rights to respect, privacy, reliability and confidentiality.

IFSW (2012):

4.1 Social work is based on respect for the inherent worth and dignity of all people, and the rights that follow from this. Social workers should uphold and defend each person's physical, psychological, emotional and spiritual integrity and well-being.

5.3 Social workers should act with integrity. This includes not abusing the relationship of trust with the people using their services.

5.4 Social workers should act in relation to the people using their services with *compassion, empathy and care.*

Step 2: Knowledge and critical thinking (see Chapter 5)

Traditional or standard sources of social work knowledge might come immediately to mind if asked to apply knowledge to Aayisha's situation. Knowledge of her attachment to the baby, her life-stage (adolescence) and knowledge about her own childhood, lack of attachment and identity and assumed consequences of abuse would all be standard. These are all bodies of knowledge that are important, and need to make up part of the picture, but, in good lazy radical style, you would first turn to the knowledge required to understand her environment. Can this be improved in order to help Aayisha flourish? She perhaps should not be pathologised, and were we able to improve her circumstances, might manage well enough. Given that lazy radicals attribute responsibility for social problems to structural difference, addressing these structural issues would unashamedly be the starting point.

So, taking the suggested 'foregrounded knowledge' from Chapter 5, you would think about the following:

➤ Inequality and poverty: you know what grinding poverty can do to people and believe that this is not caused by behaviour, but that poverty is the cause of people being desperate. You understand that poverty and inequality leads to increased anxiety, stress and substance misuse, and understand that Aayisha has been susceptible to those influences. If Aayisha, like many people, likes to post selfies on Instagram and to portray a 'perfect' life, whilst complaining about wanting the latest phone, clothes etc. you, again, do not condemn her for that. Turning to Wilkinson and Pickett (2018), you really have a grasp of how inequality leads to people feeling stress to appear perfect and to be vulnerable to social evaluative stress. What people think of us is so important, and if we make huge efforts to avoid being looked down on.

➤ Economics: you are outraged at the poverty Aayisha is in. You also know that single parents, especially young ones like Aayisha, have been hit by austerity measures more than any other group. She is significantly poorer than she might have been a couple of decades ago, whilst the richest in the country have increased their wealth several-fold. You are angry about that and understand, politically, that neoliberalism has deliberately engineered this state of affairs to increase the wealth of those at the top of the hierarchy.

➤ Hegemonic neoliberal narratives: people could easily work if they want to; work is the way out of poverty; people are not really poor, look at the things they have; and, there is no real poverty in this country. See Chapter 5 to deconstruct these statements more fully, but suffice to say that you understand the real causes of unemployment; that 'the working poor' are a new group of people who cannot afford the 'normal' things in life even when working very hard; that employment rights have been eroded to the extent that people find it very hard to get good quality, secure work; that there is real pressure on people to buy things and 'keep up'; and what relative poverty means and why it is the ethical measure of poverty in our rich country. Just 'getting a job' is not necessarily the solution for Aayisha – it will not give her enough money, it will take her away from her child and child care is very expensive.

You would synthesise the above knowledge and apply it to Aayisha, thereby moving beyond simple system 1 thinking (Kahneman, 2011) and employing the critical faculties of system 2. This might mean that the first work you do would be to make sure she is, economically, getting everything she is entitled to. Are there any charities or other organisations that could help? Can the housing department do anything – is advocacy there required? What does she say she needs? Can you help her get it? Can you find a way to help her have a night out with friends (even to a nightclub? Shock, horror!)? Are there babysitting services? Can you get funding for that? You would also need to be prepared to justify and account for why you are taking these actions as a priority rather than referring her to a counsellor or parenting class. Draw from the above knowledge, and see step 3, to make your case.

Underpinning thinking and ethical principles for step 2

In Chapter 5, we drew on Mill and Arendt. John Stuart Mill was a passionate advocate for free thinking and free talking, and, obviously, this *must* feature if critical thinking is to be promoted. It is easy to conform in a way that is, according to Mill, a dumbing down of thinking and debating to a sort of mediocre form of compliance where everyone trots out the same 'party line' and agrees with a simplified, polemic understanding of complex situations. Social media can exacerbate that with encouragement to 'like' or comment with the 'right' side of the argument or risk censure or insults by offering a different view. So, for example, a person who might have concerns about levels of immigration might want to discuss that. Rather than actually discuss (and perhaps change a mind or two), often the reaction is to shout 'racist!' It is often the case that those shouting 'racist' are also unable to argue against the person's views, because they have not done any actual thinking or learning about the situation, but have simply jumped on the bandwagon of which their friends are all passengers. This is exactly the kind of hollow exchange that Mill warns against.

Thinking about things, and engaging in discussion about unpopular ideas, has been a theme throughout this book. Some of the material presented might be challenging for the reader and might, in fact, oppose some deeply held and valued ways of thinking. However, *that is the point!!* You don't have to agree with everything I have suggested – but you do have to know why you disagree and you do have to be able to engage in the learning and critical thinking required. As Mill said:

> There is the greatest difference between presuming an opinion to be true, because, with every opportunity for contesting it, it has not been refuted, and assuming its truth for the purposes of not permitting its refutation (Mill, 1859 [2011], p. 30).

In other words, only through discussing and debating opinions can we begin to see that one has more validity than another. Not allowing debate, due to certainty of 'truth' is a far lesser method of finding out what might actually be 'truth'.

Hannah Arendt has also provided this book with the theme of the importance of thinking. Eichmann was not a thinker, and in fact Arendt states that he demonstrated a real inability to actually think. He followed bureaucratic rules to the letter, and did not question or consider any moral content or critical consideration of what he was being asked to do. He wanted to do a good job of carrying out his tasks. Arendt helps us understand just how dangerous this narrowing of ethical consideration is. An element of the task-doing mentality of Eichmann, and one important to social work is to be unquestioning about instructions from those higher up the organisational hierarchy. So, as covered at length in previous chapters, just taking instructions from, or asking for decisions to be made by managers or formal meetings, again, hollows out one's own ethical consideration of the bigger picture. At one point, for example, Eichmann had reservations about the 'bloody solution through violence' but when:

He could see with his own eyes and hear with his own ears that not only Hitler, not only Heydrich or the 'sphinx' Muller, not just the SS or the Party, but the elite of the good old Civil Service were vying and fighting each other for the honour of taking the lead in these bloody matters. 'At that point I sensed a kind of Pontius Pilate feeling, for I felt free of all guilt'. *Who was he to judge?* Who was he 'to have [his] own thoughts on the matter?' (Arendt, 1965, p. 114)

In conclusion, then, Mill and Arendt bring home the importance of thinking critically for ourselves. Bringing knowledge to bear on the situation and on the tasks we are asked to do *and,* perhaps, questioning and challenging those tasks. This should apply even when managers and others in authority design things in certain ways or ask that things be done in certain ways. Do not just uncritically and unquestioningly accept that. It is not enough to just do what you are told, you must think about it. Don't be an Eichmann!

Once again, BASW and IFSW also provide rationale for step 2 of lazy radical social work.

BASW (2014b):

> 2.3 4 Social workers should make judgements based on balanced and considered reasoning, maintaining awareness of the impact of their own values, prejudices and conflicts of interest on their practice and on other people.

> 2.3 5 Social workers should be prepared to account for and justify their judgements and actions.

Ethical principle 12: Social workers should reflect and critically evaluate their practice.

Ethical principle 14: Social workers should develop and maintain the attitudes, knowledge, understanding and skills to provide quality services and accountable practice. They need to keep up to date with relevant research.

Ethical principle 15: Social workers should strive to create conditions in employing agencies ... where the principles of the Code are discussed, evaluated and upheld in practice. *They should engage in ethical debate with their colleagues and employers to share knowledge and take responsibility for making ethically informed decisions. They should endeavour to seek changes in policies, procedures, improvements to services or working conditions as guided by the ethics of the profession.*

Ethical principle 16: Social workers should contribute to the education and training of colleagues and students by sharing knowledge and practice wisdom. They should identify, develop, use and disseminate knowledge, theory and practice.

IFSW (2012):

> 5.1 Social workers are expected to develop and maintain the required skills and competence to do their job.
>
> 5.11 Social workers should be prepared to state the reasons for their decisions based on ethical considerations, and be accountable for their choices and actions.

Step 3: Moral courage

So, you have managed to get to know Aayisha a bit, and are optimistic about her managing with, maybe, some help. You want to act in accordance with knowing her, hearing her voice and thinking critically about her situation, in other words you want to take the actions identified at step 2. You are under pressure, however. Your team manager says she knows lots of 'Aayishas' and what this one needs is close monitoring, attendance at a parenting class, referral for sexual abuse counselling ('that always looks good in the case notes') and regular drug testing.

You are unhappy about all of that and feel significant ethical stress – you simply do not believe she needs any of the above, and neither does Aayisha. In fact, the action plan from the manager seems to be only be about making the agency look good. It won't do anything whatsoever for Aayisha, and, in fact, will distance her further from help just by the futile, bureaucratic and punitive 'feel' of the plan. You go to see her. You agree to undertake the actions previously discussed: talking to the benefit office, the housing department and trying to access babysitting. You also talk about her plans and aspirations for the future, she tells you more as she begins to trust you. You suggest some future actions like college and she is pleased with that – she seems to have a burgeoning hope that things might work out OK. Of course, you need to fill in the forms – and you do, *with* Aayisha. You tell her about the manager's instruction for drug testing. She attends a drug centre anyway, and testing is part of that and she has no problem with allowing you to access her results each month. There is a real 'partnership' feel to the work, and an authentic sense of care that Aayisha is responding to. The baby is still thriving.

So, on returning to the office, you feel that you are doing something quite difficult by going to knock on the manager's door. However, if you just unthinkingly did what she said, you would feel real ethical stress, so you are using that as a guide to doing the 'right' thing. You explain your action plan, including regular home visits, and the regular drug tests (the manager is very happy about that) and, to your surprise, really quite disinterested in the other 'extra' advocacy work. The manager smiles a bit wryly and says she 'loves your optimism' which you smile about later as you understand the condescension inherent in her meaning. You absolutely do not worry however, you know you are doing the right thing, know it's lazy radical practice (or whatever you want to call it – or maybe no names are necessary!) at its best, and finally, you know that if your manager needed an example of good social work, you might well be the choice regardless of her managerial imperatives.

OK, so things might not always work out quite that well, but you can see the kind of social worker you can be? You always have that choice. Do the managerial, process driven work, but do not *only* do that!

Underpinning thinking and ethical principles for step 3

Do you remember Arendt's work on 'cog-theory' and how just being a cog in a machine ('If I didn't do it, someone else would') was not good enough? You needed to be able to answer questions like 'well why be that kind of cog?' Or 'Why continue to be a cog?' etc. Having moral courage makes for the opposite type of practice to 'cog' work. Arendt suggests that whatever you do, you are responsible and accountable, and this leads to questioning and putting alternative ideas forward where required. The Sheppard et al. (2018) study that has been used in several previous chapters, as well as finding poor critical thinking skills among social work graduands, also found poorer than average scores for assertiveness. This, again, is concerning for step 3 of lazy radical practice, even if we are thinking quite modestly, as in the example of Aayisha above. The important message is that step 2, knowledge and critical thinking, is the fuel for moral courage. Knowing your actions or decisions are 'right' in terms of values and knowledge is so important, and will help you have confidence in any impending debate or discussion, or speaking out in a decision-making meeting. Knowledge and thinking will let you expose the moral content in your actions and in the interpretation of situations, and *this* will lead to feeling ethical stress and thus to action. Have faith, learn, think and listen to your heart.

In *Personal responsibility under dictatorship* Arendt (1964, p. 45) says:

> The dividing line between those who want to think and therefore have to judge by themselves, and those who do not, strikes across all social and cultural or educational differences. In this respect, the total moral collapse of respectable society during the Hitler regime may teach us that under such circumstances those who cherish values and hold fast to moral norms and standards are not reliable: we now know that moral norms and standards can be changed overnight, and that all that then will be left is the mere habit of holding fast to

something. Much more reliable will be the doubters and skeptics, not because skepticism is good or doubting wholesome, but because they are used to examine things and to make up their own minds.

Finally, in terms of formal codes:

BASW (2014b):

> 2.1 1 Social workers should respect, uphold and defend each person's ... well-being.

> 2.1 2 Social workers should promote and support people's dignity and right to make their own choices and decisions.

> 2.2 5 Social workers, individually, collectively and with others have a duty to *challenge social conditions* that contribute to social exclusion, stigmatisation or subjugation.

> 8 Challenging the abuse of human rights.

> Ethical principle 15: Social workers should strive to create conditions in employing agencies ... where the principles of the Code are discussed, evaluated and upheld in practice. They should engage in ethical debate with their colleagues and employers to share knowledge and take responsibility for making ethically informed decisions. *They should endeavour to seek changes in policies, procedures,* improvements to services or working conditions as guided by the ethics of the profession.

IFSW (2012):

> 10. Social workers should foster and engage in *ethical debate* with their colleagues and employers and take responsibility for making ethically informed decisions.

Conclusion

It is difficult to know how to bring this book to a close. It might be worth just looking a little further at the Codes above, for their support of overall lazy radical social work as an holistic approach to practice:

BASW (2014b):

> 2.2 Social justice: social workers have a responsibility to promote social justice, in relation to society generally, and in relation to the people they work with.

Lazy radical practice is, of course, more concerned with this in connection to 'the people (we) work with' but, nonetheless, there is the requirement to practice with social justice in mind.

2.2 4 Challenging unjust policies and practices. Social workers have a duty to bring to the attention of their employers, policy makers, politicians and the general public situations where resources are inadequate or where distribution of resources, policies and practice are oppressive, unfair, harmful or illegal.

Thus, when we witness oppressive, neoliberal policies and practice actually causing harm (such as austerity measures, benefit cuts and sanctions, for example) we should be challenging that, rather than supporting the hegemony. *Exactly* what lazy radical practice sets out to do.

IFSW (2012):

12 Social workers should work to create conditions in employing agencies…where the principles of this statement and those of their own national code … are discussed, evaluated and upheld.

Discussing and debating ethical matters is essential, therefore seeing social work as an ethical, rather than technical, endeavour is fundamental.

Ok, so you can justify adopting a lazy radical approach to practice to anyone who might challenge you on it. And, if there is one statement from the Codes that most appropriately sums up lazy radical practice, it might be the following:

2.2 5 Working in solidarity (BSAW, 2014b).

From the Oxford English Dictionary (2018), 'solidarity' means: 'Unity or agreement of feeling or action, especially among individuals with a common interest; mutual support within a group'.

Think back to Chapter 6 when we considered moral courage within an ethics of care framework. The suggestion was made that moral courage is more likely to be activated when the worker feels that the service user belongs to the same group as themselves. So, acting oppressively or unethically puts the 'collective vitality' at risk (Simola, 2014, p. 33). Solidarity means that we are in it together *with* people who use services, that we can see the oppressive nature of the hegemony and want to do something about it. We know the answer to the question *Whose side are we on?* (SWAN, 2018). Having said that, lazy radical practice has a fight on its hands to make an impact on contemporary social work. Wilkinson and Pickett (2018) draw on research into solidarity and levels of inequality in different countries. They found that in more equal countries, people were significantly more willing to help others, driven by feelings of sympathy and moral duty. It is more difficult to feel for and with others when divisions between people are stark, but it is the job of a social worker to overcome those divisions, understand the exacerbating effect of inequality, and to make that vital human connection.

Still staying with that fundamental premise of lazy radical practice, we might return to Zygmunt Bauman for the last words.

> The future of social work ... does not depend on classifications, on procedures, nor on reducing the variety and complexity of human needs and problems. It depends, instead, on the ethical standards of the society we all inhabit. It is those ethical standards which, much more than the rationality and diligence of social workers, are today in crisis and under threat.... Rational arguments will not help; there is, let us be frank, no 'good reason' why we should be our brothers' keeper, why we should care, why we should be moral – and in the utility-oriented society the function-less poor and indolent cannot count on rational proofs of their right to happiness. Yes, let us admit – there is nothing 'reasonable' about taking responsibility, about caring and being moral. *Morality has only itself to support it: it is better to care than to wash one's hands, better to be **in solidarity** with the unhappiness of the other than indifferent, and altogether better to be moral, even if this does not make people wealthier and the companies more profitable* (Bauman, 2000b, p. 11, emphasis added).

So, here's to the future generation of Lazy Radical Social Workers. In solidarity.

Glossary of Terms

Austerity: Right wing governmental economic policy adopted to deal with the deficit in public funds (attributable to the financial crash), which involved cuts to public spending such as public services (local councils, education, care services, NHS) and quite drastic cuts to welfare benefits.

Hegemony: A term coined by Gramsci (1971) to describe the mechanisms that allow a political ideology to be accepted by a society (via civic institutions such as the media) and to become unquestioned 'common sense'.

Keynesian economics: The economic system that preceded neoliberalism (from post-World War 2 until Thatcher's government in 1979). After World War 2, the Labour Government introduced the welfare state, the national health service and the ideology that the state would look after people's basic needs from cradle to grave. This meant that the government would also regulate businesses, protect workers' rights and provide a buffer against the fluctuations of the market by borrowing to invest in business when necessary.

Lazy radical social work: Radical social work without the need for activism (going on marches, signing petitions etc.). 'Practivism' i.e., being radical in your practice!

Left wing: A political position that has 'equality' as its priority and, thus, will regulate and control business in terms of profit, will tax rich people more and will redistribute wealth to poorer people by protecting wages and working conditions, spending on public services and paying reasonable benefits.

Managerialism: Imported from the private sector and sometimes known as 'new public management', managerialism involves quality assurance through quantitative measures such as targets, performance indicators and audits. Policy and procedures are developed at the level of management and workers are expected to follow these with little autonomy.

Neoliberalism: The political ideology since the late 1970s. Economically right wing, neoliberalism seeks to change the role of government by freeing up markets and banks to make as much money as possible, whilst providing a role for government in opening up markets, selling public services to the private sector and promoting tough law and order policies. The public sector is subject to severe cuts (including cuts to benefits) whilst tax breaks are provided for the wealthiest people, corporations and businesses. The economics of neoliberalism are supported by a hegemonic culture of individualism (each person out for themselves), competition, independence and individual responsibility for success or failure. In this brave new world, structural forces such as poverty are excuses, and everything is understood as being the responsibility of the individual person.

Poverty – absolute: When people do not have the resources required for survival.

Poverty – relative: When people have less than 60% of the median income (JRF, n.d.).

Radical Social Work: An approach to social work that roots society's problems in structures and policies rather than attributing all of the 'blame' to individual behaviour or personality. There is always likely to be an interplay between society and individuals, so radical social work may be more easily understood as a paradigm which understands structural difference, like poverty and inequality, to *have an effect* on people. This is in contrast to neoliberal social work that would concentrate only on the individual's choices and behaviour as if wider factors are of no relevance.

Right wing: A political position that has 'freedom' as its priority. This means that business is freed from the interference of government and allowed to do what it will to make profit. The small role of the state in right wing economics also means that the private sector is allowed access to traditionally publicly owned areas of life. Tax breaks are allowed for the wealthiest individuals and for businesses and corporations. These policies ultimately mean that inequality increases as the rich get richer (businesses making profit for owners and being taxed less on those profits) and the poor get relatively poorer (benefit cuts; privatisation of, and budget cuts to, services they rely on; and businesses paying low wages and providing insecure temporary work for which it is cheaper to employ people; etc.).

References

Arendt, H. (1964) *Personal Responsibility Under Dictatorship*. https:// grattoncourses.files.wordpress.com/2017/07/arendt-personal-responsibility-under-a-dictatorship.pdf (accessed 1 March, 2018).

Arendt, H. (1965) *Eichmann in Jerusalem: A Report on the Banality of Evil*. London: Penguin Books.

Bailey, R. and Brake, M. (eds) (1975) *Radical Social Work*. London: Edward.

Banks, S. (2012) *Ethics and Values in Social Work* 4th Ed. London: Red Globe Press.

Barak, A. (2016) 'Critical consciousness in critical social work: Learning from theatre of the oppressed', *British Journal of Social Work*, 46, 1776–1792.

Barnard, A. (2008) 'Values, ethics and professionalization: A social work history', in A. Barnard, N. Horner and J. Wild (eds) *The Value Base of Social Work and Social Care*. Maidenhead: OU Press.

Barsky, A. (2009) 'When Right is Not Easy: Social Work and Moral Courage' https://blog.oup.com/2009/12/social-work-moral-courage/ (accessed 11 December, 2017).

BASW (British Association of Social Workers) (2014a) *Croisdale-Appleby report combines deep academic rigour with deep understanding of the social work profession*. www.basw.co.uk/news/article/?id=681 (accessed 11 October, 2017).

BASW (British Association of Social Workers) (2014b) *Code of Ethics for Social Work*. Birmingham: BASW.

BASW (British Association of Social Workers) (2018) *The Professional Capabilities Framework*. www.basw.co.uk/professional-development/professional-capabilities-framework-pcf (accessed 14 June, 2018).

Bauman, Z. (1989) *Modernity and the Holocaust*. Cambridge: Polity Press.

Bauman, Z. (2000a) *Liquid Modernity*. Cambridge: Polity Press.

Bauman, Z. (2000b) 'Am I my brother's keeper?', *European Journal of Social Work*, 3 (1), 5–11.

BBC (2015) 'Children's social services staff "altered report"'. www.bbc.co.uk/news/uk-england-hampshire-34898799 (accessed 9 March, 2018).

BBC (2018a) 'Labour could renationalise railways in five years – McDonnell' www.bbc.co.uk/news/uk-politics-45609604 (accessed 25 September, 2018).

BBC (2018b) 'Teachers "need help" tackling poverty impact on education' www.bbc.co.uk/news/uk-scotland-44295465 (accessed 20 June, 2018).

BBC (2018c) 'Met Police "use more force more often" against black people' www.bbc.co.uk/news/uk-england-london-44214748 (accessed 19 June, 2018).

Beddoe, L. and Keddell, E. (2016) Informed outrage: Tackling shame and stigma in poverty education in social work, *Ethics and Social Welfare*, 10 (2), 149–162.

Beresford, P., Croft, S. and Adshead, L. (2008) '"We don't see her as a social worker": A service user case study of the importance of the social worker's relationship and humanity', *The British Journal of Social Work*, 38 (7), 1388–1407.

Bloom, P. (2016) *Against Empathy: The Case for Rational Compassion*. London: Bodley Head.

Bowlby, J. (1969) *Attachment and Loss*. New York: Basic Books.

Brady, D. (2005) 'The welfare state and relative poverty in rich western democracies, 1967–1997', *Social Forces*, 83 (4), 1329–1364.

British Social Attitudes (2017) 'Paper summary: Welfare'. www.bsa.natcen. ac.uk/latest-report/british-social-attitudes-32/welfare.aspx (accessed 9 March, 2018).

Brown, K. and Rutter, L. (2008) *Critical Thinking for Social Work*. Maidstone: Learning Matters.

Calder, G. (2016) *How Inequality Runs in Families*. Bristol: Policy Press.

Casey, L. (2012) *Listening to Troubled Families*. https://assets.publishing. service.gov.uk/government/uploads/system/uploads/attachment_data/ file/6151/2183663.pdf (accessed 19 January, 2018).

Catholic Herald (1978) 'The Thatcher Philosophy'. https://margaretthatcher.org/ document/103793 (accessed 25 February, 2015).

Cohen, D. (2017) 'How London's knife culture is being fueled by jargon, social media and music'. *London Evening Standard* www.standard.co.uk/news/crime/ how-londons-knife-culture-is-being-fueled-by-jargon-social-media-and-music-a3579396.html (accessed 10 January, 2018).

Community Care (2013) 'The Munro report two years on: Social workers find little has changed'. www.communitycare.co.uk/2013/02/19/the-munro-report-two-years-on-social-workers-find-little-has-changed/(accessed 10 March, 2018).

Croisdale-Appleby, D. (2014) 'Revisioning social work education'. www.gov. uk/government/uploads/system/uploads/attachment_data/file/285788/ DCA_Accessible.pdf (accessed 9 December, 2017).

Crouch, C. (2011) *The Strange Non-Death of Neoliberalism*. Cambridge: Polity Press.

Cunningham, B. (2008) *Exploring Professionalism*. London: University of London.

Daily Mail (2009) 'What made Baby P's mother Tracey Connelly so wicked?' www.dailymail.co.uk/news/article-1206629/What-Baby-Ps-mother-Tracey-Connelly-wicked.html#ixzz4w2xHRcR0 (accessed 12 October, 2017).

Doel, M. (2012) *Social Work: The Basics*. Abingdon: Routledge.

Donnellan, H. and Jack, G. (2015) *The Survival Guide for Newly Qualified Social Workers*. London: Jessica Kingsley Publishers.

Dreger, A. (2016) *Galileo's Middle Finger*. New York: Penguin.

Duncan-Smith, I. (2017) 'The CSJ Story' www.centreforsocialjustice.org.uk/ about/story (accessed 27 February, 2018).

Eagleton-Pierce, M. (2016) *Neoliberalism: The Key Concepts.* Abingdon: Routledge.

Edmondson, D., Potter, A. and McLaughlin, A. (2013) 'Reflections of a higher specialist PQ group on the Munro recommendations for children's social workers', *Practice: Social Work in Action*, 25 (3), 191–207.

Evetts, J. (2003) 'The sociological analysis of professionalism: Occupational change in the modern world', *International Sociology*, 18 (2), 395–415.

Fazzi, L. (2016) 'Are we educating creative professionals? The results of some experiments on the education of social work students in Italy', *Social Work Education*, 35 (1), 89–99.

Featherstone, B., Broadhurst, K. and Holt, K. (2012) 'Thinking systemically – thinking politically: Building strong [artnerships with children and families in the context of rising inequality', *British Journal of Social Work*, 42, 618–633.

Featherstone, B., Morris, K. and White, S. (2014) 'A marriage made in hell: Early intervention meets child protection', *British Journal of Social Work*, 44, 1735–1749.

Featherstone, B., Morris, K., Daniel, B., Bywaters, P., Brady, G., Bunting, L., Mason, W. and Mirza, N. (2017) 'Poverty, inequality, child abuse and neglect: Changing the conversation across the UK in child protection?', *Children and Youth Services Review, (in press).* DOI: 10.1016/j.childyouth.2017.06.009.

Feeley, M. and Simon, J. (1992) 'The new penology: Notes on the emerging strategy of corrections and its implications', *Criminology*, 30, 449–474.

Fennig, M. and Denov, M. (2018) 'Regime of truth: Rethinking the dominance of the bio-medical model in mental health social work with refugee youth', *British Journal of Social Work*, https://doi.org/10.1093/bjsw/bcy036.

Fenton, J. (2014) 'Can social work education meet the neoliberal challenge head on?', *Critical and Radical Social Work*, 2 (3), 321–335.

Fenton, J. (2015) 'An analysis of 'ethical stress' in criminal justice social work in scotland: The place of values', *British Journal of Social Work*, 45 (5), 1415–1432.

Fenton, J. (2016) *Values in Social Work: Reconnecting with Social Justice.* London: Red Globe Press.

Fenton, J. (2018) 'Putting old heads on young shoulders: Helping social work students uncover the neoliberal hegemony'. *Social Work Education* https://doi.org/10.1080/02615479.2018.1468877.

Fenton, J. (2019) 'Social work education and the neoliberal challenge', in Webb, S. (ed) *The Routledge Handbook of Critical Social Work.* London: Routledge.

Fenton, J. and Kelly, T. (2017) '"Risk is king and needs to take a backseat!" can social workers' experiences of moral injury strengthen practice?', *Journal of Social Work Practice*, 31 (4), 461–475.

Ferguson, H. (2018) 'How social workers reflect in action and when and why they don't: The possibilities and limits to reflective practice in social work', *Social Work Education*, doi: org/10.1080/02615479.2017.1413083.

Ferguson, I. (2008) *Reclaiming Social Work: Challenging Neo-liberalism and Promoting Social Justice.* London: Sage.

Ferguson, I. (2013) 'Social workers as agents of change', in Gray, M. and S. A. Webb. (eds) *The New Politics of Social Work.* London: Red Globe Press.

Ferguson, I., Ioakimidis, V. and Lavalette, M. (2018) *Global Social Work in a Political Context: Radical Perspectives*. Bristol: Policy Press.

Ferguson, I. and Lavalette, M. (2009) 'Social work after baby P', in Ferguson, I. and M. Lavalette. (eds) *Social Work after Baby P: Issues, Debates and Alternative Perspectives*. Liverpool: Liverpool Hope University.

Fine, M. and Teram, E. (2012) Overt and covert ways of responding to moral injustices in social work practice: Heroes and mild-mannered social work bipeds, *British Journal of Social Work*, 43, 1312–1329.

Fook, J. (2012) *Social Work: A Critical Approach to Practice*. London: Sage.

Fox, C. (2016) *I Find That Offensive*. London: Biteback Publishing.

Frank, J. M. and Rice, K. (2017) 'Perceptions of poverty in america: Using social empathy to reframe students' attitudes', *Social Work Education*, 36 (4), 391–402.

Fronek, P. and Chester, P. (2016) 'Moral outrage: Social workers in the third space', *Ethics and Social Welfare*, 10 (2), 163–176.

Funge, S. P. (2011) 'Promoting the social justice orientation of students: The role of the educator', *Journal of Social Work Education*, 47 (1), 73–90.

Furedi, F. (2004) *Therapy Culture*. London: Routledge.

Gair, S. (2013) 'Inducing empathy: Pondering students' (in)ability to empathise with an aboriginal man's lament and what might be done about it', *Journal of Social Work Education*, 49 (1), 136–149.

Garner, R., Ferdinand, P. and Lawson, S. (2009) *Introduction to Politics*. Oxford: OUP.

Garrett, P. M. (2010) 'Examining the "conservative revolution": Neoliberalism and social work education', *Social Work Education*, 29 (4), 340–355.

Garrett, P. M. (2016) 'Questioning tales of "ordinary magic": Resilience and neoliberal reasoning', *British Journal of Social Work*, 46, 1909–1925.

Garrett, P. M. (2017) '"Castaway categories": Examining the re-emergence on the "underclass" in the UK', *Journal of Progressive Human Services DOI: 10.1080/10428232.2017.1399038*.

Gilligan, P. (2007) 'Well motivated reformists or nascent radicals: How do applicants to the degree in social work see social problems, their origins and solutions?', *British Journal of Social Work*, 37 (4), 735–760.

Giroux, H. (2014) 'Neoliberalism, Youth, and Social Justice'. www.youtube.com/watch?v=KW5FRuMkQ6g (accessed 6 January, 2018).

Goldhill, R. (2017) 'Videoing supervision: Messages for probation practice', *Journal of Social Work Practice*, 31 (3), 279–292.

Gove, M. (2013) 'Michael gove speech to the NSPCC: Getting it right for children in need'. www.gov.uk/government/speeches/getting-it-right-for-children-in-need-speech-to-the-nspcc (accessed 6 November, 2017).

Gramsci, A. (1971) *Selections from the Prison Notebooks*. edited and translated by Quintin Hoare and Geoffrey Nowell Smith. London: Lawrence and Wishart.

Grant, L. (2014) 'Hearts and minds: Aspects of empathy and wellbeing in social work students', *Social Work Education*, 33 (3), 338–352.

Guardian (2013) 'Gove's wrong choices over call for social work reform'. www.theguardian.com/education/2013/nov/13/gove-wrong-choices-social-work (accessed 10 May, 2015).

Guardian (2016a) 'Privately educated elite continues to take top jobs, survey finds'. www.theguardian.com/education/2016/feb/24/privately-educated-elite-continues-to-take-top-jobs-finds-survey (accessed 9 April, 2018).

Guardian (2016b) 'The death of neoliberalism and the crisis in western politics'. www.theguardian.com/commentisfree/2016/aug/21/death-of-neoliberalism-crisis-in-western-politics (accessed 5 May, 2018).

Guardian (2018) 'Benefit sanctions found to be ineffective and damaging'. www.theguardian.com/society/2018/may/22/benefit-sanctions-found-to-be-ineffective-and-damaging?CMP=Share_iOSApp_Other (accessed 25 June, 2018).

Gupta, A. (2015) 'Poverty and shame – Messages for social work', *Critical and Radical Social Work*, 3 (1), 131–139.

Hansford, C., Ely, G. E., Flaherty, C. and Meyer-Adams, N. (2017) 'Social work is a profession not an ideology. A qualitative analysis of student perceptions of social justice discussions in the classroom', *Journal of Teaching in Social Work*, 37 (3), 199–217.

HCPC (2017) *Health and care professions council*. www.hpc-uk.org/ (accessed 2 February, 2018).

Held, V. (2010) 'Can the ethics of care handle violence?', *Ethics and Social Welfare*, 4 (2), 115–129.

Hennessey, R. (2011) *Relationship Skills in Social Work*. London: Sage.

Higgins, M. (2016) '"Cultivating our humanity" in child and family social work in England', *Social Work Education*, 35 (5), 518–529.

Higgins, M., Goodyer, A. and Whittaker, A. (2015) 'Can a Munro inspired approach transform the lives of looked after children in England?', *Social Work Education*, 34 (3), 328–340.

Higher Education Funding Council (2017) 'The TEF' www.hefce.ac.uk/lt/tef/ (accessed 10 March, 2018)

Hingley-Jones, H. and Ruch, G. (2016) '"Stumbling through"? Relationship-based social work practice in austere times', *Journal of Social Work Practice*, 30 (3), 235–248.

Horner, N. (2012) *What Is Social Work 4th Ed*. London: Sage.

Hyslop, I. (2016) 'Social work in the teeth of a gale: A resilient counter-discourse in neoliberal times', *Critical and Radical Social Work*, 4 (1), 21–37.

IFSW (International Federation of Social Workers) (2012) *Statement of Ethical Principles*. www.ifsw.org/statement-of-ethical-principles/(accessed 2 May, 2018).

IFSW (International Federation of Social Workers) (2014) *Global Definition of Social Work*. https://ifsw.org/policies/definition-of-social-work/ (accessed 15 May, 2017).

Independent (1993) 'Major on crime: "Condemn more, understand less"' www.independent.co.uk/news/major-on-crime-condemn-more-understand-less-1474470.html (accessed 14 April, 2018).

Independent (2013) 'The British public wrong about nearly everything, survey shows'. www.independent.co.uk/news/uk/home-news/british-publicwrong-about-nearly-everything-survey-shows-8697821.html (accessed 5 January, 2015).

Ingram, R. (2015) *Understanding emotions in social work*. Maidenhead: McGraw-Hill.

Ingram, R., Fenton, J., Hodson, A. and Jindal-Snape, D. (2014) *Reflective Social Work Practice*. London: Red Globe Press.

Ingram, R. and Smith, M. (2018) 'Relationship-based practice: emergent themes in social work literature'. *Insights 41: a series of evidence summaries* www.iriss. org.uk/sites/default/files/2018-02/insights-41.pdf (accessed 2 July, 2018).

International Business Times (2016) 'UK is least-generous country in Europe for unemployment benefits' www.ibtimes.co.uk/uk-least-generous-country-europe-unemployment-benefits-1544415 (accessed 3 March, 2018).

Ioakimidis, V. (2016) 'A guide to radical social work'. The *Guardian* www. theguardian.com/social-care-network/2016/may/24/radical-social-work-quick-guide-change-poverty-inequality (accessed 20 December, 2017).

Ivory, M. (2017) 'Should social workers be political activists?' The *Guardian* www.theguardian.com/social-care-network/2017/may/26/should-social-workers-be-political-activists (accessed 10 January, 2018).

Jones, O. (2011) *Chavs: The Demonization of the Working Class*. London: Verso.

Jones, O. (2014) *The Establishment And How They Get Away With It*. London: Penguin.

JRF (Joseph Rowntree Foundation) (2010) 'Credit and debt in low-income families'. www.jrf.org.uk/report/credit-and-debt-low-income-families (accessed 11 November, 2017).

JRF (Joseph Rowntree Foundation) (2011) 'Poverty and ethnicity: A review of evidence'. www.jrf.org.uk/report/poverty-and-ethnicity-review-evidence (accessed 20 June, 2018).

JRF (Joseph Rowntree Foundation) (2014) 'Public attitudes towards poverty'. www.jrf.org.uk/publications/public-attitudes-towards-poverty (accessed 24 May, 2015).

JRF (Joseph Rowntree Foundation) (2015) 'Welfare and benefits commentary - analysis of the trends'. www.jrf.org.uk/mpse-2015/welfare-benefits-intro (accessed 14 December, 2016).

JRF (Joseph Rowntree Foundation) (2016) 'In work poverty hits record high as the housing crisis fuels insecurity'. www.jrf.org.uk/press/work-poverty-hits-record-high-housing-crisis-fuels-insecurity (accessed 17 December, 2017).

JRF (Joseph Rowntree Foundation) (2017a) 'UK Poverty 2017 A comprehensive analysis of poverty trends and figures'. www.jrf.org.uk/report/uk-poverty-2017 (accessed 15 February, 2018).

JRF (Joseph Rowntree Foundation) (2017b) 'Reasons for not working among people in workless households'. www.jrf.org.uk/data/reasons-not-working-among-people-workless-households (accessed 23 March, 2018).

JRF (Joseph Rowntree Foundation) (nd) 'What is poverty?' www.jrf.org.uk/our-work/what-is-poverty (accessed 25 March, 2018).

Kahneman, D. (2011) *Thinking Fast and Slow*. London: Penguin.

Kipnis, L. (2017) *Unwanted Advances: Sexual Paranoia Comes to Campus*. New York: Harper Collins.

Knight, C. (2014) 'Students' attitudes towards and engagement in self-disclosure: implications for supervision', *The Clinical Supervisor*, 33 (2), 163–181.

Kosny, A. and Eakin, J. (2008) 'The hazards of helping: Work, mission and risk in non-profit social services organizations', *Health, Risk and Society*, 10, 149–166.

Lansley, S. and Mack, J. (2015) *Breadline Britain: The Rise of Poverty*. London: Oneworld.

Lavalette, M. (2017) 'Activism is key to healthy mind and healthy society', *Professional Social Work June 2017*.

Levitas, R. (2005) *The Inclusive Society*. Basingstoke: Palgrave Macmillan.

The Life Guide (2016) *The political spectrum explained*. www.youtube.com/watch?v=JlQ5fGECmsA (accessed 28 September, 2018).

Lilla, M. (2017) *The Once and Future Liberal*. London: Harper Colliins.

Lymbery, M. (2014) 'Understanding personalisation: Implications for social work', *Journal of Social Work*, 14 (3), 295–312.

MacDonald, R. (2015) 'The power of stupid ideas: Three generations that have never worked'. https://workingclassstudies.wordpress.com/2015/05/11/the-power-ofstupid-ideas-three-generations-that-have-never-worked/ (accessed 2 October, 2015).

Marston, G. (2013) 'Critical discourse analysis', in Gray, M. and S. A. Webb. (eds) *The New Politics of Social Work*. London: Red Globe Press.

May, D., Luth, M. and Schwoerer, C. (2014) 'The influence of business ethics education on moral efficacy, moral meaningfulness, and moral courage: A quasi-experimental study', *Journal of Business Ethics*, 124, 67–80.

McCandless, D. and Posavec, S. (2010) 'Left vs Right' www.informationisbeautiful.net/?s=left±vs±right±wing (accessed 6 January, 2018).

Mcgarvey, D. (2017) *Poverty Safari: Understanding the Anger of Britain's Underclass*. Edinburgh: Luath Press.

McKendrick, D. and Webb, S. (2014) 'Taking a political stance in social work', *Critical and Radical Social Work*, 2 (3), 357–369.

McLaughlin, K. (2008) *Social Work, Politics and Society: From Radicalism to Orthodoxy*. Bristol: Policy Press.

McLaughlin, K. (2012) *Surviving Identity: Vulnerability and the Psychology of Recognition*. Hove: Routledge.

McLaughlin, K., Leigh, J. and Worsley, A. (2016) 'The state of regulation in England: From the general social care council to the health and care professions council', *British Journal of Social Work*, 46, 825–838.

McNeill, F., Batchelor, S., Burnett, R. and Cox, J. (2005) *21st Century Social Work: Reducing Re-offending: Key Practice Skills*. www.gov.scot/Publications/2005/0 4/21132007/20080 (accessed 12 April, 2018).

Michaels, W. B. (2006) *The Trouble with Diversity: How we Learned to Love Identity and Ignore Inequality*. New York: Metropolitan Books.

Mill, J. S. (1859 [2011]) *On Liberty*. London: The Walter Scott Publishing Company.

Monbiot, G. (2016) 'Neoliberalism, the ideology at the root of all our problems'. www.theguardian.com/books/2016/apr/15/neoliberalism-ideology-problem-george-monbiot (accessed 20 April, 2017).

Morley, C. and Macfarlane, S. (2014) 'Critical social work as ethical social work: Using critical reflection to research students' resistance to neoliberalism', *Critical and Radical Social Work*, 2 (3), 337–355.

Mullaly, B. (2007) *The New Structural Social Work* 3rd Ed. Ontario: OUP.

Munday, B. (2003) *User Involvement in Personal Social Services*. United Kingdom: University of Kent.

Munro, E. (2011) *The Munro Review of Child Protection: Final Report*. London: TSO.

Murray, C. (1990) *The Emerging British Underclass*. London: IEA Health and Welfare Unit.

Narey, M. (2014) 'Making the education of social workers consistency effective'. www.gov.uk/government/uploads/system/uploads/attachment_data/file/287756/Making_the_education_of_social_workers_consistently_effective.pdf (accessed 13 February, 2018).

The National Audit Office (2016) 'Children in need of help or protection'. www.nao.org.uk/wp-content/uploads/2016/10/Children-in-need-of-help-protection.pdf (accessed 10 March, 2018).

Newham, R. A. (2016) 'The emotion of compassion and the likelihood of its expression in nursing practice', *Nursing Philosophy*, 18. DOI: 10.1111/nup.12163.

Nicolas, J. (2015) 'Why pretend social work is about social justice? It's not'. The *Guardian*. www.theguardian.com/socialcarenetwork/2015/oct/20/why-pretend-social-work-is-about-social-justice-its-not (accessed 19 July, 2017).

Norstrand, M. (2017) 'Practice supervisors' perceptions of social work students and their placements – an exploratory study in the Norwegian context', *Social Work Education*, 36 (5), 481–494.

Norton, B. (2015) *Adolph Reed: Identity Politics is Neoliberalism*. https://bennorton.com/adolph-reed-identity-politics-is-neoliberalism/ (accessed 14 may, 2018).

Oliver, C., Jones, E., Raynor, A., Penner, J. and Jamieson, A. (2017) 'Teaching social work students to speak up', *Social Work Education*, 36 (6), 702–714.

Orwell, G. (1933) *Down and Out in Paris and London*. London: Penguin.

Oxford English Dictionary (2018) www.oed.com/(accessed 10 June, 2018).

Parton, N. (2008) 'Changes in the form of knowledge in social work: From the "social" to the "informational"', *British Journal of Social Work*, 38 (2), 253–269.

Parton, N. (2014) *The Politics of Child Protection: Contemporary Developments and Future Directions*. London: Red Globe Press.

Pease, B. (2013) 'A history of critical and radical social work', in M. Gray and S. A. Webb (eds) *The New Politics of Social Work*. London: Red Globe Press.

Political Compass (2017) *The political compass*. www.politicalcompass.org/ (accessed 6 November, 2017).

Preston-Shoot, M. (2011) 'On administrative evil-doing within social work policy and services: Law, ethics and practice', *European Journal of Social Work*, 14 (2), 177–194.

Quinlan, K. (2016) 'Developing student character through disciplinary curricula: An analysis of UK QAA subject benchmark statements', *Studies in Higher Education*, 41 (6), 1041–1054.

Reamer, F. and Shardlow, S. (2009) 'Ethical codes of practice in the US and the UK: One profession, two standards', *Journal of Social Work Values and Ethics*,

6 (2), n.p. www.socialworker.com/jswve/content/view/120/68/ (accessed 10 October, 2016).

Reimer, E. C. (2013) 'Relationship-based practice with families where child neglect is an issue: Putting relationship development under the microscope', *Australian Social Work*, 66 (3), 455–470.

Reisch, M. (2013) 'What is the future of social work?', *Critical and Radical Social Work*, 1 (10), 67–85.

Riley, J. (2015) *The Routledge Guidebook to Mill's on Liberty*. Abingdon: Routledge.

Rogers, C. R. (1966) 'Client-centered therapy', in S. Arieti (ed) *American Handbook American Handbook of Psychiatry*. New York: Basic Books.

Rogowski, S. (2015) 'From child welfare to child protection/safeguarding: A critical practitioner's view of changing conceptions, policies and practice', *Practice: Social Work in Action*, 27 (2), 97–112.

Scottish Government (2003) *The Framework for Social Work Education in Scotland*. Edinburgh: Scottish Executive.

Scottish Government (2008) *Scotland's Choice: Report of The Scottish Prisons Commission*. www.gov.scot/Publications/2008/06/30162955/0 (accessed 23 February, 2018).

Segal, E. (2011) 'Social empathy: A module built on empathy, contextual understanding and social responsibility that promotes social justice', *Journal of Social Services Research,* 37, 266–277.

Sheedy, M. (2013) *Core Themes in Social Work: Power, Poverty, Politics and Values*. Maidenhead: Oxford University Press.

Sheppard, M. and Charles, M. (2017) 'A longitudinal comparative study of the impact of the experience of social work education on interpersonal and critical thinking capabilities', *Social Work Education*. Advance online publication. [DOI: 10.1080/02615479.2017.1355968].

Sheppard, M., Charles, M., Rees, P., Wheeler, M. and Williams, R. (2018) 'Interpersonal and critical-thinking capabilities in those about to enter qualified social work: A six-centre study', *British Journal of Social Work*, doi: 10.1093/bjsw/bcx143.

Simola, S. (2014) 'Understanding moral courage through a feminist and developmental ethic of care', *Journal of Business Ethics*, 130, 29–44.

Skorupski, J. (2011) 'John Stuart Mill's On Liberty'. www.policy-network.net/pno_detail.aspx?ID=4003&title=John±Stuart±Mill%E2%80%99s±On±Liberty (accessed 10 October, 2017).

Smith, M. (2011) 'Reading Bauman for Social Work', *Ethics and Social Welfare*, 5 (1), 2–17.

Smith, M. and Woodiwiss, J. (2016) 'Sexuality, innocence and agency in narratives of childhood sexual abuse: Implications for social work', *British Journal of Social Work*, 46, 2173–2189.

Smithson, R. and Gibson, M. (2017) 'Less than human: A qualitative study into the experience of parents involved in the child protection system', *Child and Family Social Work*, 22, 565–574.

Social Work Action Network (SWAN) (2018) https://socialworkfuture.org/ (accessed 11 November, 2017).

SSSC (Scottish Social Services Council) (2016) *Codes of Practice for Scottish Social Service Workers and Employers*. Dundee: SSSC.

Stanford, S. N. (2011) 'Constructing moral responses to risk: A framework for hopeful social work practice', *British Journal of Social Work*, 41, 1514–1531.

Stickle, M. (2016) 'The expression of compassion in social work practice', *Journal of Religion and Spirituality in Social Work: Social Thought*, 35 (1–2), 120–131.

Sullivan, W. M. (2005) *Work and Integrity: The Crisis and Promise of Professionalism in America 2ⁿᵈ Ed*. San Francisco: Jossey-Bass.

Telegraph (2010) 'We are all middle class now, darling'. www.telegraph.co.uk/news/politics/7053761/Were-all-middle-class-now-darling.html (accessed May 2017).

Telegraph (2016) 'Paul Gascoigne to face racism charges over comedy show gag'. www.telegraph.co.uk/news/2016/06/04/paul-gascoigne-to-face-racism-charges-over-comedy-show-gag/ (accessed 24 May 2017).

Telegraph (2017) 'One in four care homes unsafe, says watchdog as experts criticise 'Russian roulette' in social care'. www.telegraph.co.uk/news/2017/07/05/one-four-care-homes-unsafe-says-watchdog-experts-criticise-russian/ (accessed 10 February, 2018).

Thompson, N. (2001) *Anti-Discriminatory Practice* 3ʳᵈ Ed. London: Red Globe Press.

Thompson, N. (2016) 'Social workers not bureaucrats', *Professional social work magazine*, May 2016.

Tirado, L. (2014) *Hand to Mouth: The Truth about Being Poor in a Wealthy World*. London: Virago.

Trevithick, P. (2012) *Social Work Skills and Knowledge: A Practice Handbook*. Maidenhead: Oxford University Press.

Tronto, J. (1993) *Moral Boundaries: A Political Argument for an Ethic of Care*. London: Routledge.

Trotter, C., Evans, P. and Baidawi, S. (2017) 'The effectiveness of challenging skills in work with young offenders', *International Journal of Offender Therapy and Comparative Criminology*, 61 (4), 397–412.

Turbett, C. (2014) *Doing Radical Social Work*. London: Red Globe Press.

University of Glasgow (2012) *The Road From Crime*. DVD. Lagan Media Production for the University of Glasgow.

van Breda, A. D. (2018) 'Reclaiming resilience of social work: A reply to Garrett', *British Journal of Social Work*, 0, 1–5.

van Heugten, K. (2011) 'Registration and social work education: A golden opportunity or a Trojan horse?', *Journal of Social Work*, 11 (2), 174–190.

Varoufakis, Y. (2017) *Talking to My Daughter about the Economy*. London: Penguin.

Verhaeghe, P. (2012) *What about Me? the Struggle for Identity in a Market-Based Society*. London: Scribe.

Wacquant, L. (2009) *Punishing the Poor*. Durham and London: Duke University Press.

Warner, J. (2015) 'Social work, class politics and risk in the moral panic over Baby P', *Health, Risk and Society*, 15 (3), 217–33.

Weaver, A. (2008) *So You Think You Know Me?*. Hampshire: Waterside Press Limited.

Webb, S. (2006) *Social Work in a Risk Society: Social and Political Perspectives.* London: Red Globe Press.

Webb, S. (2009) 'Against difference and diversity in social work: The case of human rights', *International Journal of Social Welfare*, 18 (3), 307–316.

Wedge, M. (2012) 'Why French Kids Don't Have ADHD'. www.psychologytoday. com/us/blog/suffer-the-children/201203/why-french-kids-dont-have-adhd (accessed 2 April, 2018).

The Week (2016) 'Benefit fraud v tax evasion: Which costs more?' www.theweek. co.uk/62461/benefit-fraud-v-tax-evasion-which-costs-more (accessed 10 April, 2018).

Weinberg, M. (2016) *Paradoxes in Social Work Practice: Mitigating Ethical Trespass.* Abingdon: Routledge.

Whincup, H. (2017) 'What do social workers and children do when they are together? A typology of direct work', *Child and Family Social Work*, 22 (2), 972–980.

Whittaker, A. (2011) 'Social defences and organisational culture in a local authority child protection setting: Challenges for the Munro review?', *Journal of Social Work Practice: Psychotherapeutic Approaches in Health, Welfare and the Community*, 25 (4), 481–495.

Whittaker, A. (2018) 'How do child protection practitioners make decisions in real-life situations? Lessons from the psychology of decision making', *British Journal of Social Work*, 0, 1–18.

Whitaker, L. and Reimer, E. (2017) 'Students' conceptualisations of critical reflection', *Social Work Education*, 36 (8), 946–958.

Wilkinson, I. (2017) 'The controversy of compassion as an awakening to our conflicted social condition', *International Journal of Law in Context*, 13 (2), 212–224.

Wilkinson, R. G. and Pickett, K. (2010) *The Spirit Level: Why Equality Is Better for Everyone.* London: Penguin.

Wilkinson, R. G. and Pickett, K. (2018) *The Inner Level: How More Equal Societies Reduce Stress, Restore Sanity and Improve Everyone's Well-Being.* London: Penguin.

Wills, J., Whittaker, A., Rickard, W. and Felix, C. (2017) 'Troubled, troubling or in trouble: The stories of "troubled families"', *British Journal of Social Work*, 47, 989–1006.

Woodiwiss, J. (2014) 'Beyond a single story: The importance of separating "harm" from "wrongfulness" and "sexual innocence" from "childhood" in contemporary narratives of childhood sexual abuse', *Sexualities*, 17 (1–2), 139–158.

Woodward, R. and Mackay, K. (2012) 'Mind the gap! students' understanding and application of social work values', *Social Work Education: The International Journal*, 31 (8), 1090–1104.

Index

Printed in the United States
By Bookmasters